PROPERTY OF THE
Public Library of the Town of Beverly.
PUBLIC LIBRARY OF THE TOWN OF BEVERLY.
1855.
WITHDRAWN

FUTURE WATER

FUTURE WATER

An Exciting Solution to America's Most Serious Resource Crisis

John R. Sheaffer and
Leonard A. Stevens

WILLIAM MORROW AND COMPANY, INC.
New York / 1983

Grateful acknowledgment is extended to the following for permission to reproduce photographs and other illustrative material: County of Muskegon Wastewater Management System, Denver Water Department, Forest Preserve District of Du Page County, Lubbock Parks and Recreation Department, David C. Lutter, Charles A. Manganaro, the Metropolitan Sanitary District of Greater Chicago, Captain Albert A. Swanson, Tramell Crow Company and Valmont Industries.

Library of Congress Catalog Card Number: 83-61855

ISBN: 0-688-01575-1

Printed in the United States of America

First Edition

1 2 3 4 5 6 7 8 9 10

BOOK DESIGN BY FRANK CANGELOSI

Contents

LIST OF ILLUSTRATIONS

FUTURE WATER

I

Linear Versus Circular

Of all the engineered wonders on the American landscape—from gantries that guide rocket ships into space to nuclear reactors seething with radioactivity—probably the most numerous are the least known. They are large water purification systems, factorylike plants, some covering hundreds of acres with elaborate assemblies of pipes, pumps, filters, tanks and towers. There are thousands around the country. Many of these treatment works were constructed and continue to be built at enormous public expense, in the country's most costly public works program. The plants are supposed to separate unwanted material from the nation's water in order to clean up our streams and lakes.

However, few of us who pay the bill recognize that the money supports one of the most costly failures of the twentieth century. The failure has been documented by the leading expender of the wasted funds, the federal government, through its comptroller general, its inspector general and the investigative staff of the Appropriations Committee of the House of Representatives. Although the complex works take the lion's share of the billions upon billions spent on clean water for America—as much as $50 billion since 1972—the citizens who provide the funds are warned in the 1980s that before the year 2000 we could run out of potable water, that "water is the most serious, long range problem now confronting the nation—potentially more serious than the energy crisis."

How could we spend money for clean water in amounts ordinarily associated with national defense and exploration of the moon, yet find ourselves in the ultimate of a long series of water crises? This embarrassing query is generally avoided despite all that is said about the impending disaster, but the question must be raised and explored if we are to understand the menacing water crisis in America and develop alternative solutions in place of more costly, futile measures.

An attempt to understand the water debacle necessarily leads us back to the turn of the century, when there was an earlier phase of the present crisis—which, by the way, has a history of at least 150 years. Around 1900 a debate was in progress over how the country should save its freshwater from increasing pollution. On one side, those described as the linear-system proponents claimed the nation had enough water to serve indefinitely, both as water supply and to dilute municipal sewage discharged into streams and other natural bodies of water. Where there was too much wastewater (sewage) for dilution, these people claimed the discharges could be cleaned up enough with technological treatment systems to overcome the problem. Simply put, the linear-system proponents saw water flowing in a straight line from sources to users to receiving streams, and on out to sea.

Arguing to the contrary were those who can be called the circular-system proponents, who advocated obeying nature's inviolable law of return by sending our used water back to the natural cleansing systems of soil, plants, air and sunshine for reclamation and reuse, over and over again. They warned that the discharge of wastewater into natural bodies of water disregarded powerful forces of nature and amounted to a grand plan for disaster. They also refused to believe that man-made machinery would ever match nature's reliable water-cleaning capabilities. The validity of their cyclical point of view was demonstrated by many remarkable European farms that used nature's purification system to reclaim both the water and the waste it carried from some of the world's largest cities. Such a farm system was considered for Chicago, but was turned down in favor of a far more expensive canal. It at once opened up shipping between the Great Lakes and the Mississippi River and diverted sewage away from the city's Lake Michigan water supply to a point on the Mississippi near St. Louis's water-supply intake.

The linear-system proponents, who favored the canal, also won the national debate, and their philosophy guided the growth of America's water establishment, a complex conglomeration of government agencies, industries, engineering curricula, professional societies, laws, health standards and budgets determining how we acquire, use and dispose of our water. For decades the establishment seemed to prove the rightness of its case, building America's amazing water supply systems, ending the fear of typhoid fever, the most virulent of waterborne diseases, and serving the nation with an abundance of "safe water" unmatched anywhere on earth.

The widespread delivery of reliable water set the public at ease—too much so, it can be argued. Healthful drinking water in the United States seemed as free and plentiful as air, a cornucopia of potable supplies to be used for everything from a table beverage in the country's finest restaurants to flushing toilets and streets, from quenching fires and red-hot steel to cooling offices and electric power plants and irrigating lawns, shrubs and millions of acres of crops for food and fiber. Wherever the flow fell short of the demand, whether in rain-rich or in arid regions, the remarkable waterworks engineer was usually able to find new sources on or below the surface of the earth. Water always seemed to be somewhere for the taking, and it could be delivered by pipes, mountain tunnels, aqueducts, canals, pumps, whatever was required, for a few cents per 1,000 gallons.

To the average citizen the inexpensive availability of good water became practically a constitutional right, and regardless of where he settled he demanded more and more water. Indeed, he was likely to consume the most in arid lands with the least supply. For example, freshwater use in the nation increased about 160 percent between 1955 and 1975, to the point where the national per capita consumption was some 150 gallons per day—however, during the summer months in California's hot Central Valley, the average suburbanite consumed as much as 660 gallons per day.

But slaking this rising thirst with linear supply systems had an immeasurable impact on the country's natural water systems. If, as one hydrologist put it, the construction of a dam is "man's ultimate way of thumbing his nose at God," the magnitude of the insult is evident when we consider how many thousands of dams and comparable alterations have been imposed upon the surface of the United States for municipal water supplies. Our tamperings with nature's waterworks became so extensive and complex that they were often acclaimed as engineering wonders of the world—for example:

- the huge water tunnels of New York City that reach out to reservoirs as much as 125 miles away to bring 1.5 billion gallons of pure water per day by gravity flow to 6,100 miles of in-town pipelines, supplying 600,000 commercial and residential buildings;
- the California water system that, in meeting citizen demands for water at the dry end of the state as well as at the wet end, has become "one of the most massive rearrangements of the natural environment that has ever been attempted."

If such renovations constitute an affront to the Creator of the natural environment, the gesture may be eliciting a response with the crisis of all water crises. Regardless, the debacle is of our own making, and the classic solution that held it off—reach out and reach out some more for new water sources—is at the root of this ultimate of resource problems. The leading motivation has been to provide water wherever it is desired, regardless of costs from gross inefficiencies or from the destructiveness sometimes associated with the effort. Water is overused where it should be least used; dislocations of natural sources have serious environmental consequences; and water-induced wealth is unfairly distributed—generally with eastern states paying their own way while western states thrive on federally financed water projects.

But the opportunity to continue in this manner diminishes, for we are close to the end of the linear reach. The truth of this contention is pointed up by how a few of the many experts who cling to the old, expiring solution have gone to the wild blue yonder for fanciful ideas to extend the linear reach—such as:

- towing icebergs from Antarctica to the California coast, where water from the melting ice would be pumped ashore for human consumption;
- using nuclear-powered pumps to shuttle water by pipeline across North America from water-rich to water-short areas—like borrowing from the Columbia River to augment the Colorado, or contributing to irrigation on the Great Plains with water from the Great Lakes;
- smearing stretches of the Arctic with carbon black, causing the ice cap to melt in the sun, and then piping the water to the United States; or producing the same meltwater with massive nuclear-bomb-fired steam chambers carved in the ice;
- desalting the oceans to provide the world's most expensive potable water;
- extending pipelines into the far north to transport iceballs that would be melted by friction with the pipes on their southward journey, so as to arrive as freshwater at arid destinations.

But while these and other visionary schemes die of impracticality, a minority of experts argue that, practical or not, such solutions concentrate on the wrong end of the problem, that the real answers to the water crisis are to be found not in the continued search for new sources but in the efficient management of existing supplies in closed, circular systems, where used water is kept and reclaimed along with the wastes it carries.

The misuse of existing supplies is largely neglected, although this is where major causes for the growing crisis are found. A profligate disrespect for freshwater is ingrained in many consumers and even promoted by the construction, financial and operational barons of water supply and sewage disposal. Trillions of gallons of good water are needlessly wasted every day, multiplying the demand on potable supplies and adding to the volume of sewage discharged, which in turn increases the contamination of other potential supplies.

The fruits of our carelessness with water have shown up more recently in our most sacrosanct of reservoirs, the nation's aquifers, water-bearing geologic formations. Aquifers supply half of all American citizens with their water, from a total volume four times that of the Great Lakes. The subterranean supplies are threatened in two ways. Some are having their water withdrawn faster than nature can "recharge" them, and are thus being forced toward depletion. Other aquifers, including those where natural recharge balances withdrawals, are endangered by contamination from the disposal of traditional wastes and the poisonous residues of the nuclear age and chemical revolution.

Before solutions to this growing crisis can be realistically considered, we must confront a national ethic condoning the idea that used resources are wastes to be disposed of at any cost. We are so caught up by this mentality that we willingly make non-returnable investments of tens of billions of dollars to be rid of the use-tainted resources of sewage by dumping them in our streams and lakes. Most of the investment pays for the nation's thousands of treatment works, which are designed not to reclaim the wastes or the used water but to keep their disposal from becoming a public nuisance. The immense investment in disposal may reduce the obnoxiousness and help move the wastes unobtrusively out of sight and out of mind, but the practice continues to contaminate vast water supply sources and leads us deeper and deeper into the water crisis. There are huge profits in the business of disposal, but no public dividends for the large public investment, only ever-increasing losses for all of us.

The downward spiral will continue until there is a change from our present ethic of water use to another, based on the understanding that the pollutants of water are really valuable resources out of place. When this is understood, we can consider wastes as raw materials, and through proper capital investments turn them into valuable resources to enhance the production of food, fiber and energy, all with the incidental byproduct of clean water. Seen in this light, wastewater and iron ore are analogous in that both can become valuable resources when proper capital investments are made. The dividends from wastewater investments can be substantial. Besides dealing effectively with the water crisis by preserving and enlarging upon supplies, the returns include a healthier economy through more efficient use of resources, with a practically free bonus of improved environmental quality. Unlike towing icebergs and carbon-blacking the polar ice cap, replacing our throw-away mentality with concern for reclaiming and reusing our resources offers not only a practical solution but really the only solution to the water crisis.

No pipe dream, this overdue ethic is already backed by the innovative clean water law passed overwhelmingly by the Congress of the United States in 1972 and strengthened in 1977. The father of the legislation, Senator Edmund S. Muskie, hailed the law as a new direction that could unshackle the nation's water from the wastes that spoil its purity and diminish potable supplies. But the change from a linear to a circular direction was too much for the powerful forces locked into traditional systems, so the mandate, fought, thwarted and disparaged, was not implemented by succeeding administrations. However, the ethic behind the mandate is proven sound by working examples—including:

- 13 Michigan municipalities, including a large industrial city, that convert over 30 million gallons of sewage a day into safe, clean water by filtering it through the soil and crops of a huge farm, from which over $1 million a year from the sale of feed corn is returned to the taxpayers;
- a new 274-acre office-hotel complex in Illinois that is water self-sufficient, using and reusing water both from wells and from precipitation to supply the employees and hotel guests, heating and cooling systems, fire protection, and landscape beautification with man-made lakes and irrigated lawns and gardens;
- a Colorado city that breaks the confrontational tradition that often forces farmers out of business by legal condemnation of their irrigation water for use as urban supply; now, in a cooperative mode, the community only borrows irrigation water and—after municipal use and partial cleaning—returns the supply to the farm owners with the valuable fertilizing nutrients of sewage remaining for added enrichment of the crops;
- one of America's largest, most beautiful city parks, which

for a half century has been irrigated, fertilized and beautified with lakes and waterfalls using nutrient-enriched water reclaimed from the municipal sewage;

- a Texas city in one of the most water-troubled areas of the country that sends its wastewater to a large farm where it is cleaned while irrigating and fertilizing crops, and then returned for use in a downtown beautification and recreation project;
- an attractive midwestern recreation site, with three man-made lakes surrounding a mountain built of solid waste collected from one million people over a decade and designed not to poison the groundwater as do hundreds of public landfills in the United States;
- the remarkable case of a California city in one of the nation's most arid regions, where for 20 years citizens have been swimming in, fishing from and picnicking around eight freshwater lakes, every drop of which has been reclaimed from the community's sewage by filtering it through simple beds of soil;
- a New Jersey city that is investing in its municipal wastewater as a raw material to produce (1) salable crops, like corn, hay and Christmas trees, (2) electricity from engine-generators run on biogas, a fuel developed from sewage sludge, (3) alcohol fuel distilled from corn irrigated and fertilized by the wastewater, in the process using waste heat from the biogas system, (4) poultry and livestock feed from distillers' dry grain, a byproduct from the alcohol still, and, above all, (5) reclaimed potable water for reuse in the community and region.

As such examples indicate, the national water crisis is not a shortage of water, but the mismanagement of ample supplies that we already have. The most effective solutions can be found in changing from the linear to the circular management of new and existing supplies. But change is virtually a stranger to the granitic world of water and wastewater. Three authorities who know firsthand of this unyielding state of affairs were quoted on the point in a 1981 *Audubon* magazine article:

Thomas Jorling, one of the draftsmen of the famous clean

water law of 1972 and later the administrator for water at the U.S. Environmental Protection Agency (EPA), explained, "The biggest problem comes from where the program is driven and it is driven by consulting engineers."

David Zwick, director of the Clean Water Action Project, expanded on the explanation: "The conventional industry has gotten so large and gained so much momentum that it just continues, having surrounded itself with this infrastructure of bureaucratic, governmental, academic and business groups, all feeding on each other. It is an orthodoxy—and it's backed by billions and billions of dollars, and it just keeps rolling along."

And Andrew Ellicott, director of public affairs for the powerful Water Pollution Control Federation, confirmed, "Engineers tend to go with processes they are most familiar with."

Many who might be described as today's circular-system proponents have concluded this orthodoxy will, indeed, just keep rolling along. If there was ever reason for it to change, the potential was found in the innovative clean water laws of the 1970s, first in the Federal Water Pollution Control Act amendments of 1972. But the motivation was blunted, and billions and billions in federal construction grants and matching funds allowed by the law paid for a lot more of the same crusty linear systems that did little to delay the water crisis of the 1980s.

The disappointment of the 1970s teaches that we can find solutions for the crisis only by going around the "infrastructure of [various] groups, all feeding on each other." The opportunity undoubtedly lies in the private sector, where open minds may still recognize that the wastes fouling and diminishing our crucial water supplies are really resources out of place. As such they can become raw materials for bankable private ventures that can produce goods, services and employment, reduce inflationary, nonproductive expenditures of tax dollars on construction grants and return America's precious water, cleaned and ready for reuse.

Even though the circumstances of crisis are pressing for such a change, it is unlikely to come until a great many people know about the world of water, particularly that of wastewater, and proceed with the solutions we badly need.

II

Reach Out and Reach Out

When the American historian Francis Parkman was gathering material for his famous work *The California and Oregon Trail,* he stopped for water one hot summer morning at the junction of the South Platte River and Cherry Creek, where settlers would soon begin forming the city of Denver. "No water in the Creek," Parkman wrote in his journal for August 15, 1846; "dug holes and got some." A few years later the founders of Denver chose the same location for the same reason, water supply. The evolution of this supply can be viewed as a model of how waterworks developed for most American towns and cities as they obtained, used and threw away ever-increasing volumes of water. An understanding of how this pattern evolved in Colorado, and elsewhere, is fundamental to an understanding of how today's water crisis developed and how it may be solved.

The first citizens of Denver took their drinking water by buckets from Cherry Creek and the South Platte, in the company of their horses, cattle and dogs. The quality of the water soon deteriorated, and people turned to springwater hauled from outside of town. Others dug private wells in town and quickly lowered the water table, forcing them to go deeper and deeper; nevertheless, the water quality continued to decline because the locations of wells relative to outhouses were ill planned.

The amenities of indoor plumbing arrived around 1872, increasing demands for public water supplies pure enough to drink and plentiful enough to carry off the wastes of kitchens, laundries, baths and the greatest luxury of all, modern toilets (politely called water closets). The need was first met by an Irish immigrant, Colonel James Archer, whose distribution mains were supplied from an underground source with pressure provided by a New York–made "Holly direct pumping system." At inauguration ceremonies for Archer's new "Holly water," it was shot 100 feet into the air from a hose on F Street.

The colonel's Denver Water Company immediately needed to double its supply to satisfy demand, but even then consumers had to confine their uses to domestic purposes. In 1880, with Denver's population having multiplied by seven in the past decade, Archer said he would settle the water supply problem forever by going to a source that would always be plentiful enough for Denver. He tapped the South Platte three miles upstream from the city, only to find on delivery that the purity of the water was less than expected. In fact, it came through customers' faucets bearing an occasional fish.

However, the impurities of this public supply and private wellwater alike included more than fish. Both were increasingly contaminated by the insidious typhoid bacillus. Denver's sewage disposal was still left to individuals who inevitably fouled their own and neighbors' water supplies with waterborne disease germs. At the time terrible typhoid epidemics were striking towns and cities across the country, and Denver was no exception. Hoping to rid itself of the germs, the Colorado city built its first public sewers in 1880. They led to a downstream discharge point on the South Platte, where, according to the common belief, the free flow of the river would purify the infectious sewage in a hundred yards.

With freshwater flowing in and wastewater flowing out, Denver's linear supply pattern was now intact. In the century since then the pattern has become longer, larger and more complex, but the same inflow-outflow configuration remains.

In roughly the first half of this 100 years, the water seekers from the mile-high city filled its multiplying water mains from sources farther and farther out into the South Platte watershed. As the outreach extended, private water entrepreneurs and then the Denver Board of Water Commissioners coped mainly with the vicissitudes of nature.

The water from high in the Rockies ordinarily came in a fast feast followed by a prolonged famine. In a few spring and summer weeks, the melting snowpack in the mountains swelled the rivers and creeks of the South Platte watershed as the meltwater gushed down the eastern slopes onto the Great Plains. But once the melt was over, the streams flattened out close to the vanishing point—which led the American humorist Artemus Ward to write, "The Platte would be a good river if set on edge." The stream was also described as a mile wide and an inch deep. The key to dependable water supplies was to catch the meltwater and ration it out during the long, lean remainder of the year.

The first major impoundment of the South Platte was created by Cheesman Dam, a structure 221 feet tall, completed in 1905. The dam, which became a National Historic Civil Engineering Landmark, formed a reservoir 40 miles southwest of Denver holding 25 billion gallons of water. Since then three other impoundments have been constructed on the Platte, adding another 40 billion gallons of storage for Denver. The two largest of these reservoirs, Antero and Eleven Mile Canyon, are far from and high above Denver in the mountains west of Pikes Peak.

While these two were under construction, the city's waterworks engineers had their eyes on another rich mountain watershed, that of the Colorado River, on the western slopes of the Rockies over the continental divide. The opportunity to draw from the Colorado came with the construction of a famous railroad tunnel driven through the mountains under the divide. The 6.2-mile Moffat Tunnel, 50 miles west and some 4,000 feet above Denver, actually consisted of two bores, one large enough for a train, the other a parallel eight-by-eight-foot "pioneer bore" that gave construction workers lateral access to the main tunnel. When the railroad project was finished in 1928, Denver converted the pioneer bore to a water tunnel, and on June 10, 1936, the city's first transmountain supplies flowed through the cut from the Fraser River.

The Moffat was only the first of three tunnels that now carry some 37 billion gallons of water per year to Denver. One of the newer bores is the Harold D. Roberts Tunnel, "the world's longest major underground tunnel." It is over 23 miles long, with stretches lying 5,000 feet beneath the 13,000-foot peaks of a mountain range, and it draws from the vast Dillon Reservoir supplied by the Blue River system. The reservoir's construction even required transplantation of the town of Dillon, Colorado. Two other tunnels, the Gumlick and the Vasquez, transport water from the Williams River system under one section of the continental divide, then back under, to deliver it to the Moffat Tunnel system and hence to Denver.

One could easily assume that all the mountain water would be as pure as the driven snow producing most of it, but as the early vendor of Holly water learned, supplies, even from points distant to the city, were never as pure as needed. The city, in fact, became a pioneer in purification by installing one of the nation's earliest water treatment plants in 1890. Over the years Denver constructed, enlarged and improved upon a total of three water treatment plants to purify the increasing volumes of supply.

In 1980 the vast, sprawling water system—with computers helping to maximize efficient withdrawals—delivered over 76 billion gallons of water through more than 2,000 miles of transmission lines and mains. Nearly 1 million people over the metropolitan area drew the water from nearly a quarter-million taps. Like their fellow Americans, Denverites used great amounts of water, an average of 213 gallons per day per person. And like so many waterworks officials in America, Denver's felt they were on the edge of not enough. Aware that they were unlikely to obtain rights to more new water, the Water Department was nourishing its existing supplies. Citizens were pressed to conserve—for example, to irrigate lawns only at designated times or risk fines. And the department was conducting a $29 million, seven-year water reuse project using complex technology to convert some of the city's sewage effluent to potable water, hoping it could increase Denver's drinking water 15 percent by the year 2000. If it were all purified the percentage, of course, would be much higher.

A comparable history of sewage, at the disposal end of Denver's linear supply system, can be told in brief by virtue of its sameness. From the day in 1880 when sewage was first dumped directly into the South Platte, the practice never stopped, though the volume increased tremendously. Indeed, at times of low natural flow, the Platte downstream from Denver was as much sewer as river. The wastewater deluge became such a serious source of pollution that the city was forced to build costly sewage treatment plants that removed some (but not all) of the waste ingredients to reduce the damage to the river. Eventually many of the sewage works were consolidated under the Metropolitan Sewage Disposal District, which collected wastewater from 13 area municipalities, partially cleaned it and dumped the effluent in the Platte.

The story from Colorado is one of engineering heroics, driving tunnels through the highest, most rugged mountains of the United States and altering entire watersheds with massive dams. It was done to meet the demands of citizens on the arid lap of the Rockies who grew accustomed to the profligate water consumption of all Americans in territories dry or wet. The story is also one of heroics performed to escape the practice of carelessly contaminating good water with the wastes of the people served. This less palatable component of the saga—sewage contamination—was often ignored, not only in the telling, but in the actual course of events. The avoidance was the bad seed of repetitive water crises that often motivated the heroics. The same plot has been played out in America for at least a century and a half and is still the program of the water crisis at the end of the twentieth century.

In October 1844 a member of Boston's famous Channing family wrote and published a long, passionate letter entitled "A Plea for Pure Water." Walter Channing began by saying, "Perhaps at no time in the history of this long vexed question, has the public want of water been so deeply and widely felt, or so strongly expressed. It has reached all classes, and is daily becoming more pressing and more emphatic."

Boston's water, he explained, was neither pure nor plentiful, and both quantity and quality were dropping. With the exception of a minor supply by a decrepit aqueduct from Jamaica Pond, the city's water came from springs. As the springs were lowered from heavy use, they suffered infiltration of seawater from Boston Harbor. The intrusive sea not only introduced dissolved salts and thus hardness to the springs, but it returned the city's sewage dumped into the harbor.

"It will not combine with soap," Channing complained of

the contaminated spring water, "but decomposes it, and so is only made more impure by the soap mixed with it. It cannot be used for washing either the skin or the clothes of people. . . .

"Then for cooking, how wholly unfit is our spring water. . . . It hardens the meat you attempt to boil in it. It alters the character of vegetables, often making them unpalatable, hard and heavy, and so difficult of digestion, and unfavorable to the health."

As the polluted sea found its way into Boston's springs, so did the leakage of badly constructed sewers—"gutters beneath the surface," said Channing, claiming they carried "the whole filth of the city." He felt the earth was impregnated with sewage and illustrated by telling of how "a very valuable mineral spring somewhat suddenly burst up into a well, in Hawkins street." Thousands came to see and drink from the celebrated spring, and many were "cured of very grievous maladies"—until it was discovered that the source was a leaky sewer and "that some serious mistake must have been made concerning the medicinal qualities. . . ."

The abandonment of Boston's springs increased demands on Jamaica Pond. The Aqueduct Company overextended its already leaking pipes, and consumer supplies dwindled to dribs and drabs. Even wealthy Bostonians sat with candles in their dank cellars late into the night, waiting to catch the trickles that might come down the wooden service pipes from the aqueduct.

Channing said Boston should get on with the solution that he claimed was obvious: build more aqueducts to the sources of untainted supplies outside the city, plentiful enough for both drinking needs and flushing away the city's wastes—which Channing claimed "directly promotes health and longevity and . . . tends to diminish pauperism." He thereby recommended what would become a main element in developing the water supplies of the whole nation: seek good and bountiful sources as far away from your own wastes as possible—a maxim followed in Denver.

The Massachusetts capital abandoned its springs and began a long series of out-of-town water acquisitions. A century after Channing's plea, in the greatest single project of that effort, Boston impounded the entire flow of a 186-square-mile watershed 60 miles west of the city. The 16-mile-long Quabbin Reservoir, which took up 74,886 acres in 3 counties and 12 towns, was the main structure in the project. The towns of Enfield, Greenwich, Dana and Prescott were completely eliminated, and the remains of 7,606 persons in 35 cemeteries were moved during construction. The Quabbin increased the Metropolitan Water District's safe yield from 133 million to 330 million gallons a day. But with most of another half century past, Boston's water still remains in trouble. Oddly enough the problems are amazingly similar to those described in Channing's complaint. Both water and sewer lines are leaking badly, the supply is close to falling short, and officials continue thinking in terms of Channing's solution, to look for new supplies outside the city. They are doing so with a multimillion-dollar, highly controversial study that, among other possibilities, considers diverting 72 million gallons per day of the Connecticut River into the Quabbin Reservoir via a 10-mile aqueduct.

And as Boston has gone so has the historical course of water supply in much of the nation. The case of New York City is probably cited more than any other metropolis. Like Denver's and Boston's, New York's water first came from springs and wells that were spoiled by human wastes—until 1842, when the city celebrated delivery of water from the Croton River 40 miles away. From there the outreach extended until supply lines touched the headwaters of the Delaware River basin, and an interstate commission had to be assembled to advise on how to divide up the basin's waters among New York City, Philadelphia and other communities in New York State, Pennsylvania and New Jersey. But no matter how far out the great waterworks of New York were stretched, increasing consumption kept the city on the heels of a water shortage, especially when droughts dropped the reservoir levels. The condition became so bad in 1950 that a professional rainmaker, Dr. Wallace E. Howell, was hired to seed clouds with dry ice from aircraft and to introduce silver oxide smoke from the ground. Torrential rains fell upon the reservoirs' watersheds—sending nearby residents to court over the flood damages—and Dr. Howell proudly took the credit, claiming he had increased rainfall 14 percent. Whatever the cause, the reservoirs recovered—until the next and the next of many such crises.

FUTURE WATER

For sheer expansiveness in reaching out for water, no area can compare with southern California. In 1900 Los Angeles's 102,000 citizens obtained their water from the Los Angeles River and local wells, which were soon unfit for public supply. The answer was a remarkable 233-mile aqueduct delivering water from the Owens River on the eastern slopes of the Sierra Nevada. The flow from the Owens seemed ample enough to supply both Los Angeles and agricultural irrigation of the San Fernando Valley. But that was a bad estimate, for population growth, as well as crops, was stimulated by the water, so much so that in about a dozen years the city annexed over 250 square miles to provide for the influx of people. Los Angeles engineers went back to the Owens River for additional diversions, but were fought off by watershed residents. The water seekers were then accommodated by the Colorado River basin and construction of two great impoundments, the Hoover Dam, the then highest dam on earth, and the downstream Parker Dam, which formed a storage reservoir for the California supply. On June 17, 1941, the first water from Colorado arrived in southern California through the 242-mile, $220 million Colorado River Aqueduct. The cost was shared by a consortium of communities that formed the Metropolitan Water District of Southern California.

Again the new flow—four times that of the aqueduct from the Owens—was a growth stimulant; and the population of Los Angeles shot upward, doubling in three decades, while surrounding areas tripled. In the first of these decades the water district spread out its lines to include San Diego, Long Beach, Pasadena and numerous smaller communities. By 1950 the district supplied 4 million people, and the main line of the Colorado River Aqueduct plus the distribution network totaled 672 miles. It was the largest single water system on earth and could deliver 1 billion gallons of water a day. But then a return to the same old story: more water was needed, so the engineers lengthened their old Los Angeles Aqueduct to the Owens River with a 100-mile extension to the Mono basin, added another barrel to the original main line and increased the supply back home.

In California the struggle for water goes on forever. No sooner is one immense problem solved than a bigger one arises. In a 1964 decision of the Supreme Court of the United States,

Arizona v. *California,* Arizona won rights to a big share of the Colorado River water that flows westward to southern California. It will be diverted eastward upon completion of the Central Arizona Project, a long series of aqueducts from the Colorado to the Phoenix-Tucson area. Thirsty Californians of the south will then, they hope, have their lost waters replaced by supplies from the northern, wetter end of their state. The southbound flow will be carried by still another great distribution system, known as the State Water Project.

Such changes in waterworks are perpetual. In 1951 the Irrigation Districts of California published an illustrated, topographical map showing the state's water developments. In less than 20 years the map had to be revised five times to stay current with the complex of massive changes imposed upon the face of the earth by the state's increasing tangle of canals, aqueducts, dams and reservoirs.

Even as waterworks engineers were beginning to astound the nation with their feats of outreach at the turn of the century, evidence was accumulating that this way to untainted sources was not enough to guarantee safe drinking water for consumers. A tragic piece of evidence had developed in 1885 from a most unlikely place, Plymouth, Pennsylvania, in the Appalachians on the eastern side of the state. The town supply was thought to originate from the best possible of sources, fast-flowing, self-purifying mountain streams entering the public reservoirs. But that spring, Plymouth was hit by a horrible epidemic of typhoid fever. Of 8,000 citizens, 1,200 were stricken and 130 died. The typhoid germs had come to town with the mountain water, which had remained clear and odorless throughout the crisis. The origin of the epidemic was traced to a single case of typhoid in a lone dwelling on a distant mountainside. The house stood next to one of the streams leading to the Plymouth water supply.

The tragedy occurred only three decades after drinking water had been implicated in the spread of disease, and practically at the time when the germ theory of disease was established. In the 1850s one of the most famous studies in the history of epidemiology was published, showing that cholera could be transmitted by polluted water. Dr. John Snow found that people using the contaminated Broad Street pump in London were subject to cholera more than nonusers. Snow also studied the cholera incidence associated with two water companies, serving neighboring customers through separate mains in the same area of London. He found that customers of the company drawing water from the Thames at Battersea—in the middle of London, where many sewage discharges entered the river—suffered an unusually high incidence of the disease. Their neighbors buying from the second company enjoyed an unusually low incidence of cholera, but their Thames water came from upstream of the discharges. Snow's work was most impressive because it came decades before Louis Pasteur, Robert Koch and others established the germ theory of disease.

While cholera never struck hard at the United States, typhoid fever did. Through the latter half of the nineteenth century and first decades of the twentieth, typhoid was an American nightmare. The horror of the disease was characterized in 1888 by a committee of the American Public Health Association: "Uncertainty hangs over us like a cloud. Danger is as present with us in the daily routine of our peaceful lives as on the battle-field, only that embodiment of evil is an invisible and intangible germ instead of a fast-flying bullet. Danger flows beside us in our streams, in our mains, from the taps in our houses. The germ of the disease may not be in this pitcherful or in that, in this tumberful or in that, but it will find us some day if we continue to use the water which contains it."

At the root of this evil was the haphazard—for that matter, insane—manner in which the nation handled its growing volumes of sewage. While great engineers stood front and center to be praised for astounding accomplishments in supplying citizens with potable water, they had little reason for exultation down at the sewage end of the water line. Here the motto was "Out of sight, out of mind."

The least expensive, gravity-assisted way to live by the motto was to dump the town's sewage into the nearest river—downstream, of course, as they did at Denver with the Platte. The nauseating mix could then be put out of mind, in the belief that the river would dilute the waste and banish it from existence in a few hundred or thousand yards of flow. But the fallacy of this assumption was written in the death statistics of cities and towns sharing the same rivers for both water supply and sewage disposal. The once grand Ohio River, flowing from Pittsburgh to the Mississippi, was a prime victim of the fallacy.

Pittsburgh drew its water from the Allegheny and Monongahela rivers, which converge in the city to form the Ohio. In its 283 miles the Allegheny received the sewage of 53 cities with populations of 1,000 to 25,000. The shorter Monongahela entered Pittsburgh with the sewage of 33 cities. The big industrial metropolis then withdrew the unsavory mixture for its water supply—and in a three-year period after the turn of the century, according to a local newspaper's estimate, the treatment of typhoid fever cost $3,335,000. Then Pittsburgh did unto its downstream neighbors what others upstream had done to it: dumped the sewage of a quarter-million people into the top of the Ohio. Hundreds of miles downstream Louisville, Kentucky, drew its water from the burgeoning mix of river and sewage. One commentator pointed out that "some four and a half million people send sewage to Louisville!"—from Cincinnati, Pittsburgh and hundreds of smaller communities on the big stream and its tributaries. And one of America's most beautiful rivers became known as "a thousand miles of typhoid."

At the time hundreds of growing population centers were caught in a double bind by the linear pattern their engineers had adopted for water supply and sewage disposal. Ridding one place of its sewage devastated the health of another. Fulton, New York, for example, began discharging sewage to the Oswego River around 1900, and the typhoid rate of Oswego County more than quadrupled, from 20 to 90 deaths per 100,000, between 1895 and 1905.

Across the country rivers called upon to supply increasing volumes of domestic water were simultaneously depended upon for carrying off expanding loads of sewage. A chart presented to the 1908 White House Conference on the Conservation of Natural Resources showed the high correlation between typhoid fever deaths and the use of polluted riverwater for drinking purposes. Between 1902 and 1906 the mean death rate from the disease in 19 river-supplied cities was 61.6 per 100,000 people. Pittsburgh, with 120 deaths per 100,000, topped the list, which included Wheeling, Harrisburg, Philadelphia, Cincinnati, Richmond, Toledo, New Orleans and Seattle.

While these communities were plagued by sewage from upstream, the cities and towns bordering the Great Lakes were beset with their own sewage mingling with their own water supplies. The lakes were bountiful sources of pure water, but gravity and municipal habit meant that wastewater was most easily disposed of right back in the lakes. To keep the bad away from the good, cities like Cleveland spent millions of dollars driving tunnels out and under the Great Lakes to draw in fresh bottomwater free from sewage contamination.

Chicago's ultimate solution was different and the most dramatic of all. As the city grew, and shallow wells and outdoor privies were abandoned in favor of public water and sewerage, the city was plagued by cholera, typhoid fever and dysentery. Public sewage was discharged to the Chicago River, which flowed into Lake Michigan. For clean water Chicago tunneled under the lake beyond the pollution, only to have the increasing volumes of contamination migrate to the water intakes. New tunnels to more distant points suffered the same fate—and the death rate from waterborne diseases increased. Then on August 2 and 3, 1885, more than six inches of rain fell upon the city, washing all its filth into the sewers and on into the Chicago River. The stream belched forth a black, disease-ridden mass of pollution, and it engulfed the city's newest water intakes, two miles from shore. The public outcry led to what has been described as one of the engineering wonders of the world.

The big, burly midwestern city actually reversed the flow of the Chicago River by connecting it to the Des Plaines River via a 28-mile canal. The channel, 160 feet wide and 24 feet deep, was excavated by over 8,000 workmen laboring from 1892 to 1900. In moving more than 40 million cubic yards of earth and rock, the Chicago engineers developed new machines and techniques that were said to have made feasible the digging of the Panama Canal in the next decade. The project attracted thousands of tourists, who rode out from the city on excursion trains to see the mammoth steam shovels, dredges, derricks, hoists and rubber belt conveyors carve out the canal that would transport Chicagoans' sewage away from their drinking water. On January 16,

1900, the appropriate gates were opened and water from Lake Michigan flowed into the Chicago River, down through the new canal to the Des Plaines, on into the Illinois River and finally to the Mississippi just above St. Louis. Besides ridding Chicago of its wastewater, the new channel was designed so ships could navigate between Lake Michigan and the Mississippi. Interestingly enough, the sewage-laden canal followed the route portaged by Louis Joliet and Father Jacques Marquette two centuries earlier. Because of its dual role the channel was named the Sanitary and Ship Canal.

But while the project sanitized Chicago by draining away the sewage from some 2 million people, the contrary was the case for the downstream recipients. In the five years following completion of the canal, the typhoid fever death rate in St. Louis increased 73 percent. The following year, 1906, found the city at the Supreme Court of the United States with a case against Chicago's canal. But St. Louis lost and was forced to go on suffering the Windy City's sewage, along with discharges from dozens of Mississippi River towns all the way up to Minneapolis and St. Paul.

America finally emerged from the nightmarish decades of typhoid crises, but the solution was not to rid the rivers of sewage —which was the proposal of the circular-system proponents, who were introduced earlier. The answer was to filter and disinfect the fouled waters until they were free of the typhoid germs. One of the earliest successes at filtration was the result of experiments at Lawrence, Massachusetts, where typhoid deaths were exceptionally high. The research enabled Hiram F. Mills to develop and install a filter for the city's water in 1893, and in the next five years the typhoid death rate dropped 79 percent compared to the previous five years. Public filtration, which became known as water treatment, was improved and widely adopted across the country. In most systems the water seeped, or was forced, down through beds of sand. The filters became more and more effective, so that in 1910 a survey of 78 American cities showed that typhoid deaths were down to 20.5 per 100,000 from a ratio of 58 per 100,000 found in an earlier survey of 47 American cities.

In 1908 the typhoid germs that had threatened Americans for decades were dealt another blow when a small quantity of bleaching powder (chlorine) added to a reservoir serving Jersey City, New Jersey, sharply reduced the bacteria count of the water. Research then revealed that large colonies of bacteria could be wiped out by chlorine in amounts so small as to have no serious odor or taste problems. Most important, the minute quantities appeared to have no health effects on human consumers of the water. Disinfection of Philadelphia's water supply was initiated in 1910 with liquid chlorine, and the practice spread quickly around the country. With it the typhoid death rate soon dwindled to a meaningless statistic.

The end of the nightmare was measured not only by a declining death rate, but by a new testing procedure. Until the early days of the twentieth century, the criteria for judging the safety of drinking water were simple and long-standing: taste, odor, color and the most reliable of all, "Does it cause sickness or death?" With improved understanding of the germ theory and microscopy, a more scientific assay of water was developed. It was a count of fecal coliform bacteria, harmless organisms found in the large intestines of humans and animals. The count, made in water samples with a microscope, could warn of pollution by fecal matter, and thus of possible contamination by dangerous pathogens associated with sewage. The test, which could indicate that typhoid germs were present in water, was a propitious development that worked handily with the new water treatment technology. The fecal coliform count was widely adopted, and it became the primary test for safe drinking water—indeed, in practice, virtually the only test used on water supplies for the greater part of the century. However, it did not detect all the pathogens and poisons that may contaminate drinking water.

The effectiveness of filtration, disinfection and the coliform count in reducing typhoid fever was a triumph for the proponents of linear water supply systems. They now could claim there was no serious reason of health to prevent the disposal of sewage in the nation's streams and lakes, even in those serving as sole sources of water supply for the communities along their banks. It was a blow to the circular-system proponents, who wished to ban sewage disposal in natural waters in favor of sending the wastes back to the soil. Some of the victorious linear-system proponents now even discounted the need for sewage treatment works that would partially purify sewage before dumping it into the rivers—unless the works were essential for reasons other than health, such as pollution severe enough to kill fish or so obnoxious it would create a political ruckus.

The conviction that the miracles of technology had made possible the simultaneous use of rivers for drinking water and sewage disposal was found in the writings of Allen Hazen, a Bostonian who had become one of the world's leading authorities on water supply. In 1914 the second edition of his book *Clean Water and How to Get It* included a new chapter on disinfection of public water supplies. It was written, said Hazen, in light of the great advances made since publication of his first edition in 1908:

> It is . . . both cheaper and more effective to purify the water and to allow the sewage to be discharged without treatment, so far as there are not other reasons for keeping it out of the rivers. It seems unlikely that a single case could be found where a given and reasonably sufficient expenditure of money wisely made could do as much to improve the quality of a given water supply when expended in purifying sewage alone, as could be secured from the same amount in treating the water. Usually I believe that there would be a wide ratio: that one dollar spent in purifying the water would do as much as ten dollars spent in sewage purification.
>
> The water works man therefore must, and rightly should, accept a certain amount of sewage pollution in river water, and make the best of it. Taking it up in this way he will master the situation by purifying the water. Success in supplying good water cannot be otherwise reached.
>
> The general prospect of keeping all sewage out of rivers is attractive, and it will always have its earnest advocates, but it is not a practical proposition and it is not necessary. It is not even desirable, when the greater good to be secured by a given expenditure in other directions is taken into account.

Hazen's advice became the rule of the twentieth-century waterworks man. For many it still remains their maxim, even when the exotic, extensive contaminants of modern times make the continuation a folly.

III

The Furrow or the River

By the turn of the century "the sewage difficulty" had become an emotional topic for public speakers, novelists, journalists and pamphleteers in both America and Europe, for rivers from the Seine and the Thames to the Housatonic and the Mississippi had been turned into stinking, disease-ridden disasters with the free-for-all dumping of sewage. The public outrage had become explosive and authorities were looking for solutions to the ungodly mess.

They relied mainly on experts with the aseptic title of "sanitary engineer." At the top of their profession were men like Allen Hazen at the leading American center for research on water purification, the Lawrence (Massachusetts) Experiment Station, located on the badly polluted Merrimack River. These engineers were devoted to the creation of technology that could ensure the purity of the nation's developing water supplies and gain public acquiescence for the use of rivers for sewage disposal. They accepted the basic premise of linear supplies and strove to make it work.

At their heels was a small, fervid band of protestants, the proponents of circular supplies. They maintained that rivers should never be the receptacles of sewage. In making their case many spoke eloquently of human excretion, describing it as a God-given treasure that could only be wasted to the rivers and the sea at the risk of divine retribution. Along with support from such references as Deuteronomy 23:13–14 ("As part of your equipment have something to dig with, and when you relieve yourself, dig a hole and cover up your excrement. For the Lord your God moves about in your camp to protect you. . . . Your camp must be holy, so that He will not see among you anything indecent and turn away from you"), these people quoted, of all sources, Victor Hugo's *Les Misérables.* In the manner of nineteenth-century novelists, Hugo wrote a 6-part, 15-page description of the sewers of Paris, where his hero Jean Valjean was about to hide. It began with an impassioned plea for Paris to stop wasting its sewage to the sea, when science "after long experimentation" had proven that "the most fertilizing and the most effective of manures is that of man." The Chinese, added Hugo, "to our shame knew it before us. Thanks to human fertilization, the earth in China is still as young as in the days of Abraham."

"To employ the city to enrich the plain would be a sure success," the author proclaimed. "If our gold is filth, on the other hand, our filth is gold." And Hugo asked, ". . . these fetid streams of subterranean slime which the pavement hides from you, do you know what this is? It is the flowering meadow, it is the green grass, it is marjoram and thyme and sage, it is the satisfied lowing of huge oxen at evening, it is perfumed hay, it is golden corn, it is bread on your table, it is warm blood in your veins, it is health, it is joy, it is life."

But instead of enriching the earth, Hugo bemoaned, France was annually sweeping one hundred million francs worth of waste into the sea by way of its rivers. "The cleverness of man," he wrote, "is such that he prefers to throw this hundred million into the gutter. It is the substance of the people which is carried away . . . by the wretched vomiting of our sewers into the rivers, and the gigantic collection of our rivers into the ocean. . . . From this two results: the land impoverished and the water infected. Hunger rising from the furrow and disease rising from the river."

Victor Hugo was a forerunner to an emerging group protesting the public folly of destroying rivers at the expense of the land. The problem was taken up by royal commissions, leading engineers, architects and scientists, who invariably arrived at the same conclusion reached by the great French novelist. For example, the renowned English chemist and physicist Sir William Crookes wrote in his book *The Wheat Problem* that £16 million worth of fixed nitrogen was "annually lost to agriculture by the reckless discharge of sewage to our rivers and sea." He agreed with one of his contemporaries who complained that the collection and disposal of human waste was "making a sewer of the sea and a desert of the dry land." Such spokesmen were often dismissed by public authorities as impractical visionaries who would putrify the countryside by spreading the excremental odors and diseases of the city upon the fields. Victor Hugo denounced the critics: "You have the power to throw away this wealth, and to think me ridiculous into the bargain. That will cap the climax of your ignorance." Proof of their ignorance was soon found at a growing number of towns and cities where urban-rural cooperation was solving the sewage difficulty.

By 1890 anyone interested in how wastewater could be profitably applied to the land might visit any of a number of farms near the capital cities of England, France and Germany. The investigators were likely to return most impressed by four remarkable farms around Berlin.

When plans were first made for the sewering of the German metropolis, they called for the conventional discharge of wastewater to the Spree River, running roughly east and west through the city. The plan was rejected, and the Berlin city council turned to sewage irrigation. A collection system was built in two separate parts, and each carried wastewater away from the Spree to large farms outside the city, two at Falkenberg and Malchow to the north and two at Osdorf and Gross Beeren to the south. The four farms totaled 19,000 acres, which had been purchased by the city council.

Sewage was pumped from Berlin to storage ponds at the highest points of the farms. The ponds of 5 to 22 acres served two purposes: to absorb and store for slow release large gushes of stormwater flushed into sewers from city streets; and to store the normal flow of sewage when brief spells of winter cold interfered with irrigation. The ponded wastewater, with the worst of its solid ingredients settled out, was released as needed to extensive systems of irrigation ditches and thus distributed to croplands. After the irrigant had percolated down through the soil and nourished the roots of the plants, it was collected by small underdrainage pipes, which conducted the earth-filtered water by gravity flow to the lowest points of the farms. The effluent from the two northern farms moved via natural courses back to the

Spree in Berlin. The outflow from the southern farms found its way to the Havel River at nearby Potsdam.

The secret of the farms' success was scrupulous management, which was described as follows by an English civil engineer, Herman Alfred Roechling, who visited Berlin around 1890:

> Everything in connection with the irrigation of the land is done in military order; the day and night sewage-men parade at 6 A.M. and at 6 P.M. at an appointed place . . . whence after the calling of the roll and the examination of kit and tools, they march each to his particular district. Every man carries in a tin case over his shoulder a book containing minute directions of what he is to do, and what punishment he will get if he does not carry out his instructions. He must fill up a form attached to the book stating what sluice-valves he has opened during his shift . . . the time of opening and closing each, how many revolutions he gave to the spindle of each valve . . . and what plots he irrigated. . . . To Englishmen it might seem that such arrangements were over-elaborate, but in Berlin they work remarkably well.

The success of all this was measured by the sale of crops stimulated with the fertilizing nutrients from the wastewater, by the purity of effluent flowing back to the Spree and the Havel and by public acceptance of the farms as nuisance-free, healthy, attractive places to work at, visit and live by.

The irrigated crops included hay for the farms' cattle, wheat, barley and oats, as well as root crops and vegetables like turnips, potatoes, carrots and cabbages. Proceeds from the sale of produce in Berlin offset, or nearly offset, the large capital investment for the four-farm system.

The crops thrived on the irrigation for one obvious reason—they were thoroughly watered—and one less obvious reason—they were well treated to the primary elements of fertilizer (nitrogen, phosphorus and potassium), and many "micronutrients." These ingredients were, in a sense, back from town, returning to work on the farm. They were nutrients that had once been taken up by the roots of growing plants, which had then been consumed as food and returned with the sewage to fertilize more crops.

And thus around and around the food chain they traveled in a cycle ordained by nature. At Berlin this cycle was completed to the advantage of the city, its citizens, the farms and especially the rivers. The conventional use of the rivers for sewage disposal would have wasted the valuable nutrients to the seas. At Berlin the water with the waste filtered out by the farms came back to the rivers, adding to, instead of polluting, the potable supply.

The farms' visitors became aware that effluent drawn directly from the underdrains was safe drinking water. The earth and plants had not only taken up the nutrients, but had also filtered out the undesirable ingredients of public wastewater and used them to improve the soil. On his several visits to the farms the English engineer, Roechling (referring to himself in the third person), was impressed by the effluent. "The water was in almost every case perfectly clear and transparent," he reported, "and only in one or two instances could the author notice a slight, earthy smell. In Gross Beeren he was informed that, during 1886, 80 good-sized pike were caught in effluent ditches. Had he not known that the streams contained the effluent from the farms, he would have been unable to detect it, as there was absolutely no trace of contamination . . . and . . . it cannot be distinguished by the senses from clear spring water."

Roechling noted at Malchow that six ponds made of the effluent from some 500 irrigated acres were stocked with various species of fry. When the fish were harvested, the sewage authorities of Berlin received a prize from the German Fishing Club.

Many of the visitors, still skeptical of such good reports, went to the farms expecting to find expanses of odoriferous filth worked by sickly men suffering the zymotic maladies of the city. The opposite was true. There was no odor. The rich beauty of the fields bordered by roads with over 70,000 fruit trees attracted hundreds of Sunday visitors from the city, who came to see four of the most beautiful, bountiful farms in Germany. And the greatest surprise of all was the good health of the workers. Indeed, many were "misdemeanants," whom Roechling described as "men impoverished in health by bad and irregular habits of life," but working on the farms seemed to improve their health.

As the four projects developed, concerned authorities kept careful records of the sicknesses and deaths among the hundreds of workers and their families, who lived on the farms, ate from their produce and drank from wells dug on the sites, and, in the case of field hands, from the effluent of the irrigated plots. The conclusion was that these rural handlers of urban sewage were as healthy as, if not healthier than, the population producing the waste. Moreover, the health studies could never trace the causes of farm illness and deaths to illnesses in the city. This was dramatically illustrated one time when typhoid fever struck eastern and northern Berlin, the first epidemic in the many years since establishment of the farm system. The expected failed to happen: not a single case occurred on the farms using the sewage that was unquestionably contaminated with the dread disease. Understandably the farms gained the reputation of being among the healthiest places around Berlin. So convinced were the authorities of their healthful ambience that they built four convalescent homes, one on each farm. The institutions had a total of 286 beds, and the water for the convalescing patients came from wells on the properties.

The visitors to Europe's remarkable purification farms found another one on the Plain of Gennevilliers north of Paris. Not long after the publication of *Les Misérables* a relatively small portion of Parisian sewage was pumped to Gennevilliers and to a farm that eventually covered 2,000 acres. It more than confirmed Victor Hugo's high hopes for application of sewage to the land.

One of America's leading authorities on sewage disposal, George W. Rafter, visited the French farm in 1894 and declared it was "perhaps, on the whole the most successful case of profitable utilization in agriculture to be found anywhere." The American engineer went on to report, "The crops grown under sewage irrigation at Gennevilliers have been successful in the highest degree. They comprise absinth, artichokes, asparagus, beans, beets, cabbage, carrots, celery, kohlrabe, cucumbers, leeks, melons, onions, parsnips, peppermint, potatoes, pumpkins, spinach, tomatoes, turnips, clover, rye grass, mangolds, wheat, oats and Indian corn." Rafter stressed there was nothing puny about any of this produce: stalks of corn 9 to 10 feet high, great cabbages running more than 34 tons per acre, carrots over 22 tons per acre and mangolds 53 tons per acre. The crops sold in Parisian markets made the farms a profitable venture, a highly unusual result for the business of sewage treatment, which was ordinarily a total loss, with polluted water to boot. Rafter was also convinced that effluent from the French farms was perfectly safe to drink, as his report revealed: "The author visited the Plain of Gennevilliers on a rather warm day in December, 1894. The effluent was bright and sparkling and as he was exceedingly thirsty after a long walk he had no hesitation in dipping up water from the effluent channel and drinking it, the gentlemen accompanying him having made the positive assurance that no harm would result therefrom."

Rafter also visited England, where, he concluded, there were more sewage-purification works than in any other country. They included all the technological methods of purification then known, but Rafter stated that "the consensus of opinion . . . was decidedly in favor of the land purification process." He was surprised to find that the Royal Agricultural Society awarded prizes for the best sewage farms, and competition was keen. Visiting farms at Beddington, Leamington, Birmingham and Doncaster, the American engineer found results comparable to Berlin's (which Rafter had also visited). The irrigated acreage produced a wide variety of grain and root crops. As elsewhere, the effluent was like springwater and there were no health or odor problems. At Beddington the visitor found beautiful country homes on roads through and around the 525-acre farm. Rafter talked to one of the owners, who had arrived there 25 years before, rented and then bought the property, explaining that the sewage-irrigated croplands did not injure the value of his holdings.

The visiting engineer left England convinced that land purification was by far the best way to treat sewage. "So overwhelming is this evidence," he concluded, "that we must in the future consider this part of the subject as what the lawyers call res adjudicata—a proposition absolutely settled and no longer to be called in question."

On returning home Rafter made a survey of American purification works, which he published in 1899. Compared to his earlier report from Europe, his new report indicated that sewage purification in America was seriously lagging and severe pollution of streams and of the Great Lakes was the result. He included numerous references to communities using land purification systems, but they were sad and minor examples compared to the exemplary works he had seen in Europe. The American projects were often located at insane asylums and poor farms, the first known attempt at sewage irrigation in the United States having been at the state insane asylum in Augusta, Maine. If any American land purification systems could compare to those in Europe, they were the ones at Brockton, Massachusetts, and Pullman, Illinois.

At Brockton some 30 irrigated acres produced a variety of crops, like peas, beans, tomatoes, sweet corn, cabbage and turnips. Rafter had learned that the previous season's pea crop had been very successful, and one of the city's leading hotels had bought the entire harvest. Plots of field corn had astonishing yields, as high as 144 bushels per acre. Nearby South Framingham, Massachusetts, also grew corn "with the greatest luxuriance" that brought exceptional prices, from $30 to $40 an acre. The effluent from this farm, which flowed into the Boston water supply, was "kept up to the proper standard of purity," said Rafter.

The farm at Pullman, Illinois, served the model town developed by the Pullman Palace Car Company 14 miles south of Chicago. The sewage irrigation works had been designed as an integral part of the community by Benezette Williams, a Chicago engineer. According to Rafter, the design, then 16 years old, was "in line with what is universally considered to be the best practice of the present day." While the Pullman farm was a model design that turned an 8 to 10 percent profit from the sale of produce in Chicago, its record was blemished when unpurified wastewater escaped from the system into nearby Lake Calumet, a source of ice for the big city to the north.

Rafter spoke sadly of the deficiency in what he felt was the best-designed system in the United States. "In view of the large experience gained elsewhere," he wrote, "failure to purify the sewage effluent at all times must, as has already been pointed out, be attributed to the management, rather than the method. . . . The American farms, generally speaking, have not realized their full agriculture capacity by reasons of defects in management." He added two recommendations: the United States needed to develop "a class" of managers specializing in the methods of sewage irrigation, and the management should be separate from local politics.

Later study and experience would show that more than good management was required to make the process, to become known as land treatment, succeed. Above all, a great deal of engineering attention was needed to provide year-round dependability and to take full advantage of the obvious benefits the European farms were beginning to demonstrate. Mainly the designers, who often developed their systems haphazardly under public pressure, failed to work out storage systems that could provide round-the-clock acceptance and controlled application of wastewater in all seasons of the year. The continuous flow of sewage had to be accommodated regardless of weather, temperature or any other condition that might demand the interruption of irrigation. In winter months European farm systems generally relied on the fact that town sewage remained above freezing and kept the soil free of frost, which could turn the surface into an impermeable crust, ruining its filtration capabilities. Of course, intense cold spells could, and often did, solidify the soil, and the farms were flooded with the unceasing flow of raw sewage. The unholy messes—particularly prevalent in America—tarnished their image, and the term "sewage farm"—a dubious description at best—was used to advantage by opponents promoting alternative ideas for purifying sewage. The demise of the farms, which was also the result of their being overrun by spreading suburbs, contributed to a defeat for their advocates, the circular-system proponents, and a victory for the linear-system advocates and their technological processes.

IV

Dilution, the Nonsolution

The engineering effort that might have made land treatment a widespread success went instead into the alternatives that channeled the nation's wastewater, as raw or partly purified sewage, into rivers and lakes. Chicago with its Sanitary and Ship Canal was a bellwether for the direction Americans would follow with their sewage. The canal was actually one of two alternatives studied by the city's Drainage and Water Supply Commission. Land treatment was the other, and two sites some 20 miles south of Chicago were considered. But the commission rejected the land alternative, claiming it would be impractical because of the need to level large expanses of farmland. With that the commissioners settled for one of the largest earth-moving projects in the history of the world. At a fraction of the cost and effort Chicago might have led the way with a land treatment system that could have demonstrated how the nation might use its wastewater as a resource without contaminating crucial water supplies.

Instead, American engineers became leaders in the development of technological means of sewage disposal in streams and lakes, including essential water supplies. The effort fitted comfortably into a growing sense that machines could be designed to solve almost any problem, water purification included. But replicating nature's process—and that was what the sewage engineers tried to do—turned out to be far more difficult than nature made it appear.

The difficulty was unintentionally demonstrated during the World's Colombian Exposition at Chicago in 1893. The fair's 6 million to 9 million gallons of sewage a day was run through a much-acclaimed treatment plant with tanks of sand acting as filters. The discharge flowed into Lake Michigan. But when the fair was over, Allen Hazen, who had personally operated the plant, admitted in the 1893 annual report of the Massachusetts State Board of Health that the system's filtration was inefficient.

The search for an effective filter continued for another 20 years. At first researchers thought the answer would be chemical precipitation, in which chemicals mixed with sewage caused sedimentation of the wastes so they could be easily removed. But when chemical precipitation plants were built in many communities, they failed. Meanwhile scientists at the Lawrence Experiment Station tried to understand how nature cleaned water when it percolated into the earth. After two years, with over 4,000 chemical analyses and countless microscopic examinations, they concluded that in addition to the purely mechanical removal of particles from dirty water, bacteria played a key role in the purifying process. The living organisms formed thin films on the surfaces of filtration material and enhanced purification. The process worked best if sewage was held in contact with the filmy surfaces for brief periods of time. And then it was recognized that the most purification occurred when the porous areas of the bacteria-laden material were thoroughly exposed to oxygen.

From this discovery came the trickling filter, a bed of coarse material, like crushed stone or clinkers, which was intermittently sprayed with wastewater and oxygenated with air blown from underneath. As the sewage trickled to underdrains, it contacted bacterial film formed on the filter material; the biological action removed a portion, but not all, of the pollutants. The trickling filter was widely adopted for sewage treatment and is still used in many American municipalities.

Other researchers felt the answer to relieving the obnoxious condition of sewage was to oxidize it by blowing air through the water. The idea was to stimulate bacterial activity that would stabilize the pollutants and cause them to settle out of the water as sludge. In 1914 two English engineers at the Manchester, England, sewage works explained how they had returned a small amount of sludge to the aeration tank from which it had come and found it "activated," and thus increased, the bacterial growth. This became the basis of the activated sludge process, the most widely used sewage treatment method of all, but it still did not completely purify sewage water. Moreover, it produced a great deal of sludge that had to be disposed of—by burial in landfills, by burning, or even by dumping into the water that the system was supposed to be keeping clean.

Activated sludge units became the second stage in what were known as primary-secondary treatment plants. In such a system the primary, or mechanical, component screened the liquid when it had entered and was being held briefly in a simple tank. Here some of the solids settled to the bottom of the tank, and eventually the accumulated sludge had to be removed. Meanwhile the "primary effluent" flowed from the tank on to the secondary, or biological, stage for further purification by an activated sludge unit.

With development of this process in 1915, conventional sewage treatment passed the major milestone of its history. Of course, refinements were made—tertiary stages were added to try to complete the water-cleaning process—but for practical, round-the-clock use, the designers of commercial-scale sewage treatment systems never matched the purification capabilities that most engineers knew existed in the common dirt under their feet. Sewage treatment by man-made technology was never a full measure. No one dared say the effluent was potable water because it still contained pathogens and a good portion of the chemical contamination. The chemicals included the fertilizing nutrients nitrogen, phosphorus and potassium, which could stimulate crops when applied to land, but which overstimulated aquatic growth (like algae, a contributor to pollution) when discharged to streams and lakes.

If these systems planners ever intended to clean up sewage enough to serve as potable water, their sights had been lowered long before. Instead, the goal was to keep the receiving waters of sewage tolerable to the public view and sense of smell, and, if they were pressed hard enough, acceptable to those who insisted on public bathing and fishing. The tolerance level also took account of public health, but not so far as to assure the health of anyone who drank directly from the receiving waters. Indeed, the standard tests for water pollution were adapted to these diminished goals and were essentially designed to measure the offensiveness of water, not its potability. The main test revealed whether or not the organic matter in sewage was demanding so much oxygen that biological life essential to water quality was choked to death. Technicians described the test as a measure of BOD (biochemical oxygen demand).

The diminished goal and standards to accommodate it allowed decision makers to keep the discredited practice of discharging sewage into natural bodies of water, although they dressed up their transgressions in formal, technical apparel and entitled it "dilution." They proposed that dilution alone could get rid of wastewater in many instances without any public nuisance, but if dilution alone was not enough, it could be helped by partially cleaning up the sewage before discharge. In this way thousands of water sources were consigned to remain nonpotable supplies that could be consumed by the public only if purified by costly water treatment plants.

In 1922 a leading textbook, *Sewage and Sewage Disposal,* by Leonard Metcalf and Harrison P. Eddy of Boston, led off its discussion of sewage treatment methods with a chapter entitled "Sewage Disposal by Dilution":

> The most natural method of disposing of sewage is to discharge it into the nearest body of water. This is called disposal by dilution. It is not a makeshift, but just as thoroughly a scientific process of purification as any other, if it is intelligently practiced within the safe limits of the digestive capacity of the water. When the processes of nature by which the water is kept inoffensive are overworked, the sewage-laden waters become offensive and it is necessary to treat the sewage in some way to assist the forces of nature which had previously prevented any nuisance—the primary object in studying methods of sewage treatment being to find ways of changing the character of sewage so that the effluents from the treatment works will neither cause offensive conditions nor be a menace to health when they are discharged into some body of water.
>
> If the floating matter alone is objectionable, it is necessary to remove that only. If deposits of suspended matter are the source of complaint, the removal of settling solids may be sufficient. Where dilution fails because of lack of oxygen, the treatment of sewage may be carried far enough to reduce its oxygen demand to the point where the natural water is able to provide an adequate supply of oxygen.

Metcalf and Eddy's prescription for sewage disposal—dilution with treatment if necessary to avoid obnoxiousness—was already the conventional approach to the problem. They pointed out that of an estimated 28 million American citizens served by public sewers in 1905, dilution alone took care of 96 percent of their raw sewage while only 4 percent was treated before discharge. Ten years later, the authors estimated, 84 percent of the sewage from nearly 42 million Americans was disposed of by dilution alone; thus the amount of treated wastewater had increased 12 percent. Regardless, the dilution prescription was not what a doctor would order for safe drinking water, but essentially a protective measure against the public ire that severe water pollution could unleash.

No matter how "thoroughly a scientific process of purification" the proponents might call it, dilution was fundamentally wrong, and American rivers rebelled at being enlisted as extensions to the nation's sewage systems. Water pollution became increasingly worse as the twentieth century wore on, so that a 1939 text on sanitation reported that the average river or stream in the United States was continuously and grossly polluted.

How serious the problem had become was evident in the 1941 report of a Philadelphia symposium on water pollution abatement in the Delaware River basin. As the Delaware approached Philadelphia, it contained raw and treated sewage from a series of upstream towns. It was a question whether the river diluted the sewage or the sewage the river. The dissolved oxygen so essential to the freshness of water dwindled to the vanishing point as the Delaware arrived at the City of Brotherly Love—which incidentally was adding 350 million gallons of raw sewage to the river daily. At the foot of Chestnut Street on a summer day, testers could find no oxygen at all in the water. The potent mixture ate the paint off the hulls of ships and corroded their brasswork and steel plates. Ships' engineers refused to take on the water for their boilers. They would not even use it as ballast for fear of injuring the crew's health. Shipping companies often refused to make this, "the largest freshwater port in the United States," a port of call, because the water was anything but fresh. But harbor workers had no choice. They were forced to stay and suffer the nauseating sewage odors. Meanwhile the morale and efficiency of shipyard workers in the new defense effort were "lessened by these pungent odors." No respectable fish would have been caught dead in this environment, so the once extensive fishing industry on the Delaware downstream from Philadelphia was all but gone.

Thus, in one of the most historic American cities, a few blocks from Independence Hall and off Penn's landing, Philadelphians and millions of visitors could see and smell the legacy of the linear proponents who had captured the right to integrate America's rivers into her sewage disposal systems. These "experts," who had opposed going back to the land with wastewater because of the unhealthy mess they claimed it would make, had themselves delivered the disaster predicted for the countryside to the downtowns of hundreds of American communities with waterfronts. Not only had they fouled what should remain the most beautiful, the most treasured amenity of a town, its river, but they had dumped the flushings of the population into their own water supplies. Dilution alone and dilution aided by treatment, bad ideas at best, were forever outstripped by the always increasing flows of wastewater. Dilution was but a frivolous way of saying pollution. At the water supply intakes on such rivers, treatment plants with filters, aeration machinery and chemicals were said to make the putrid water safe to drink, but the product was so tainted in taste and odor that consumers could understandably believe it was unsafe.

Perhaps the greatest pity of all was the loss of respect for one of our most valuable resources, our rivers. They were stigmatized as sewers and were treated accordingly. They attracted the town's dumpers, and others stood back, hiding behind their queasiness. The mountain-supplied South Platte in the heart of Denver was typical. At a six-acre riverside site that should have been a serene part of downtown Denver, the polluted Platte attracted a horrendously noisy automobile wrecking yard that chewed up discarded heaps and shipped the metal back to steel mills. Downstream a short distance, a railroad changed the oil of diesel engines at a spot where the black gunk could find its way into the South Platte. The city and county of Denver went to the river with everything from street sweepings to pumpings from storm sewers and heavily salted snow from the streets. Joe

Shoemaker, who was once Denver's manager of public works and later the head of a remarkable effort to clean up the Platte, saw the city's habit of dumping in the river as being "lodged there like the instincts of animals."

The sewage stigma had its influence on the sanitary engineers who were claiming the nation's natural waters should be part of their sewage works. As they developed professionally, they needed to publish technical papers on sewage research and on outstanding collection and treatment systems. But when they looked for a professional home, sanitary engineers were treated like pariahs. They found limited interest in such organizations as the American Society of Civil Engineers, the American Chemical Society and the American Public Health Association. The avoidance of sewage was most pronounced in the society that should have been most interested, the venerable American Water Works Association (AWWA). Its province, supplying safe water, was profoundly influenced by sewage disposal. But the AWWA didn't care to make the connection—as was illustrated by a magazine dispatch from the Association's 1927 convention. WATER WORKS ASSOCIATION STICKS TO WATER, announced the headline of an *Engineering News Record* story, which opened by saying: "That the American Water Works Association has all it can handle in its own field and therefore will not form a sewage section was decided at its Chicago Convention last week."

The rebuffs led to various local and state groups of sanitary engineers forming their own national organization in 1928. It was first called the Federation of Sewage Works Associations, and it published the *Sewage Works Journal.*

Over the next 20 years the organization's name often plagued the members. The word "sewage" was their albatross, and they frequently considered eliminating it from the association's title. However, they did not do so until prompted by an odd event in the late 1950s, when the federation's president, Mark Hollis, suffered from an embarrassing problem during a television interview in Dallas. The station had a list of words banned from its airwaves; "sewage" was one, and Hollis was unable to give the name of his organization. Shortly after that the title was changed to the Water Pollution Control Federation.

This caste system imposed upon the nation's linear water-supply systems, where the Brahmins were associated with the clean side and the pariahs with the unspeakable end of the line, had a significant impact on the state of water in America. It cultivated the public's complacent notion that there was a world of potable water and another separate and apart world of sewage. The kitchen faucet drew from the first world, and the toilet flushed into the second. The idea that the first might be drawing from the second was unthinkable to millions of Americans, although that was precisely what was happening. Their drinking water was really recycled sewage. Furthermore, the recycling systems ran counter to nature's and were not dependable. Given the increasing amounts and added potency of wastewater, millions of people were, in fact, being served some of the worst ingredients of their own sewage.

V

The Cancer Connection

If the American water crisis maturing in the 1980s had a birthday, it would be May 26. That day in 1965 marked the beginning of the end for a half century of self-satisfaction that the United States was one of the few nations on earth where safe drinking water was found everywhere in plentiful supply. Henceforth evidence would pile up exceedingly fast that our national water ethic, allowing the wanton mistreatment of sources and profligate consumption of supplies, was leading to one of the greatest resource crises of all.

On May 26, 1965, the director of public health for Riverside County, California, was warned by a group of pediatricians that they were seeing an unusual number of patients with severe gastroenteritis. The symptoms were diarrhea, abdominal cramps and, in the worst cases, bloody stools. A quick survey by the public health staff revealed that about 1,000 people had sought medical care for the problem in the past few days. In a matter of hours an investigation team was searching for the cause—which they first suspected was a new dry-milk product being introduced with free samples. But a telephone survey of patients quickly ruled that out. Other commonly consumed foods, like eggs and dairy products, were then systematically surveyed for the cause. Meanwhile the investigators virtually ignored the county's public drinking water—which served the city of Riverside and came from the purest of sources, wells driven deep into the earth. To suspect the water seemed useless, for it was a matter of history that epidemics spread by municipal water supplies had been eliminated long ago in America. Furthermore, team members were aware that fecal coliform counts were continuing to show that the Riverside supply was not contaminated.

As the days went by, the pressure for a solution increased because the epidemic was worsening. School absenteeism was double its average. Increasing numbers of patients complained of the intestinal malady at clinics, doctors' offices and the March Air Force Base dispensary. Then a quick demographic survey of the patients revealed that practically all of them lived within the city limits of Riverside. This finding forced attention to the water supply; it almost had to be the common denominator. Tests specific to the disease run on water samples from the city revealed the culprit, a certain type of salmonellosis. The test of coliform counts, which had continued to indicate the supply was safe, had missed the disease-producing contamination. Chlorinating the public wells ended the problem, but by then some 16,000 people had been stricken, 170 had been hospitalized and 3 had died. How the guilty pathogens had arrived in the wells remained a mystery.

The Riverside outbreak, like the typhoid epidemic at Plymouth, Pennsylvania, 80 years earlier, became a historic event in the annals of public health. It obviously surprised the nation's water and health officials. They had been resting on their laurels for nearly half a century, believing they had conquered the formidable enemy of epidemics spread by water. But discomforting surprises were only beginning.

Soon after Riverside two more disturbing events occurred. In 1968 a disinfection system failed in the water supply of Angola, New York, and another epidemic of gastroenteritis blemished the nation's record for good drinking water. But a year later a more dramatic event happened at Worcester, Massachusetts. With eight more games to go in the season, the College of the Holy Cross football team was suddenly put out of commission by infectious hepatitis. Following a weekend game with Dartmouth College, 20 players, including 7 starters, became ill with the viral disease. Blood tests showed that 55 other players were infected. In addition to the team itself, hepatitis struck down 7 coaches, 4 managers, the trainer and the college's sports information director. Homecoming was canceled and Holy Cross was beaten for the remainder of the 1969 season. The Dartmouth players feared they might have contracted the bug during the previous Saturday's game with Holy Cross, but they had not. Obviously the viral infection had been confined to the Holy Cross varsity team—and the reason became clear when Worcester public health officials traced the cause to a water fountain on the unlucky team's practice field. The fault turned out to be an ineffective "cross-connection control procedure," meaning that contaminated water had accidentally bypassed the city's treatment plant and found its way to the fountain on the varsity practice field.

As had been true with the gastroenteritis germ, the dangerous viral organisms were not detected by the standard coliform test that was so heavily relied upon to warn of health hazards in water supplies. At the time, tests for viruses had not been perfected for routine use. The problem was one of numbers. For approximately every 100,000 coliform bacteria in raw sewage there was only 1 virus. Detecting viruses meant searching for a few in great volumes of water, truly a matter of finding needles in haystacks. For example, one viral testing device, though cumbersome, was praised for its ability to search through 300 gallons of water per hour. Still, as lonely as viruses might feel per gallon, their national population was growing with the burgeoning flow of sewage. The likelihood of their getting into drinking water supplies was increasing.

In 1969, the year that Holy Cross was beaten so badly by these microorganisms, the Bureau of Water Hygiene, an agency under the Public Health Service of the United States, conducted a nationwide study on the status of drinking water in the country. In addition to a survey of quality, the Community Water Supply Study looked at facilities and bacteriological surveillance programs. The research covered 969 public supplies across the country, including the entire state of Vermont, seven relatively small areas around the nation and one fairly large section of southern California. The study sample, 5 percent of all public supplies in the nation, covered both surface and groundwater systems, serving about 18,200,000 persons. The sample was considered to be "reasonably representative of the status of the water supply industry of the United States." The results dealt one more serious blow to the smug idea that Americans could rest at ease with the assumption that pure water always flowed from their faucets—and a large portion of the study's test samples were, in fact, drawn from people's faucets.

Defects in quality and health risks were discovered everywhere the surveyors went. The deficiencies were found in big cities and small towns alike, but the most serious failures turned up in communities of less than 100,000 persons. Of all the systems studied, 41 percent were delivering water of an inferior quality, to 2.5 million consumers. Of these people, 360,000 were supplied with potentially dangerous water. In a part of the study where 2,600 samples were drawn from consumers' faucets, 36 percent were delivering water with one or more bacteriological or chemical constituents exceeding limits set by the Public Health Service. Nine percent were contaminated with bacteria potentially dangerous to consumers. The results translated statistically indicated that millions of Americans served by water utilities were not only receiving water of poor quality, but their health was jeopardized in the bargain. James H. McDermott, director of the Bureau of Water Hygiene, concluded, ". . . there can be little doubt that this situation warrants major national concern."

There were several reasons for the startling state of affairs. Among them was plain laxity. The Brahmins of water supply were not only resting on their laurels, but in many instances seemed to be asleep. More than half the water supply systems studied had physical deficiencies, like groundwater sources poorly protected from contamination, and inadequate capacity to disinfect public supplies. More than three quarters of the system operators were ill trained in fundamental water microbiology, and nearly half were deficient in chemical knowledge relating to their operations. The study showed that while consumers blithely assumed their drinking water was rigorously monitored for impurities, even rudimentary protective measures simply didn't exist in the vast majority of systems. In 85 percent of the cases, insufficient numbers of bacteriological samples were analyzed to ensure safe water. In over two thirds of the systems, not even half the sampling recommended by Public Health Service standards had been done.

Who represented the public here? Who were the guardians of the people's drinking water? Supposedly state and county authorities in most instances, but they seemed to be missing. More than three quarters of the systems studied had not been inspected by public health officials during 1968, the last full calendar year prior to the survey. In half the water supply plants, operators were unable to recall when a health department had last inspected their systems, if ever.

The study report, issued in July, 1970, made it clear that this was no time for such gross laxity. At best, water systems were generally old and lacking the capacity to serve America's growing population. The traditional opportunity to reach out for new sources was rapidly diminishing, and existing supplies were suffering from increased contamination all over the country. Even the nation's hallowed groundwater could no longer be trusted for purity. Nearly 10 percent of the wells sampled in the federal study were contaminated with coliform bacteria.

Worst of all, hazardous chemicals were turning up with increased frequency in both surface water and groundwater, reflecting the dramatic expansion of the chemical industry. New compounds, appearing everywhere from the farmer's furrow to the housekeeper's cleaning cupboard, were bound to find their ways down sinks, gutters and geological pathways to the water that people consumed. One authority said we had opened a "virtual Pandora's box of chemical agents." In 1970 industry was using about 12,000 different toxic chemical compounds, a number increasing by more than 500 per year. They posed the possibility of the homeowner opening a faucet for a glass of fresh water, only to be delivered a black widow cocktail mixed with the residue of some miraculous new cleaning fluid. The extended hangover could be death by cancer or genetic distortions of one's children. Such fates made a few feverish weeks of typhoid look desirable.

Against this formidable array of poisons and elusive diseases, the waterworks man was still betting on dilution, followed by tin-lizzy filters designed in an age when removal of coliform bacteria from relatively good water was a victory to brag about. But this level of accomplishment was no longer enough to cope with the exotic contaminants of water in the latter decades of the twentieth century. Surveillance and water treatment systems of World War I vintage might as well have been fishnets when it came to detecting and eliminating toxic compounds and viral organisms from drinking water.

Oddly enough, the Community Water Supply Study was done at a time when increasing sums of money and a great deal of attention were being devoted to clean water in America. But the big drive was to clean up the nation's filthy lakes and streams, and the people behind it seemed relatively unaware of the growing problems related to drinking water. They complained of "water pollution," and, as was frequently quipped, the health concern seemed to be more for fish than people. Certainly there was grievous water pollution. A walk beside nearly any river in the country offered evidence, with water choking to death from green algae blooms stimulated by the burgeoning sewage discharges. Cries of protest were coming from the powerful new environmental movement, and politicians were responding with antipollution money. In 1970 the flow of federal money to water pollution control was over $1 billion. Meanwhile the agency responsible for safe drinking water (now called the Office of Water Hygiene) had a total budget of only $2.8 million, and of that, only $235,000 went into research to improve the surveillance, treatment and distribution of water supplies. The disparity was an odd twist on the classic division separating the water people from the sewage people. The pariahs, now characterizing themselves as water pollution control experts, had practically become the Brahmins and were taking the largest sums ever spent in the name of clean water.

In 1971 the Congress of the United States conducted what were described as "the most exhaustive Congressional proceedings relating to an environmental issue in the history of the nation." And from them came the Federal Water Pollution Control Act Amendments of 1972. The goals and policies to be pursued by the new law were spelled out on its first page. The basic goal was for the discharge of pollutants to the nation's waters to be eliminated by 1985, with a mid-1983 interim goal of providing "for the protection and propagation of fish, shellfish and wildlife and . . . for the recreation in and on the water. . . ." The law made it national policy "that the discharge of toxic pollutants in toxic amounts be prohibited." And it was national policy "that Federal financial assistance be provided to construct publicly owned waste treatment works. . . ."

The lay reader of these lofty aims might have assumed that by 1985 the nation's waters would be pure enough to drink directly from their sources, but a close look at the 1972 law revealed no goals for drinking water quality. Strange as the layman might find it, the question of water to drink was addressed by another, contemporary set of federal measures—again displaying the idea that there was a separate world of water from that troubling the fighters of sewage pollution. Indeed, in May, 1971, as Senate hearings were being held on water pollution control, the House of Representatives was conducting hearings on two almost identical pieces of "safe drinking water" legislation. Both addressed concerns stirred up by the debacles at Riverside, California; Angola, New York; and Holy Cross, and by the Community Water Supply Study. And both measures would bring the force of federal law into the business of ensuring safe drinking water for American consumers.

Members of the House Subcommittee on Public Health and Environment were warned that the nation's water suppliers were generally unaware of the effects newly discovered contaminants could have on the health of present and future generations. Instead of confronting and dealing with these dangers, the congressmen were warned, the nation was allowing public water supplies to deteriorate until human illness forced officials to find remedies. This trend was condemned as immoral because of the "involuntary use of citizens for bioassay."

Oddly, the most relaxed witnesses at the hearings were representatives of the utilities most responsible for supplying safe drinking water. They opposed federal regulations of their industry, arguing that public supplies were generally in good hands and the best antidote for faults in purity was publicity to stir up public protests. If there had to be government regulation, the waterworks representatives felt, state laws were ample. The only trouble with the states, they claimed, was inadequate staff work, and that offered the opportunity for the only federal intervention they would condone: sending money for upgrading staffs. But even if the states fell down on the job, the private water suppliers had no great worries because they would fill the gaps, they said.

This line of testimony came from the foremost water supply organization of all, the American Water Works Association, representing some 30,000 water utilities serving more than 175 million citizens. The AWWA's executive director, Eric Johnson, was asked how he would expect an aroused public could deal with cases of hazardous water delivered by the utilities. "Well, in places," he replied, "local committees, that is, people, get concerned. The League of Women Voters is a very strong organization in the local community to organize an effort.

"I think I would fire the local water superintendent and hire a new one, and certainly the city council can, in most places, take care of this and see that the job is done.

"I think the strongest political advantage the local mayor or council can have is a good water utility, and I do think we ought to use this [for enforcement]."

If Johnson's reply lacked the ring of conviction, it was possibly because his organization felt the nation's problems of water contamination were minimal, that they were under control by utilities kept in line by state surveillance, such as it might be. He admitted that the federal government had a lot more power to correct water problems than did his association, but claimed national intervention wasn't needed because ". . . we don't feel there is a real crisis as far as water supply is concerned at the present time, despite the Community Water Supply Study." He felt there could be such a crisis in ten years, and that research and training money provided by the legislation at hand could help avert it—but no thanks if the funds had to come with federal teeth enforcing national standards.

Johnson had been preceded in the hearings by that year's AWWA president, Thurston E. Larson. He was also sanguine about the state of America's drinking water, despite the growing evidence that quenched the optimism of others. After listening to Larson, an incredulous congressman, Tim Lee Carter of Kentucky, remarked, "I notice that you are not alarmed by the chemicals or viruses which have been found in water throughout the United States. Is that true?"

"We are concerned," replied Larson, who, in his regular job, had worked for the Illinois State Water Survey for nearly 40 years, "but I'm not personally particularly alarmed. . . ."

"You have not been to the right places," the congressman chided, "because many of the water supplies are not as pure as they should be, and I believe if you will go a little bit further you will find this to be true. Personally, I think that we must emphasize more the standards and the purity there."

"We don't deny this," said the association president. "We do have some supplies that are not up to snuff."

The relaxed outlook—helped by vigorous lobbying—soothed enough members of Congress to keep any safe drinking water bill from becoming law for three years. Such a measure did make it through the Senate, but it only gathered dust in the House of Representatives. However, something happened on November 7, 1974, that caused the House staff members to blow off the dust so the legislation could be promptly considered on November 18, when Congress returned from recess.

On that November 7 the Environmental Defense Fund, based in Washington, D.C., released a study revealing that high cancer death rates in Louisiana were statistically related to drinking water obtained from the Mississippi River. The environmental organization had undertaken the study for two reasons: (1) earlier investigations had shown the riverwater, even after conventional treatment, contained traces of cancer-causing chemicals, and (2) 9 Louisiana parishes (counties) had been listed among 45 cities and counties with the nation's highest cancer death rates for white males. Furthermore, Louisiana offered the opportunity of comparing the consumers of riverwater with those supplied from wells.

The defense fund research showed that the deaths from cancer could be associated with drinking chemically tainted water. The report claimed, "The statistical analysis in this study provides the first evidence in this country, to our knowledge, that carcinogens in drinking water are in sufficiently high concentrations to endanger human health."

A most disturbing offshoot of the study was the implication that chlorination of drinking water might be a cause of human cancer. The suggestion came from finding more chloroform in the chlorinated drinking water from the Mississippi than the river itself contained—and chloroform was a known carcinogen in rats and mice, and potentially in humans. How did so much of the dangerous compound get into the chlorinated water? It was known that free chlorine acting upon certain organic compounds produced by decaying vegetation (which could be found in surface water, such as rivers) formed other organic compounds identified by the tongue twister "trihalomethanes." Chloroform was a trihalomethane usually found in high concentrations. Putting this evidence together now made chlorination—the great, widely used protector of the public health since 1908—a suspected cause of cancer.

Within 24 hours the U.S. Environmental Protection Agency ordered a nationwide study of chemical contamination of drinking water. The EPA also explained that a study already completed had shown 66 chemicals were present in the Mississippi River water used by New Orleans and nearby communities. And the EPA revealed that such chemical contamination had been found in surface drinking water supplies all across the United States.

If the word "typhoid" had political impact around the turn of the century, it was only a wisp of that produced by the word "cancer" in 1974. The reaction reached a crescendo in the ten November days before Congress returned from recess. Meanwhile opponents of the safe drinking water bill issued their battle cry once more. Robert B. Hilbert, then the AWWA president, charged that the nation's water supply was being "impugned" by the report from Louisiana. Repeating his Association's thesis, Hilbert said there was no crisis, that hasty action could bring massive and unwanted federal intervention into water utilities. The federal role, he reiterated, should be limited to research and training and kept out of surveillance and enforcement.

This time Congress did not listen, and the day after members returned from recess the House passed the Safe Drinking Water Act by 296 to 84. To avoid any chance of a pocket veto by President Gerald Ford after Congress had adjourned for the year, the Senate and House quickly reconciled the differences between their measures, and the legislation went to the White House, where the President signed it into law a few days later.

The final product had a number of teeth dreaded by the water utilities. For example, citizens were guaranteed the right to bring suits against public systems that failed to provide safe water. And in turn the law mandated that officials of public waterworks had to notify the media and consumers whenever purity dropped below federal standards.

Dr. Robert Harris, the author of the Environmental Defense Fund study in Louisiana, saw the results and ensuing legislation as a landmark in the history of water supply. In a television interview Dr. Harris explained, "Disclosures in New Orleans regarding cancer-causing chemicals in drinking water [were] really the first battleground [where] drinking water and water pollution came face to face with public health problems in this country."

VI

The New Direction Not Taken

On October 18, 1972, champagne corks were popping on Capitol Hill as members of the U.S. Senate and House of Representatives, their staffs and others celebrated passage of the great, new clean water law, PL 92-500, the Federal Water Pollution Control Act Amendments of 1972. That day Congress had overridden President Richard Nixon's veto of the bill.

Those celebrating believed we finally had a law that could be used to clean up America's water. Since passage of the Water Pollution Control Act of 1948, a series of new acts and amendments had gradually increased the federal role in dealing with the ever more serious pollution of streams and lakes. Now the amendments of 1972, setting a 1985 goal for clean water across America, gave the federal government the dominant role in controlling water pollution.

But more important, the amendments called for a dramatic change in direction to reduce pollution. The father of the new law, Senator Muskie, had explained the change on submission of the bill to the full Senate, saying, "These policies . . . simply mean that streams and rivers are no longer to be considered part of the waste treatment process." One of the chief drafters of the amendments, Thomas C. Jorling, said it meant that "we must apply our technological genius to achieve recycling, or to confine pollutants so our water will be restored to the role that nature intended." The law looked like the death warrant for dilution.

The celebration was not only premature, it revealed the celebrants' naïveté. Dilution was not dead. The country's sanitary engineers proceeded as if the only difference made by the new law was the immense amounts of money it authorized to do the same old thing. For example, in Connecticut two years after the 1972 amendments were passed, a proposed new plan for water supply indicated that with minor exceptions the state's rivers were not to be used for drinking water because they had to continue as wastewater-receiving streams. They could possibly serve for recreation, but not for human consumption. Connecticut's top water-pollution control official, a sanitary engineer in the classic mold, simply did not take seriously the new direction set by Congress—nor did his counterparts in other states and, indeed, in the very agency administering the new law, the EPA. In the few years of its life, the agency had filled up with traditionalists.

A similar fate befell the Safe Drinking Water Act of 1974. Two and a half years after its passage, the law's impact was appraised by Nicholas Wade of *Science* magazine. Alluding to the Louisiana study that had prompted the legislation, Wade asked what difference the law had made about the way New Orleans was treating its water supply from the Mississippi.

"Absolutely nothing!" replied Dr. Robert Harris, author of the study. Stewart H. Brim, director of the New Orleans Sewage and Water Board, agreed. Harris called the Mississippi "the colon of America—in essence our industrial society flushed its wastes through New Orleans." But Brim said, "That is an asinine statement!"—and pointed out that the river's sheer volume at New Orleans had enormous powers of dilution. As to the fear that chlorination of supplies from the Mississippi could be responsible for the area's high cancer rate, the New Orleans waterworks man said, "It is one thing to sit in a lab and play with mice; it is another to live in the real world where you have to keep water clean and safe and do it in a way that people can pay for."

The real world of clean and safe water was surely something that people paid for—and they paid dearly, but did not receive their money's worth. The federal amendments of 1972 funded what became the largest public works project in the land, and as 1982 arrived, nearly $50 billion in federal, state and local funds had been spent. But with all the investment for clean water, the nation was now being warned that it faced the greatest water crisis ever.

The sense of the crisis was sharpened by nationwide droughts. One of them dried out the three-state area around New York City, the capital of the national media, and the water crisis alarm was sounded across the country by newspapers, magazines, radio and television. For example, in a "Special Report" entitled "The Browning of America," *Newsweek* magazine warned that "drought, waste and pollution threaten a water shortage whose impact may rival the energy crisis." A major, five-article series in *The New York Times* worried about crucial water supplies "being squandered through poor management and inefficient use to such a degree that water is running short in many areas." And a *U.S. News & World Report* article, "Water: Will We Have Enough to Go Around?," declared, "Signs of the impending crisis are everywhere."

The components of this, the ultimate of water crises, remain essentially those described a century and a half ago by Walter Channing of Boston when he warned that the city's supply was "neither pure nor plentiful and both quantity and quality are dropping." The modern crisis, of course, is far more extensive and complicated, for clean water is demanded in unprecedented quantities by the intricate circulatory system of modern America. Channing's Boston now uses over 50 billion gallons of water a year, and the piddling leaks that he complained about have become billion-gallon floods. The water pipes of America's aging cities are leaking, and Boston, with 20 percent of its lines built before 1900, leads all the others by losing an estimated 17 percent of its water supply.

The nation's pipes, good and bad, carry much more than the domestic supplies used for drinking, bathing, laundering, flushing toilets, watering lawns and the like. As we go to the wells, lakes and rivers, we withdraw about 300 billion gallons of water per day, with the largest share going to indirect consumption, including food production, which is about the greatest water user of all. The *California Water Atlas* explains, for example, that the 1,500 pounds of food consumed annually by the typical American requires 1,000 gallons of water per pound to produce—or in a year's time the water it would take to fill a one-acre pond five feet deep (1.6 million gallons). The beef Americans love is one of the most water-intensive foods in the world, requiring around 4,000 gallons a pound. The water goes into irrigation, processing, cooling and all the other water-demanding activities associated with modern food production. But any concern over today's intensive use of water requires a look at virtually everything around us. The newsprint in the local newspaper may come from a moderate-size mill where the 1,000-ton paper production per day takes the equivalent of the freshwater used by a city of 1 million people. Producing the pound of cotton in a pair of jeans uses some 1,300 gallons of water. The ton of steel in the family automobile requires about 30,000 gallons of water to manufacture.

One could go on asking: what is the freshwater cost for everything from the concrete stoop to the kitchen sink? And each item would have its surprise answer. The gross national product takes a tremendous amount of water to produce—and often of the same quality that people drink. Statistics from the past and projections for the future by a host of private and governmental organizations show the demand has increased dramatically in the past 25 years and may grow a great deal more by 2000—as much as four times again, according to one of the highest projections. This growth crunch, coupled with dwindling supplies of freshwater, lies at the root of the threatened water crisis.

However, the nation as a whole has far more water resources than we are ever likely to withdraw. The average precipitation for the conterminous United States (all but Hawaii and Alaska) is 30 inches per year, which feeds a stream flow of some 1.2 trillion gallons a day. But this daily flow would have to continue for 50 years for the total to approach the amount of groundwater calculated to underlie the surface of the United States. This immense, dark, still reservoir provides 25 percent of the nation's freshwater for all purposes, which includes drinking water for about one half of all United States residents.

If the 30-inch annual precipitation were evenly spread across the country and around the calendar, the problem of water availability would be nil. But of course it does not always rain or snow where needed. Nor do American demands always fit availability. With our national image of ubiquitous supply, we move about in smug assurance that potable water will either be at our destination or follow fast upon our arrival, regardless of humidity or aridity. An old motto is expected to work at all locations: "Pudnik grows where water goes, or water goes where Pudnik grows."

United States citizens are presently acting out an astonishing demographic anomaly by shifting in droves from the wet snow belt to the arid sun belt, despite water signals warning that the migration is foolhardy. The growing numbers of people settling in the most arid regions of the country are not only testing groundwater reserves far beyond reasonable limits, but they are even banking on surface supplies that actually may not be available.

Arizona is a prime case, with population growth well above the national average. The state's development has actually been dependent on using groundwater reserves much faster than nature can replenish them. Even at Arizona's 1970 level of development, underground reserves were being reduced by nearly 700 billion gallons a year, while the annual replenishment by nature was less than 100 billion gallons. Flaunting this stark depletion statistic, Phoenix, the state capital, grew 31 percent from 1970 to 1980, while real estate developers projected an image of a water wonderland with man-made lakes and streams—including the development Fountain Hills, sporting the world's highest fountain, rising 560 feet in the air. With such abandon at the heart of the desert, the water consumption of Phoenix climbed to 260 gallons per day per person, more than 100 gallons above the national average. So it is no surprise that by the 1980s one of Arizona's most perplexing problems was groundwater overdraft, or "groundwater mining."

Meanwhile water-nervous officials are anxiously awaiting the Colorado River water that Arizona won from California at the Supreme Court in 1964. The supply is slated to arrive via the Central Arizona Project, a 300-mile series of pipes and aqueducts diverting nearly 4 trillion gallons of water per year from the Parker Dam to the Phoenix and Tucson areas. The project, authorized by Congress in 1968, is scheduled for completion in the late 1980s with an escalated price for the nation's taxpayers of $1.5 billion. But even so the question remains as to whether enough Colorado River water will be available to supply the system all the way to Tucson. The river has become an endangered species, because it is "overappropriated." If all the claims on the Colorado—a vast jumble of water rights going back many decades but still binding—were exercised, they would add up to some 6.5 billion gallons a year more than presently flows into the Southwest. Arizona's proportionate share of the leavings, if any, might be very meager.

Other evidence of the callous overdraft of groundwater at the start of the 1980s helped set off the national media's crisis alarm. For the first time millions of people learned of the Ogallala, a vast aquifer under the Great Plains, extending from the Texas High Plains north through Nebraska. Moreover, a great deal of the irrigation water that maintains the United States leadership in world agricultural production is pumped from this underground supply. But the Ogallala, like Arizona's aquifers, is being mined. Farmers are pumping up more groundwater for irrigation than is returned either by themselves or by nature. The problem is most acute on the Texas High Plains, where a billion-dollar-plus agricultural economy was built on the overdraft of the Ogallala. A strange ostrich complex seems to comfort many of the groundwater depleters with the false assumption that their wells tap a mysterious, endless source. The notion is cultivated by state and federal policies, such as price supports for commodities depending on irrigation, low-interest loans stimulating questionable water-use practices and even a depletion allowance encouraging pumpers to deplete rather than conserve groundwater.

Besides drying out wells, the groundwater overdraft in some areas causes what may be the most dramatic symptom of the impending crisis: subsidence. In the afflicted areas, when water that saturates subsurface layers of sand and clay is withdrawn and the liquid pressure drops, the clay particles squeeze together, the earth contracts and the surface sinks, or subsides. In California's San Joaquin Valley, utility poles display signs that mark the level of the land's surface in years gone by and reveal it has subsided as much as 30 feet. Heavy groundwater withdrawals for irrigation are to blame. The city of Tucson has settled some seven feet along with its descending water table, and the desert community continues downward eight to ten inches a year.

Texas, with its national superlatives, may have the greatest subsidence of all, in Houston. As boosters of the "super city" brag of its population growth, they might also suffer queasiness caused by a sinking feeling. The metropolitan area, which depends heavily on groundwater, has been slowly losing altitude, to the point where some sections are dropping below sea level. Parts of Baytown on Galveston Bay have descended (along with real estate values) so far that a dozen attractive homes stand abandoned in ponds of saltwater. The sinking symptom is spreading across the metropolitan region as newcomers arrive—as many as 1,300 a week—and settle primarily in areas dependent on wells for water. The U.S. Geological Survey monitors the subsidence of Houston with sensitive instruments called borehole extensometers, and these data, compared with water-use figures, confirm that as groundwater consumption rises the land falls.

But for the sheer drama of subsidence, Texas loses to Florida. Here pieces of land have dropped implosively when water overdrafts caused underground limestone caverns to collapse. The most dramatic of Florida's "sinkholes" occurred at Winter Park in May, 1981. The chasm, 125 feet deep and 400 feet across, devoured a house, parts of other buildings, six expensive Porsches, a camper, a sycamore tree and a chunk of an Olympic-size swimming pool. About 125,000 truckloads of dirt would be needed to fill the hole. The Water Park implosion was, of course, national news, and it dramatically reminded the country that we are using so much water that we could run out.

The loss of precious groundwater reserves that may have taken thousands of years to collect is extremely serious, but a more deadly component to the national crisis is the depletion of potability by contamination of both surface and underground supplies. While the authors of the Safe Drinking Water Act of 1974 had reason to believe Americans were consuming water tainted with health-threatening chemicals, they could not name, quantify or assess the risks many of the pollutants held for people. The lawmakers therefore assigned the National Academy of Science the job of identifying contaminants and determining their threat to human health. From the data the EPA was to establish quality standards that would be federally enforced for the nation's public drinking water supplies. The academy published its study in 1977 and an updated version in 1979. It further confirmed that United States citizens were being served hundreds of chemicals with their drinking water, and the number was increasing. By 1980 the count of identifiable contaminants exceeded 1,000, and the figure was believed to be only a small fraction of all the chemicals in the country's supposedly potable water.

But compared to identification, assessing the threat to human health was a far more difficult assignment. The scientists could point to some substances posing "substantial and imminent danger" and others of "virtually no danger." But the risks from a great many chemicals in between these extremes were the most perplexing to assess. How much of each could humans tolerate in drinking water? The question had to be researched, one substance at a time, often with animal studies requiring as long as two years at a half-million dollars apiece. Yet scientists recognized the one-at-a-time approach overlooked the fact that people were consuming many chemicals and the mixtures themselves could damage health. In view of such complexities the academy was unable, within the scope of its mission, to provide the risk assessments needed for the EPA to assign safe limits for the hundreds of potential poisons.

The research prompted by the Safe Drinking Water Act was, indeed, a case of Pandora who out of curiosity opened the box given to her by Zeus, to find it contained all human ills, which then escaped over the earth. In the half-dozen years following the law's passage, the scientific curiosity it stimulated showed that threats to drinking water could be grouped under four headings.

First, a rapidly increasing number of chemicals in groundwater were coming from industrial discharges to seepage pits, badly constructed dumps and landfills; from the misuse of fertilizers and herbicides in agriculture and forestry; from the bad design and poor maintenance of millions of septic systems; from the out-of-sight-out-of-mind practice of injecting potent wastes from oil drilling and other such activities into deep disposal wells, assuming the poisons would not migrate—and only the Lord knows from what else. The greatest pity of all was the permanency of most groundwater contamination. While a stream stands a chance of flushing itself out in a reasonable time, chemicals entering a vast, all but still aquifer will slowly spread into a plume that may remain to defile the water for thousands of years. In the 1980s we still lacked capabilities for monitoring and controlling most of the contaminants. One category that could be monitored included industrial solvents, like trichloroethylene (known to cause cancer in mice), and these were being found in groundwater nationwide, often in high concentrations.

Disinfection was confirmed by scientists as a second source of health risks. As suspected in the 1974 Environmental Defense Fund study in Louisiana, chlorination acting upon natural humus was proven to be forming trihalomethanes, including the known carcinogen chloroform. The threat was found in treated water from both surface and groundwater sources. Three studies reported by the EPA found chloroform in nearly 100 percent of treated surface supplies and surprisingly in some 70 percent of treated groundwater.

In the third area addressed by the federal studies, it was verified that surface supplies of drinking water were also carrying heavier and heavier burdens of chemical contamination. The EPA's Eckardt C. Beck, assistant administrator for water and waste management, testified in 1980 that "industrial discharges, agricultural and urban run-off, and accidental spills combine to make many of our rivers and streams a lethal soup of organic chemicals. One survey found 700 compounds in the finished [treated] water of a single public water system." The deadly porridge was arriving at consumers' faucets because treatment systems were incapable of removing the ubiquitous residues of the chemical revolution.

Finally, investigators pointed out that "additives" used in water systems, with all good intentions for improving the supplies, were in themselves becoming contaminants. They discovered that nearly 1,000 chemicals were involved in treatment and distribution systems, and many were getting into the "finished" water. Ingredients of the paint and other coatings for pipes and storage tanks were leaching into supplies. For example, at a time when Americans were being warned to avoid asbestos because of its potential carcinogenicity, many people were (and still are) unknowingly drinking water delivered through coated asbestos-cement pipes. And chlorine (already implicated in producing trihalomethanes) was itself showing up in drinking water at undesirable levels.

This epidemic of chemical contamination posed perplexing problems for those trying to assess and regulate the risks to human health. Eckardt Beck said, "It is like opening up a henhouse, and you have a whole bunch of hens run out, you pick one up and you have to figure out whether you want to bring it back into the henhouse or chase another one."

The chemical chase intensified in the late 1970s when many local water facilities began using sophisticated test instruments newly available to them. With devices such as the gas chromatograph and mass spectrometer, complex chemicals could be detected even though they might amount to only a few parts per billion, or even per trillion, of water. The more incisive techniques led to frequent closings of public supplies, and the publicity added to the sense of national crisis. Most of the news stories were about public and private wells whose groundwater sources were found to contain substances that could cause diseases, most often cancer.

For example, from 1978 to 1981 more than 600 wells were closed in the New York metropolitan area (which includes parts of Connecticut and New Jersey). The actions resulted from finding minute quantities of chemicals from the growing list of multisyllabic names that the public mind was associating with cancer. "The names may be alien," stated *The New York Times*, "but the chemicals are pervasive. Most are petroleum-based and are found in gasoline, cesspool and septic tank cleaners, toilet bowl deodorizers, plastics, laundry degreasers and spot removers, household cleaners and disinfectants, paint and varnish removers, dry cleaning fluids, degreasing agents for machinery, metals and engines, floor and furniture strippers and car waxes." Improperly constructed, mismanaged landfills around the New York area were considered the main contributors to the problem, as they collected the chemically based paraphernalia discarded by modern society and allowed the poisonous ingredients to leach into underlying aquifers.

Daily papers and evening news programs told of more and more people cut off from good water as we entered the 1980s. More than 400,000 citizens of 13 cities in California's San Gabriel

Valley lost their drinking water when 39 public wells were closed because of the mysterious appearance of trichloroethylene at dangerous levels. On the opposite side of the nation the case of an infant, John Constantian, in Hudson, New Hampshire, made the wire services as his symptoms of arsenic poisoning led to tests that revealed many wells in the area contained hazardous levels of the chemical. A Michigan study found 268 sites with known contamination in groundwater sources, 381 more with suspected contamination and over 50,000 where activities threatened groundwater. Massachusetts discovered that a third of its 351 communities were affected by chemical contamination of both surface and groundwater supplies. And the national prevalence of the problem was confirmed when a countrywide survey by the federal Council on Environmental Quality found there was evidence of drinking water contamination in 34 states. "The data show," the council reported, "that almost all states east of the Mississippi have major problems and that even relatively nonindustrial, lightly populated western states, e.g., Idaho, Arizona, and New Mexico, have major problems."

To reveal what people were possibly consuming in drinking water, the council published a list of 33 toxic organic compounds, the pronunciation of which could lame a tobacco auctioneer's tongue—like tetrachloroethylene and dibromochloropropane. Concentrations ranged from a few parts per billion to 27,300 parts per billion for trichloroethylene discovered in one Pennsylvania well. The health risks associated with these chemicals—most of which are tasteless and odorless in drinking water—were not completely clear, but they were not to be taken lightly. The council stated:

> No one has argued that organic chemicals in drinking water benefit human or animal health. At best, some organic chemicals may have no detrimental effects at low concentrations. But many compounds once thought safe—especially synthetic organic chemicals—can present serious and substantial health risks even in concentrations in the low parts per billion or parts per trillion range. . . .
>
> When ingested, synthetic organic chemicals . . . can cause health problems. At high concentrations and doses (acute exposures), many synthetic organic compounds can cause nausea,

> dizziness, tremors, blindness, or other health problems. . . . At lower concentrations, skin eruptions may develop, or the central nervous system may be impaired. At still lower concentrations, over many months or years (chronic exposures), some of the health problems are tolerable and some fatal. . . .

Faced with this plethora of possible threats to human health from the nation's drinking water, the EPA seemed to be stunned not only by the complexity of the problem, but by the cross fire from opponents and proponents of the Safe Drinking Water Act. Accused of foot dragging, the agency was hit with a lawsuit from the Environmental Defense Fund, which wanted action on the law it had helped bring to life. After spending tens of millions of dollars trying to assess the risks from organic chemicals and how to control them, the EPA proposed sort of an all-purpose remedy to filter organics out of water supplies, the harmless as well as the harmful. The proposal called for equipping water treatment plants with activated carbon filters, which had been used successfully at a few dozen American and European plants and in food and beverage processing systems. The idea outraged water supply industry officials who saw the filters as unnecessary, unduly expensive and an insult to their professional pride. The EPA backed off, except for promulgating a drinking water standard of 100 parts per billion for trihalomethanes. In many situations it was determined that attainment of this standard would require using carbon filters in treatment plants for water supply. This brought a lawsuit from the American Water Works Association and renewed attempts to weaken the Safe Drinking Water Act through pressure on Congress. Such squabbling only produced irresolution of the problems Americans faced with their drinking water. The news of the day went on publicizing the potential threats to their health, and the American Bottled Water Association reported that while its industry already served more than 10 million consumers, the number was increasing by 10 to 12 percent a year.

In the midst of all the arguments over filters, there came an unusual cry of despair from a New Jersey waterworks man. It reminded some people of Allen Hazen's widely adopted advice from 66 years earlier that "the water works man . . . must, and rightly should, accept a certain amount of sewage pollution . . . and make the best of it." At a 1980 congressional hearing, Richard Moser of the American Water Works Service Company of Haddon Heights, New Jersey, stated:

> Purposeful discharge of pollutants cannot be tolerated on the premise that a downstream drinking water plant can remove it. It should not be dumped into the water supply in the first place. Tolerating this dumping in the past led to the deterioration of many rivers.
>
> We are not ready to accept the responsibility of removing the myriad of contaminants which are present in most major water sources. The present concern over synthetic organic chemicals shall certainly expand in the future and we believe continuation of the present Federal, State and local efforts to abate discharges of these pollutants is the proper course of action.

Here was a familiar theme to those who had promoted and then celebrated passage of the clean water law of 1972. But by 1980 celebration had long since turned to disenchantment. The law had not worked, despite all the billions of dollars it had provided. The funds had not been spent for the new direction envisioned by Senator Muskie. They had been invested in the traditional, turn-of-the-century direction that relies on rivers and streams as part of the waste treatment process. But that rock-ribbed practice was more of a failure than ever—as Moser's plea confirmed—and it lies close to the water crisis confronting the nation in the news of the day.

We were still avoiding the solutions that the country's lawmakers had offered us and had been willing to fund.

VII

Two Pilot Projects for the Nation

Anyone seeking solutions to the problems of clean water addressed by the federal amendments of 1972 might well have traveled to two places in the United States during the early 1970s. One was Muskegon County, Michigan; the other was Lake Tahoe on the California-Nevada border. At both destinations those who made the journeys found innovative new treatment systems that purportedly would remove nearly all the pollutants of sewage, leaving effluent that could meet drinking water standards. This high degree of purification had become known as advanced wastewater treatment, a more accurate term than "tertiary treatment." But there was a big difference between the Michigan and California systems, for one was circular, the other linear. They took center stage in a growing controversy reminiscent of the circular-versus-linear debate at the turn of the century.

The Muskegon system, codesigned by one of the authors (Dr. John R. Sheaffer) with a Chicago engineer, Dr. William J. Bauer, was a circular system like the nineteenth-century farms of Berlin, but enjoying the benefits of modern soil science, agricultural engineering and land-treatment management techniques. The Lake Tahoe system, which followed the linear pattern of water supply and sewage disposal, was a highly complex physical, biological and chemical treatment plant, designed to receive raw sewage and discharge pure water. The histories of the two systems are tales of promise and disappointment reflecting the fate of the 1972 amendments. Still, Muskegon and Tahoe illuminate the choices that can lead either to solutions or to continued impotency in the face of the water crisis.

Muskegon County, which lies on the eastern shore of Lake Michigan, once thrived on timber, oil wells, foundries and recreation. But by 1968 the area's natural resources were depleted, income from forestry and agriculture was way down, and the pollution of inland lakes and the Lake Michigan shoreline had ruined the amenities that once attracted vacationers. That year, when the area's unemployment was double the national average, Muskegon officials turned for help to the University of Chicago (and to Sheaffer, who was there as a specialist in managing natural resources). A study of the problems led to the idea of using land treatment for the county's sewage to restore the area's income in two ways: (1) by revitalizing nonproductive agricultural land with crops irrigated by the wastewater, and (2) by simultaneously eliminating water pollution and bringing back tourism.

Fortunately the county had some determined, forward-looking leaders who backed the plan. The proposal also had its doubters and opponents, people who had condoned discharging sewage to the precious water in their midst, but could not envision capitalizing upon the waste as a resource that could be safely and beneficially applied to the countryside. The most serious opponents were in the city of Muskegon; they wanted simply to upgrade its conventional sewage treatment system and to continue the disposal of the partially purified effluent into Muskegon Lake, an appendage of Lake Michigan. The most they could claim for their alternative was that it would "hold the line on water pollution." But holding the lake in its present condition was hardly a responsible idea when the water was so polluted that one could see through only two or three inches of the murk.

The opposition to land treatment was undermined in two ways. Muskegon's largest industry, the S. D. Warren Paper Company, came out in favor of the land alternative. And three county judges, after taking expert testimony from all over the country, handed down a declaratory judgment sought by the county leaders. The panel had concluded that the Sheaffer-Bauer proposal for land treatment would work and that fears of odor, disease and groundwater pollution were unfounded as long as the system was carefully engineered. The opposition, which had been cultivating the fears, collapsed, and the project was soon underway. The initial engineering research was funded by a $2 million federal grant that Muskegon's congressman, Guy Vander Jagt, had helped obtain.

The land treatment system was designed for a thinly settled 10,000-acre site. Preparation of the land consisted of clearing some 4,000 acres of scrub oak and moving millions of yards of earth for building special lagoons to treat and store the wastewater and for developing the proper drainage of croplands. A sewage collection system from 13 communities around the county, including the heavily industrialized city of Muskegon, culminated in a 66-inch pipeline to the big new site. The whole system was designed to collect, treat and apply the wastewater from 140,000 residents and 200 businesses. To begin with, the flow would be about 30 million gallons of sewage a day, but the final plans allowed for county growth and treatment of 42 million gallons a day.

When the system began operation, raw sewage entered a series of three eight-acre "biological treatment cells"—each essentially a lagoon with floating churns that oxygenated the water, eliminated odors and prevented ice from forming in the winter. The simple treatment cells, with the help of bacteria and air, began purifying the wastewater, eliminating many of the pathogens, but retaining the primary fertilizing nutrients, nitrogen, phosphorus and potassium, along with essential trace elements, or micronutrients.

After a few days the water flowed out of the cells to two mammoth storage lagoons covering 1,700 acres. The lagoons served two purposes:

First, they provided storage, which could act as a buffer between the unceasing flow of wastewater and the need to interrupt irrigation of the croplands. The longest interruption was required by Michigan's coldest season, so the lagoons were made with enough capacity to impound the flow during four to five winter months when land treatment was impossible. This accounted for the large size of the lagoons. The storage lagoons also allowed for interruptions in other seasons, during heavy rains and for harvesting crops. Also, should too much of some toxic substance get into the wastewater so as to endanger crops, the storage capacity allowed the stopping of irrigation until the project manager could deal with the problem.

Second, the large lagoons provided additional wastewater treatment, which eliminated most of the remaining pathogens. Organic matter entering the lagoons from the biological treatment cells settled to the bottom, where it slowly formed a thin layer of sludge. Over the years the sludge would be dredged occasionally and applied to the land as a soil conditioner.

For nearly all of the spring, summer and fall Muskegon's nutrient-rich water was pumped from the storage lagoons and sprayed on the croplands. The application was accomplished with 55 center-pivot irrigation rigs, each with a long arm on motorized wheels, moving above the crops and around a pivot, like the hand of a great clock. The arms, with radii from 750 to 1,320 feet, carried spray heads directed downward so the wastewater sprinkled the soil and plants. Each arm took 24 hours to rotate once around its pivot, so that any given piece of cropland received only a single, brief spraying per day.

Before the system went on line, a test plot of the sandy soil revealed that extremely low yields could be expected for feed corn, the crop selected for the system. As the spray irrigation got underway, eventually covering 5,300 acres, the land responded to the enriched water, and the yield of corn increased rapidly. In the first season of irrigation, 1974, the yield was 28 bushels per acre, but in only two years the figure had increased to 80, which was about 30 bushels per acre higher than the average corn yield that season in Muskegon County as a whole. The sale of the irrigated corn brought $1 million back to the county.

Besides such earnings, a substantially upgraded environment resulted to boot, because the water benefited from a full purification system—a fabulous filter (of soil) from 5 to 12 feet thick, covering 5,300 acres (of cropland). As the spray rigs delivered wastewater, it seeped down through the soil and was cleaned by nature's remarkable treatment works. Many of the so-called water pollutants—really "resources out of place"—were removed by the soil acting as a mechanical, chemical and biological (soil bacteria) filter. Furthermore, the plants themselves became part of the filter, with the roots taking up the fertilizing nutrients and using them to stimulate the growth of corn. Finally the purified water was collected below the surface of the ground by an extensive network of common agricultural drainpipes that reclaimed the purified water and discharged it to the area's streams. The clean water began helping nature flush out the lakes and waterways previously fouled by the county's sewage disposal practices. The best sign of success was the return of fish, followed by the return of fishermen.

Muskegon was a demonstration of how a community could convert one of its most difficult problems into an asset. In nearly all other communities, sewage treatment was approached with a single, primary purpose: disposal. It was essentially a negative purpose, throwing something away. The Muskegon approach was multipurposed, with the positive goal of reclaiming and reusing not only the water but the wastes it accumulated as sewage. While other municipalities made nonreturnable investments to achieve disposal, Muskegon made a returnable investment to revitalize food production and recreation. The Michigan system offered an example of synergism at work. The total benefits of the project were greater than the sum of its parts if treated separately.

The $42 million Muskegon project had an important spin-off related to the fundamental change in direction encouraged by the Federal Water Pollution Control Act Amendments of 1972. On pages 18 and 19 of the new law there was an answer, though long delayed, to the turn-of-the-century prayers of the proponents of circular water and sewage systems. The key words here had originated with Congressman Vander Jagt, who was convinced that the project then under construction in his home district was the way to go for water pollution control. His phraseology, which he had brought as an amendment to the amendments, directed the administrator of the EPA "to encourage waste treatment management which results in the construction of revenue producing facilities." This could be accomplished, the Vander Jagt amendment continued, by "the recycling of potential sewage pollutants through the production of agriculture, silviculture [forest cultivation] or aquaculture products," by "the confined and contained disposal of pollutants not recycled," and by "the reclamation of wastewater [recovery of the purified water]."

When the Michigan congressman's contribution became part of the law, it finally recognized in a legal context that sewage was not a waste on which we should spend billions for disposal with no return, except a promise of water pollution control that was really never kept. Instead, the law recognized sewage as a combination of resources whose reclamation and reuse could be a good investment—one comparable to that required for extracting and using a valuable mineral from the earth. The return on an investment in sewage reclamation was threefold: (1) combined fertilizer and irrigation for crops, (2) reclaimed water for all kinds of purposes, and (3) an end to water pollution. The Vander Jagt amendment, which appeared in the section of the 1972 law on federal construction grants, provided the opportunity to invest in reclaiming and reusing the resources of wastewater. In a 1977 amendment to the law, such investments were further encouraged by allowing municipalities a higher percentage of federal grant money if they chose land treatment projects over conventional sewage treatment systems.

But this law that encouraged our taking a new direction in pollution control also contained a section practically demanding that we follow the same old technological approach used since the turn of the century. Under "Standards and Enforcement" the amendments passed in 1972 set up a five-year interim plan, stating that not later than July 1, 1977, the requirement for effluent from publicly owned treatment works was to be "based upon secondary treatment." The stipulation, which originated in the House version of the new federal law, proclaimed business as usual, that we would go on building conventional, staged treatment plants. The idea was to bring municipalities up to the secondary level in five years, thus partially cleaning our wastewater, and then as necessary proceed to a full cleaning with some form of advanced treatment. When the proponents of this approach were asked how the final cleaning stages might work, they pointed to an advanced treatment plant at South Tahoe, California. It had been recently constructed to avoid the sewage pollution of Lake Tahoe, which had been described by Mark Twain as the "fairest picture earth affords."

The beautiful lake, over a mile high at its surface and ringed with the snowcapped mountains of the Sierra Nevada, is one of the three clearest, deepest lakes on earth, rivaled only by Oregon's Crater Lake and Russia's Lake Baikal. The 21-mile-long body of water shared by Nevada and California is an American treasure, and the idea of spoiling its astonishing clarity was unbearable to the thousands who had fallen in love with Tahoe.

But by the 1950s the already large number of tourists was multiplied many times by gambling casinos built in State Line, Nevada, at the bottom end of the lake and adjoining South Lake Tahoe, California. A population boom hit both communities and their 2,500 citizens became more than 13,000 by the end of the fifties. The attendant rise in sewage had to be handled by the South Tahoe Public Utility District, which, at the beginning of the area's growth, had a single public septic tank treating the wastewater.

Voters soon approved construction of a conventional activated sludge plant. Ordinarily it would have discharged to the lake, but conservationists warned that the nitrogen and phosphorus in the effluent could diminish Tahoe's fabulous clarity, which was attributed to the very low natural levels of such nutrients. They feared that because of the lake's immense volume—enough to cover all of California with 14 inches of water—it could take nature a good 600 years to clean up a bad case of pollution. The conservationists demanded that no secondary effluent be discharged into the precious lake, and public sentiment backed them.

With this restriction the utility district faced an extremely difficult problem, because in the Tahoe basin everything drains into Lake Tahoe. Pumping the effluent up and out of the basin by pipeline might have been the answer, but outlying areas refused to have the waste dumped in their mountain streams. Finally the decision was to use the secondary discharge in one of the poorest, most haphazardly conceived land treatment systems possible. About 120 acres of U.S. Forest Service and municipal land was acquired for the site. Application began by spraying some 750,000 gallons of effluent daily onto the land, which was wooded, rocky and hilly. But the effort quickly turned into both an environmental and a political disaster. The soil was soon saturated. The wastewater puddled, frothed, smelled and drained toward the sacrosanct lake. Workmen frantically dug ditches and guided the mess into hastily built storage ponds. Meanwhile newspaper articles continually pointed up the precarious state of affairs, and news photographers loved to record the mountains of foam created by detergents in the wastewater. Then one Labor Day weekend—when a surge of holiday tourism caused a spurt in sewage flow—2 million gallons of effluent escaped into the lake. The discharge had a dramatic impact on the body politic, and several directors of the utility district were ousted.

Then a newly retained engineering consultant, Harlan Moyer, concluded that the only answer was to build an advanced wastewater treatment system capable of purifying the secondary effluent virtually to drinking water quality. He assumed that discharge of the high-grade effluent to Lake Tahoe would be acceptable even to the strictest conservationist. To develop such a system Moyer obtained the services of Russell Culp, a research and design specialist in sanitary engineering. Moyer and Culp then built a small pilot plant, which produced 25 gallons a minute of remarkably good water from secondary effluent. On the basis of this model, South Tahoe authorized construction of a full-scale plant, which Culp designed and constructed.

Wher completed in the late 1960s, Culp's advanced wastewater system added five treatment stages beyond the conventional primary and secondary stages. They were designed to remove the pollutants remaining in the secondary effluent, practically one ingredient per stage. The first used lime in a chemical process to extract phosphorus from the wastewater. The second consisted of a large ammonia stripping tower to remove nitrogen. Next in line was a recently invented filter with a carefully selected combination of coal, garnet and sand to remove whatever particulate matter remained in the effluent. The fourth stage was a set of activated carbon filters—an idea that Culp borrowed from food-processing industry—to decolorize the effluent and remove dissolved organic materials. Finally the water was chlorinated to eliminate pathogens that might have survived to this fifth stage and point of discharge.

Of course, the extracted materials and chemical residues from the processes themselves did not vanish from the Tahoe plant, but ended up in large quantities of sludge. In the first two years of operation (when 1.6 billion gallons of sewage was treated), the sludge included 1,500 tons of suspended solid materials, 100 tons of phosphorus, 1,700 tons of organic substances, 1,300 tons of lime mud and 170 tons of spent activated carbon. The lime and carbon were reclaimed and reused, but the remainder of the sludge was incinerated in a large natural-gas-fired furnace, equipped with air pollution control devices to protect the mountain air. The ash residue was dumped into a landfill where supposedly it would cause no environmental damage.

But when this $28 million worth of paraphernalia was ready to go, the Tahoe conservationists remained leery and opposed dumping the effluent into the famous lake. Their opposition forced the utility district to do with the tertiary effluent what they had been doing with the secondary effluent all along, spray it on the ill-fated land treatment site—but eventually the deluge virtually drowned the trees and an alternative had to be found. Going back to the earliest idea of all, the district found the answer: pump the purified water out of the Tahoe basin. This time the citizens over the mountains bought the proposal. At great additional cost a 27-mile pipeline was constructed up through Luther Pass and on into a man-made lake christened Indian Creek Reservoir. The reservoir was used for two purposes: to supply irrigation water for nearby farms and for fishing and swimming (which was approved by the state of California).

For several years the South Lake Tahoe advanced wastewater treatment plant was shown off as the sanitary engineer's dream, a magnificent machine using mechanical, biological and chemical processes to turn raw sewage into potable water. The system was heralded as a demonstration of how America would clean up its water in the future. The EPA, which had become home base for many sanitary engineers of the traditional school, joined in promoting the Lake Tahoe idea. The agency printed a colored brochure extolling the virtues of the plant. So many visitors came to inspect the engineering marvel that a tour guide was hired and a film was produced to explain the system.

"Perhaps no single project has done more to 'sell' the AWT [advanced wastewater treatment] philosophy than South Tahoe," reported the investigations staff of the House Appropriations Committee in 1979. "[It] was considered to be the prototype and the panacea for all known water pollution problems."

In administering the water pollution control law, the EPA tilted almost completely toward the Tahoe philosophy. But as new as it might have appeared, the philosophy was the same old idea dressed up in time-worn technology, trimmed with some devices new to the sewage treatment business. The Lake Tahoe plant was still a nonreturnable investment in the single-purpose disposal of what were seen as pollutants. All the tanks, towers, filters, furnaces and whatnot remained the child of the sanitary engineer's belief that the central thrust of sewage treatment was the reduction of obnoxiousness to allow the discharge of effluent to receiving waters. And Tahoe confirmed that the traditional engineer remained steadfast in his faith that man-made technology was the key to clean water.

The billions spent under the amendments of 1972 reflected that faith and paid primarily for conventional treatment plants, including a few advanced treatment systems of the Lake Tahoe variety. Meanwhile the EPA paid lip service to the philosophy set forth in the Vander Jagt amendment, but that was about it. According to the agency's regulations promulgated in the 1970s, no funds were to be granted for the construction of sewage treatment systems until alternative methods—and specifically land treatment—had been considered and found unfeasible. However, the demand was not really enforced. In many cases it was ignored by consulting engineers in their proposals for municipal sewage treatment systems. Where they did recognize the requirement, it was often tossed only a passing nod—or in some instances, considered in ways that bordered on the frivolous.

For example, the proposal of a prominent engineering consultant retained by a rural Connecticut town favored a secondary treatment plant after purporting to study land treatment. The sanitary engineers, who lacked training or experience in land treatment, said it would require an outrageously large site—far more land than would actually have been required for the town's small flow of wastewater. The site, they claimed, would have to accommodate vast lagoons to be excavated at unbearable costs. The only such site happened to be on a plateau high above the town, and sewage would have to be pumped there at a continuing cost that would break the community. In truth the system would have been feasible with much less land, which was available near and on the same level as the town. The descriptions of the oversized lagoons confirmed the consultants' ignorance of how large they should be and of how they could be constructed without massive excavations.

In a Massachusetts study similar distortions of comparative costs were so gross as to affront the intelligence of even the least-informed layman. A consulting firm supporting conventional treatment over land treatment announced that the chlorination facility for the former method would cost only $20,000, but for the latter it would cost $360,000. There was no reason why the equipment needed to be different in size, design or cost for either method.

The cases of these New England towns were typical of how things came out when conventional sanitary engineers were forced to explore land treatment. Too many acres were needed. The public would not accept it. Land treatment would be a hazard to public health. It would be odoriferous. It was an old idea discredited decades ago. All these objections had been proven groundless, but the proof was ignored because the appraisers of the land treatment alternative usually worked with neither training nor experience in the new discipline. The negativism could have come from trade journals, which carried articles with such titles as "Land Disposal: A Giant Step Backward," "Land Disposal: The Paper Tiger," and "Land Disposal: The Environmental Blunder of the 20th Century." The titles alone betrayed the authors' biases. They were so ingrained with the disposal philosophy that land treatment was beyond their comprehension. The management and use of pollutants as resources out of place was not understood. Thus, the critics gravitated to their familiar turf—disposal by dilution.

The fundamental new direction pointed to by Congress was not seriously followed by the EPA. The agency's bureaucracy, heavily staffed with sanitary engineers of the old school, bought the tickets for thousands of private engineers to ride the time-worn disposal route of partial sewage treatment and dilution. By 1980 the more than $30 billion expended had been invested in some 18,000 sewage treatment plants that were either in operation or under construction.

However, the high-priced venture was beginning to be recognized as a fiasco—labeled "The $33 Billion Misunderstanding" by *Audubon* magazine in 1981—and the taxpayers who footed the bills learned from their daily newspapers that they were being badly fleeced. "Elaborate hulks of expensive and failing machinery litter the American landscape, the wreckage of Washington's good intentions," reported the *San Francisco Chronicle* in August, 1981. "They are monuments built by one of America's largest and most idealistic public works programs: the drive to clean up America's water. And much of it doesn't work."

Such disconcerting news came from the federal government itself, in particular from three studies of the construction grants program by (1) the investigations staff of the Committee on Appropriations of the House of Representatives, (2) the General Accounting Office under the comptroller general and (3) the Office of the Inspector General at the EPA. Their reports told of billions of dollars worth of purification technology seriously out of kilter. Sewage treatment plants suffered from inferior design, poor operation, bad maintenance or combinations of all three. Continued attempts by engineers to replicate nature's water-cleaning abilities were failing.

Even the leading showplace, the South Tahoe advanced treatment plant, was in trouble as deep as the lake it was built to protect. While the EPA went on extolling the system as the way of the future, the intricate processes became more and more difficult to operate and maintain. The failure of the system was evident at Indian Creek Reservoir over the mountains. The reservoir's rainbow trout—originally used to prove the purity of the Tahoe effluent—had been wiped out by annual fish kills. Recreationists had turned away from the reservoir when it filled with unpleasant algae blooms. One time the green growth became so heavy it had to be mechanically harvested and trucked away.

Worst of all, the cost of operating the advanced plant—an expense borne entirely by local user fees—ascended like a Roman candle. Annual sewer charges per single-family residence increased from $30 to $124 between 1976 and 1978. Even so the South Tahoe Public Utility District had "nearly exhausted its financial resources," according to a study panel of consultants reviewing the problems in 1978. To meet its operating expenses the district had to raise the single-family fee to $159. The big plant had become a chemical hog, requiring 870 tons of chlorine a year at a cost of $250,000. The heavy dosage ate up machinery, so that a two-inch-thick pump impeller blade became "razor thin" in only 30 days. The system was even more of a glutton for carbon, devouring 1,750 tons a year with a price tag of $535,000. The disaster showed up on a common financial barometer, the average cost for treating 1 million gallons of wastewater. In fiscal 1973–1974 the figure was $1,546. By the 1977–1978 fiscal year the number barely missed doubling, having risen to $3,077.

As the debacle grew worse, the EPA's officials, who had advertised the Tahoe system as a dream cure for water pollution problems, failed to note it had become a nightmare. When the investigations staff of the Committee on Appropriations discovered the Tahoe troubles, they looked for EPA reports warning other communities to avoid these problems, but they found none.

By the start of the 1980s the financial horrors were even more frightening for South Lake Tahoans, with the system now costing $4,221 per million gallons treated. But the utility district had had enough, and the advanced plant was scaled back to a routine secondary system. The secondary effluent was pumped up the pipeline through Luther Pass, but it no longer filled the acclaimed Indian Creek Reservoir. The lake was now being supplied by the diversion of a natural stream, and the sewage effluent was being stored in a newly constructed reservoir. From there it was being pumped to farmlands and center-pivot irrigation rigs—like those at Muskegon—for a form of land treatment. South Tahoe had come through a great deal of unnecessary technological anguish to return to the soil as a solution.

While Tahoe with its publicity fell hardest, the failure of sewage treatment technology was widespread across the country.

The evidence showed up when the General Accounting Office investigated EPA's permit program, which established minimum pollution discharge levels for public treatment plants. Agency records showed that 50 to 75 percent of the nation's plants were discharging pollutants above permitted levels. The investigators then took a random sample of 242 plants in ten states and discovered that 87 percent were in violation of their permits, with 31 percent in "serious violation." In one case a community was discharging 100 percent more pollutants than its permit allowed.

Some case histories of malfunctioning sewage treatment could have been comic except for the costs and consequences to a nation facing a serious water crisis. For example, at Greenville, Maine, (population 1,900) a $4-million-plus advanced treatment plant was built with EPA urging. It was supposed to preserve scenic Moosehead Lake, but the plant was plagued by technical problems from the start, and the town refused to accept it. Operation and maintenance costs (which had to be carried in full by the users) rose from an estimated $28,000 to $125,000 a year—a 400 percent increase that was impossible for the few citizens to bear. With a legal suit filed against the builders and 300 residents refusing to pay their sewer bills, Greenville abandoned the system and put it up for sale—only to build another plant to satisfy the EPA.

While the federal studies detailed the grand failure of sewage treatment, none of the investigators questioned what the *San Francisco Chronicle* called "the almost blind faith in high technology solutions for water pollution problems," nor how "a few hundred engineering consultant firms in effect took the grants program captive through their ability to influence the decisions on technology." To put it another way, the appraisers of the clean water law criticized the technical failure of old ideas, but not the ideas themselves. The reports seemed to imply there were no alternatives. Thus the investigators neglected to consider that the congressional intent to find new directions was being ignored. Had the study teams addressed that failing, they almost certainly would have highlighted the Muskegon land treatment system—which they did not.

From the start-up of the Michigan project it remained effective at each of its multiple purposes. As a wastewater purification system, the biological treatment cells, storage lagoons and irrigated croplands continued their high levels of performance, purifying raw sewage and delivering potable water from the agricultural underdrainage system. Not only did the process demonstrate that it could remove the traditional pollutants of domestic wastewater, it surprised many observers by extracting and containing the exotic chemicals that were contaminating more and more of the nation's surface and groundwater supplies.

The sewage of Muskegon County, which includes the heavily industrialized city of Muskegon, contained an unusually large assortment of organic compounds like those that the Safe Drinking Water Act was supposed to control. The city had more than a half-dozen chemical-processing industries discharging their wastes into the Muskegon system. They included a number of the organics that EPA listed as "dangerous pollutants." One was the potentially carcinogenic trihalomethane, chloroform, the compound that had so much to do with passage of the Safe Drinking Water Act and with the subsequent quarrels and lawsuits over its removal by carbon filters. A study of the Muskegon effluent by the Robert S. Kerr Environmental Research Laboratory of Ada, Oklahoma, found that the earth filter was remarkably successful at removing organic pollutants from the contaminated wastewater applied to the land in large amounts. Only a few of the contaminants in minor quantities got through the soil filtration to show up in the subsurface drainage system. For example, chloroform, which arrived in the raw sewage averaging 870 parts per billion, was reduced to only 6 parts per billion in the effluent; thus 99.3 percent of the trihalomethane had been removed. Government drinking water standards allowed 100 parts per billion as a safe level for drinking water.

The Oklahoma laboratory concluded, "It is very doubtful if any other types of treatment systems, with the possible exception of those utilizing heroic and very costly measures for polishing of final effluents, would have been more effective than the Muskegon System in removing the organic pollutants occurring in waste water being treated, especially since more than 60 percent . . . was comprised of industrial components."

Five years later another study of the system revealed it was effective in treating 125 chemicals found in the Muskegon wastewater with its discharges from a variety of industries. Eight years had now passed since irrigation had started, but, said the report of the study, "the soils do not exhibit any significant accumulation of organic chemicals" and "no contamination is detected in the corn crop."

From the start the Michigan system was less expensive than its technological rival, the South Tahoe plant, and the disparity grew in more ways than one. The California system decreased in effectiveness and increased in cost, while the Michigan system did the opposite. When South Tahoe was paying $4,221 to treat 1 million gallons of wastewater in 1981, Muskegon County's cost was less than one sixteenth of that, $254 per million. While Tahoe was scaling back its system, Muskegon County's annual report announced that the year of 1981 "was the most successful ever for the Wastewater Management System." And as Tahoe's complex remained on the brink of fiscal disaster, Muskegon's accomplished what ought to be hailed as a miracle in the sewage treatment world: it turned a profit of $250,187. Feed corn from the land treatment system had brought in $1,259,736, and the county had enjoyed the creation of jobs paying $1,146,690 in salaries and fringe benefits. At the same time continued tests of the water from the system's underdrains revealed that the filtration of soil and crops remained highly effective in the removal of contaminants, including hundreds of organic compounds, from the wastewater of the heavily industrialized county.

The choice between the two routes to clean water—Muskegon or Tahoe, circular or linear—seems rather easy to make, but a great many people who exert powerful influences over the national water crisis still argue that the answer is linear. Theirs remains a call for more of the same, when it should be a call to return to the intent of the federal amendments of 1972.

Water Supply System

DENVER WATER DEPARTMENT

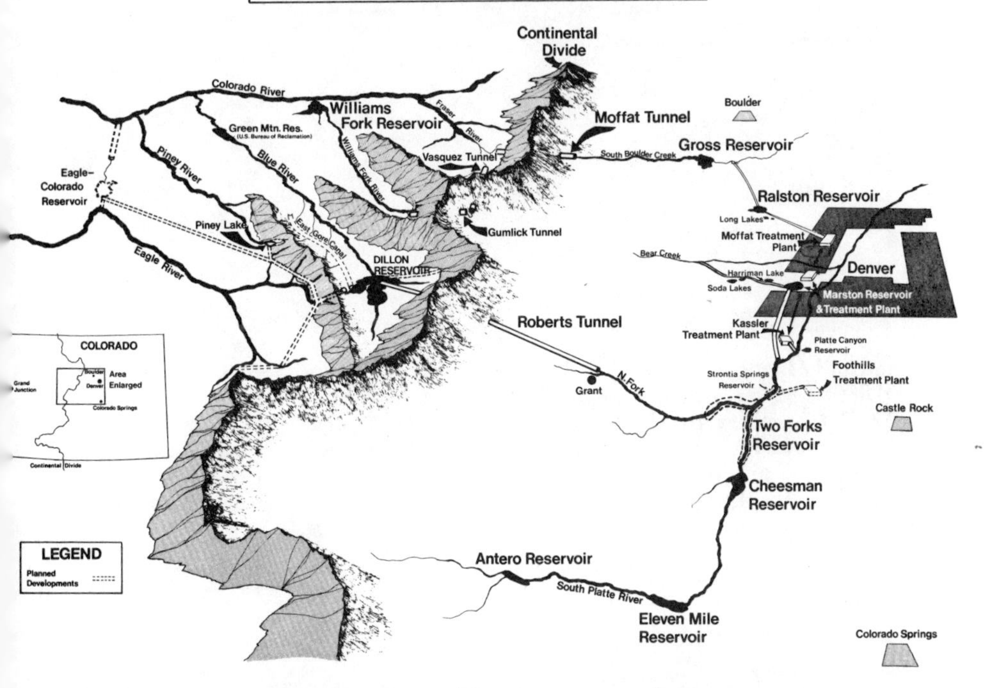

Denver's water supply system reaches out over hundreds of square miles on both sides of the continental divide to serve the metropolitan area. Like many other American cities, Denver is at, or close to, the end of its outreach for new sources to meet increasing municipal demands for water. *(Courtesy Denver Water Department)*

Boston's Quabbin Reservoir—the 16-mile-long impoundment that inundated 74,886 acres in 3 counties and 12 towns and captured the entire flow of a 186-square-mile watershed—supplies over 300 million gallons of city water per day, but it is still not enough. A controversial plan would augment the Quabbin supply with another 72 million gallons a day drawn from the Connecticut River via a 10-mile aqueduct. *(Courtesy Boston Metropolitan District Commission)*

Chicago's Sanitary and Ship Canal, shown under construction in 1896, reversed the flow of the Chicago River to lead the city's sewage off to the Mississippi and away from Lake Michigan, the endangered source of municipal water. The canal, also designed to carry ships, was excavated by over 8,000 workmen using new techniques said to have later made feasible the digging of the Panama Canal. *(Courtesy The Metropolitan Sanitary District of Greater Chicago)*

A secondary sewage treatment plant at Danbury, Connecticut—a complicated technological system designed to treat more than 12 million gallons of sewage a day for a population of over 50,000. The complex, which discharges partially purified effluent to a tributary of the Housatonic River, is typical of such plants found in America's predominantly linear water and wastewater systems. *(Courtesy Charles A. Manganaro, Consulting Engineers, New York)*

A trickling filter, the main component in a secondary treatment plant, handles sewage effluent from which the solids have been settled out in the primary stage. The liquid is sprayed from the rotating arm onto the circular bed of stones and allowed to trickle down to underdrains. In the process, microorganisms further (but not completely) clean the wastewater. Such filters, which have remained essentially the same for most of a century, are still being installed in municipal sewage treatment plants. *(Courtesy Leonard Stevens)*

Water treatment plants with large, complex sand filters (shown here) and chlorination systems are widely depended upon to purify water from public supplies. Such systems often have to treat water contaminated by effluent from sewage treatment plants that do not completely purify their discharges. *(Courtesy Leonard Stevens)*

The advanced wastewater treatment plant at South Lake Tahoe, California, was once heralded as a panacea for water pollution control. The system was designed to produce potable water from raw sewage in three stages of purification, primary, secondary and tertiary (or advanced). Though the plant worked as expected in the beginning, the effluent still had to be kept out of beautiful Lake Tahoe by pipelining it 27 miles over the Sierra Nevada (seen in the background) to a man-made lake. In time, however, the tertiary stage failed, and the plant was reduced to a conventional primary-secondary system—all at great cost to the California community. *(Courtesy Leonard Stevens)*

Effluent drawn from each of three stages in the advanced South Tahoe system reveals how they progressively cleaned up municipal wastewater (the jugs, *from left to right,* are filled with raw sewage, secondary effluent and tertiary effluent). When this picture was taken, the plant was working as designed and the final effluent was potable water, but when the system failed, the water quality diminished greatly. *(Courtesy Leonard Stevens)*

The Muskegon (Michigan) Wastewater Management System uses land treatment to grow over 5,000 acres of feed corn, which is irrigated and fertilized by partially purified sewage effluent. Some 30 million gallons of sewage arriving daily from Muskegon County municipalities are treated in "biological treatment cells," which, despite their size, are simple lagoons stirred by floating churns to introduce oxygen and stimulate biological activity. Effluent from these cells is discharged to two large storage lagoons, from which the nutrient-rich water is pumped as needed to 55 center-pivot irrigation rigs and applied to the corn crops in great circles. *(Courtesy County of Muskegon Wastewater Management System)*

The irrigation rigs have long arms that ride on wheeled towers and rotate around their pivots (like the hands of a clock) while gently spraying the corn beneath. The irrigant, which is filtered through the soil and plants, is caught by subsurface underdrains and leaves the system as potable water. *(Courtesy County of Muskegon Wastewater Management System)*

The Components of a Modern Land Treatment System

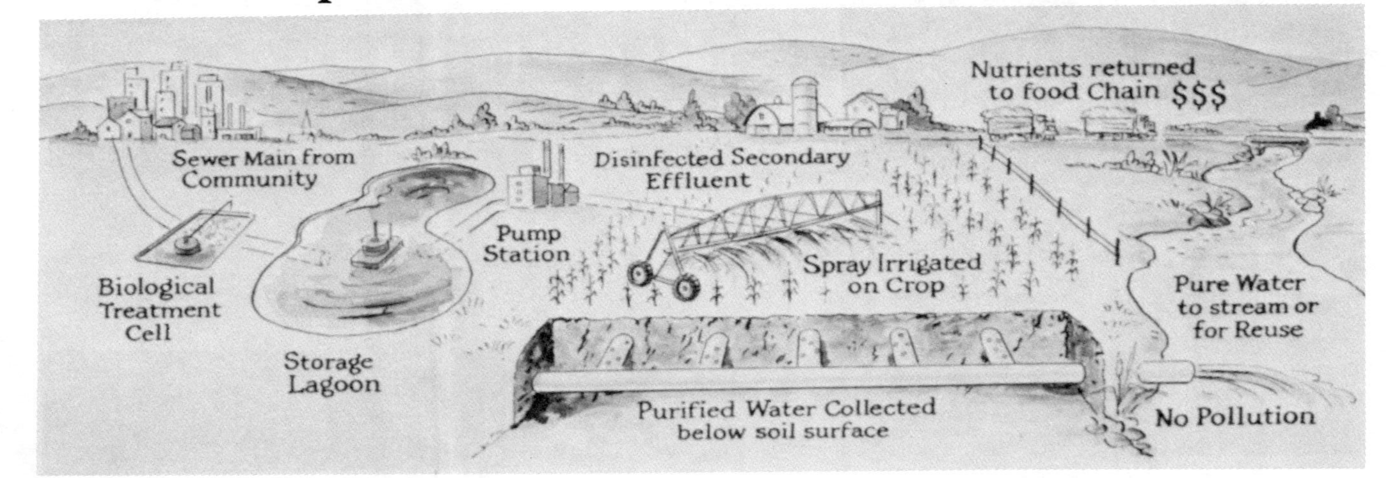

Land treatment, using modern design and management methods, offers an opportunity to convert linear water and wastewater systems to circular systems. Instead of relying on disposal by dilution in streams or lakes, wastewater is recognized as a raw material with nutrients valuable for growing crops and as a source of reclaimable water that can be reused after serving as an irrigant. This artist's conception of a land treatment system illustrates how a Muskegon-type project works, starting with municipal sewage that is treated and stored in lagoons, then used to irrigate and fertilize income-producing crops, and finally discharged as pure water. Not only can such systems reclaim a great deal of America's once-used water, they can prevent the pollution of other potential sources of supply—and in the process make money instead of wasting public funds on the disposal of potential raw materials mislabeled as pollutants.

(Courtesy Sheaffer and Roland Inc.)

The man-made Santee (California) Lakes *(above)* forming a freshwater oasis for recreation in one of the driest parts of America, are entirely supplied with water reclaimed from the city's sewage. Partially purified effluent from Santee's sewage treatment plant is filtered through "percolation beds" *(left)* of gravelly soil, collected and used to fill the lakes. *(Courtesy Leonard Stevens)*

VIII

Cleaning Water as a Bankable Business

In the fundamental difference between the Tahoe and Muskegon approaches to clean water lies the most workable long-range solution to the impending American water crisis. As the past shows and the present confirms, this ever-worsening crisis is not a matter of too little water, but of how we mistreat what we have. The linear management of water and wastewater remains at the center of the mistreatment, and this concept that has had its day—indeed, its century—continues to be largely responsible for squandering water resources. The Tahoe system, proclaimed by the sanitary-engineering establishment in and out of government as the savior of the linear approach, actually clinched its failure. Meanwhile, the circular approach to the problem, exemplified by the Muskegon system, has not yet had its day, despite dramatic proof that it can succeed when based on modern science and engineering. The license to take this new direction came with the Federal Water Pollution Control Act Amendments of 1972 and was strengthened by further amendments in 1977, but it was treated with languor by the administrators of the law, who were committed to convention. With upward of $50 billion spent, practically all for components of linear systems that depend on the discredited disposal-by-dilution theory (now referred to as "the assimilative capacity of a stream"), it is clear that clean water is not likely to come from existing legislation or more of the same kind of law in the future.

Those who were so naïve in 1972 as to believe that passage

of the clean water law was tantamount to its consummation are now wiser by more than a decade of hindsight. The failure to meet the measure's goals made it evident that a new direction for clean water is unlikely to emerge from government motivated by its own laws. Meanwhile experience and better understanding of what is involved indicate that such change has its best chance through private enterprise driven by conventional economics.

The feasibility of such a shift continues to prove out at Muskegon and is strengthened by other projects that have developed around the country. As with the Michigan project, the others are circular systems compatible with nature and the fact that much of the wastes now damaging our water resources are really raw materials reclaimable for the production of goods and services. The reclamation job can be done by bankable private enterprises that make the purification of wastewater a paying proposition. In today's linear equation, only the water supply side (often run by private businesses) produces revenue. Besides supporting the water system itself, the income frequently contributes to other public services, including the wastewater works, conventionally an all-outgo, no-income proposition. The Muskegon experience shows how to move toward balancing the equation, making wastewater produce revenue that then can even help support other services. Moreover, the Michigan project demonstrates that such systems are capable of helping out on the water supply side of the equation. First, they can truly abate water pollution, thereby revitalizing sources of supply now too dirty to use. Second, they can diminish the need for expensive purification of present supplies that require cleaning before use. And third, by returning reclaimed potable water to the community, land treatment systems can reduce the need for new sources, and the sale of the recycled water can add to traditional water revenues.

While such advantages can deal a blow to the impending water crisis, the Muskegon approach can also stimulate several indirect bonuses for society, such as:

- providing new sources of jobs and wealth;
- creating new supplies of food, fiber and energy;

- decreasing government deficits by eliminating costly treatment works now paid for by nonreturnable public construction grants raised through taxation;
- reducing inflationary spending by replacing billions of dollars in nonproductive public investments for sewage disposal with private investments that produce goods, services and employment.

If the circular approach to water and wastewater can offer a new era in managing our most precious resource, its adoption may be hastened because of its broad potential for addressing a wide range of difficulties underlying the amorphous national problem we call the water crisis.

This is really a malignant mass of crises stimulating a growing sense of public unease. It touches different people in numerous ways with various intensities. For multitudes it is a vague, minor concern that their faucets may not always flow. They worry little about the possibility except during sporadic, irritating droughts, when they are asked to conserve. For many city officials the water crisis is a worrisome danger of water shortages forcing user-rate increases, thus drawing hazardous public attention to questionable systems and practices that ordinarily go undisturbed in the world of cheap water. The crisis for more and more citizens is the gnawing, undefined fear that they are drinking the seeds of future cancers or horrid distortions of yet unborn children. For the housing industry the water crisis is the tap to the public supply, a pipe long taken for granted that now turns into the tail that wags the dog, determining whether this house or that housing development can be built at all. For farmers the crisis can be a fight for existence when urban areas reach into the countryside with political, financial and legal clout for new sources of municipal water that are old sources for crops and animals. And so it goes, each to his own water crisis, adding up to a massive national problem. But while horror stories may thrive on the difficulties, the common solutions offer slim pickings. Two are talked about most: find new supplies and/or conserve water. Both are limited at best and sometimes can even create more problems than they settle. The circular solution is hardly understood and seldom mentioned, except for occasional, undefined references to "recycling." However, this solution properly implemented can address a large number of the crisis elements and thereby become the most workable of all possible solutions. In one stroke it can offer both new sources of water and conservation of existing supplies.

For an overview of the potential to be found in the circular solution, let us discuss it in relation to two main areas of the national water crisis: first, the older snow belt cities, and second, the fast-growing sun belt cities.

The water crisis for the older cities is a matter of both decrepitude and deteriorating water quality from chemical pollution. Aging pipes leak, break and limit water pressure where years of corrosion and decay have built up interior deposits. In many communities, citizens drink water with traces of asbestos picked up from the asbestos-cement pipes once widely used in the construction of municipal distribution systems. Reports from Boston tell of pipes so old they have literally disappeared, leaving only tubes of hardened soil where the metal has worn away from decades of use. Cleveland, which competes with Boston's estimated 17 percent loss of water supply to leaks, also suffers badly from deposits (tuberculation) in metal lines laid before 1955. The resulting reduction in pressure (down as much as two thirds in one suburb) plagues the city, causing it to curb development and to suffer from lawsuits charging that low hydrant pressures contributed to the damage of several major fires. In New York City the water lifeline to the five boroughs consists of two large tunnels, one 55 years old, the other 46. Shutting them down for inspection is impossible until construction of a third tunnel, now held up by a tangle of financial and legal problems, can be completed—definitely in the distant future. Meanwhile practically all of the city's water arrives through tunnels whose conditions remain a mystery. Should either fail, the disaster for the nation's largest metropolis is hard to imagine. The aging cities' sewerage systems are also beset with leaks, but their pipes, not being pressurized, leak inward (infiltration). Often the infiltration includes good water provided by the outward leaks of pressurized water pipes (which for good reason are always laid above sewer pipes). Valuable potable water, bought but never used in the city, then flows directly to sewage treatment plants, overloading them and diminishing their already-unfulfilled promise of sewage purification. At the same time the older municipalities are troubled by "combined sewers," which mix stormwater with sewage so that in heavy rains treatment systems are literally flooded out of commission, and raw sewage passes untreated into lakes and waterways.

These are the kinds of troubles posed by the water crisis in many American cities; however, water is often only one in a package of crises sapping our urban infrastructures. They include the deterioration of transportation systems, streets, highways and bridges. The total contributes to the decline of the cities' industrial bases, with loss of jobs, population and revenues. The troubled economies are further beset with rising costs for energy, water and the treatment and disposal of waste. *The New York Times* commented that "the situation is similar to that of a family whose income has been cut, that is behind on the mortgage payments and unable to buy shoes for the children, and then learns that tree roots have plugged the drainage pipes, the furnace must be replaced and termites have weakened the foundation of the house." In the cities, capital funds to restore collapsing water and sewerage systems are far short of what their fixing would require—and this pertains to more than just the older, snow belt cities. The Urban Land Institute estimated that rehabilitation or replacement of existing water systems needed during the 1980s and 1990s would cost from $40 billion to $63 billion. Meanwhile a survey of local officials by the National League of Cities found that 54 percent believed their communities could not pay half the costs of repairing or replacing water systems.

Under this crunch the waterworks man finds himself in a perplexing maze of double binds. His decrepit works need more water, but new sources are fewer, farther away and politically more difficult to acquire. If he persuades consumers to conserve water, which always sounds good, it can trigger a political backfire: less consumption causes a drop in revenue from user fees that pay long-term debts on water systems; to meet the obligations water rates must be increased, and the conserving consumer feels he is being punished for being good. As for the leaks, breaks and constricted lines, the waterworks man cannot afford to dig up the city and fix all the pipes instantly and with the least disruption possible, so he deals only with the most critical outbreaks, forever snarling traffic here and there, but never really settling the problem.

The water crisis of the deteriorating cities is unlikely to be solved by continuing the present linear pattern of water and wastewater management, with its attendant pattern of linear economies. With this configuration, grants and revenues received are spent nonproductively in terms of solving the crises that plague the cities. Changing to a circular pattern on the Muskegon model could help convert urban economies from linear to circular, producing new revenues that stay in town to help solve the crises of aging arteries and pollution.

The wastewater streams of our troubled cities contain tons and tons of potential resources, or raw materials. This valuable cargo is generally dumped, in whole or in part, into waterways and lakes where it reduces water quality, damages essential aquatic life and diminishes recreational opportunities. If these raw materials were reclaimed through circular systems and used in the production sector of the nation's economy, it would result in new sources of goods and services, and the current costs of conventional sewage disposal would be eliminated. From these reclaimed materials we can have fertilizer for growing food and fiber, methane to generate electricity and other energy sources, as well as clean water safe to reuse. Finally these investments in resources that would otherwise be thrown away can produce new revenues, which are badly needed to restore today's deteriorating water and wastewater systems. The job can be done by traditional financing of private ventures—perhaps organized as a form of public utility—to do for profit what the clean water laws of the 1970s failed to do through government construction grants.

Opponents of the circular concept—more committed to the linear system now than ever with their immense investments in conventional plants—question the availability of land for such systems to serve urban areas, but, as will be shown in subsequent chapters, land and location are not the most formidable problem. Wastewater can be piped far out of the city of origin (in fact, pipes as long as 100 miles are employed in some of today's regional collection systems). Compared to the capital, operating and maintenance costs of short-measure treatment plants, it would take a fraction of the expenditure to transport wastewater to distant land treatment sites. Moreover, if we can pay a great deal to transport water into cities from distant sources, why can't we invest in moving it back out for reclamation, return and reuse?

Dr. Richard R. Parizek, who has long been associated with a well-known research and demonstration project on wastewater irrigation at Pennsylvania State University, concluded that land treatment need not be limited to small-scale applications. In 1972 Parizek stated, "The concept is applicable to major metropolitan centers as well. Public water supplies for these major centers are rarely derived from within city limits. Rather, water may be imported from sources 50 or more miles away. By contrast, wastewater treatment facilities have traditionally been located in the topographically low end of town for economic reasons. Large scale projects being planned or dreamed about show that these waters can be returned to their region of origin so that they might be renovated and made available for reuse. The problems involved are more apt to be political than technical or economical."

Land treatment systems do not always have to be located away from urban areas. When properly designed and operated, they are even less likely to cause nuisance and health problems than traditional treatment works, which are often sited in populated areas. Actually, land treatment systems can be amenities for the places they serve, providing open space with green growth that can even help diminish air pollution. If this advantage is understood, land certainly can be made available. For example, thousands of acres of floodplains, now being developed in urban areas, could be candidates for such sites. Today they are being built upon at startling costs to taxpayers, who are forced to fund flood control measures and to pay for flood damage to the developments. Many floodplains could be converted to attractive nutrient-recycling farms and used for other beneficial purposes. In 1975 Charles R. Ford of the Office of the Secretary of the Army asked, "Why not use our flood plains in urban areas for crop production, golf courses, forests and other uses which can capitalize on the nutrients in our wastewater and provide tertiary waste treatment at the same time? Such land-treatment sites can be located on the higher areas of the flood plains, but they can also be designed to store flood water when necessary without permitting the release of stored wastewater except through the soil filtration process." Following Ford's idea, floodplains would not only be restored to nature's intended use as buffers against high water, but would also be employed to society's benefit in reducing the costs of floods, eliminating costly wastewater treatment works, producing crop income and reclaiming clean water. In this manner the older cities—for that matter, almost any city—can use the circular solution as a weapon against their water crises.

The change from linear to circular may come about in either of two ways, or a combination of them: economic projections for the two approaches may show in dramatic fashion that it is worthwhile to replace existing sewage treatment with land treatment immediately—as happened at Muskegon; or as existing systems wear out and/or population growth requires more treatment, the demand can be met with circular rather than linear systems.

A different shape to the same water crisis is seen from the newer, rapidly growing cities across the sun belt. Here the crisis is as serious as that troubling the stagnant, older metropolises, if not more so. In the vigorous, newly developing areas of urban America, the pipes are relatively new with few breaks and leaks (Dallas, for example, leaks only 3 percent of its water from pipes, the majority of which are less than 25 years old), but the specter of crisis looms when officials and developers face up to the incessant demand that growth creates for more and more water. In these areas an increasingly anemic supply has become the lifeblood of hyped economies, and the growth on which they thrive requires constant transfusions.

While Boston may epitomize the crisis of the older cities, Tucson gets stellar billing among newer cities. Tucson is the largest American city depending solely on groundwater. Pumps lift it out of the ground five times faster than nature can restore the supply, so the Arizona municipality rides a downward spiral to depletion. The water table tapped by wells in some areas of the city dropped 110 feet in one recent decade. The descent, accompanied by land subsidence, means decreasing quality of water and increasing energy costs for pumping. When drilling straight down below the city became questionable, Tucson's water seekers went out and down by buying irrigated farms, retiring the agriculture and bringing the water into the city. By the early 1980s the insatiable quest for water had closed down 12,000 acres of farms, and officials expected to increase that acreage three times by the mid-eighties. The outreach competes with another water-intensive enterprise, the copper-mining industry of the upper Santa Cruz basin, from which comes one quarter of the nation's supply of this essential mineral. Miners have bought and closed down the farms on another 8,000 acres for the groundwater. So while the fields of cotton and pecan trees revert to desert and produce tumbleweed, the never-satisfied harvesters of their water wait and hope for the promised infusion from the Colorado River when the Central Arizona Project is completed. But that hope is often dashed by pessimists who question if the system will ever reach Tucson, and by realists who point out that if it does arrive, the city's available share of the river may soon be negligible against the ever-rising demands for water.

The most feared consequence of the water crisis in these "growth paradises" is that it could force the bridling of development. The reins on new building have already been tightened in Arizona. The 1980 Groundwater Management Act limits water usage on irrigated acreage and for municipal and industrial supplies. The aim is to have man's withdrawals equal nature's recharge by 2025. Under one part of the act, builders must assure that every house constructed has a 100-year supply of water—which leaves some areas virtually unbuildable. Water worries in other rapid-growth regions have also forced the conclusion that developers cannot proceed as if the supply of the crisis-ridden resource were infinite. Denver, as we learned earlier, came to that realization in 1977 and limited new taps of the public supply, to the builders' distress. Perhaps for developers the most startling water-based moratorium is that in force since 1973 in the Goleta valley near Santa Barbara, California. The impact was felt most in the last half of the seventies, when the valley saw only one sizable development completed (270 mobile homes with their own private water supply). Other construction in the same period was generally confined to expensive single homes on large lots with their own wells. As a result, Goleta's 1975–1980 growth in housing units was only 5.5 percent, compared to 21.3 percent in a comparable but unrestricted area to the north. A byproduct of the moratorium was a sharp price escalation for the median home, which by 1980 stood at $138,000, compared to $104,000 for the whole of surrounding Santa Barbara County.

The restraining influence of the water crisis on home building was the subject of a 14-page report in the trade publication *Professional Builder.* Its editor, Roy L. Diez, wrote, ". . . I was to find out after much staff digging, the water problem is, indeed, a national issue. It involves a whole range of quantity and quality concerns. And those concerns are already limiting or stopping growth and building in many markets.

"The problems are serious," Diez continued. "They almost assuredly will get worse. And unless they become involved now, builders stand to be among those hurt the most."

While some developers still suspect the water crisis is a political artifice of no-growth advocates, the builders' trade publication warns that the problem is real and urges its readers to look for ways to reduce water demand by promoting homes designed to conserve water or by supporting "self-contained" water systems.

This kind of awakening will sooner or later force itself upon development-prone, water-poor regions like those of the sun belt. It simply flaunts common sense to consume precious reservoirs of water faster than nature recharges them, use the supplies only once and then dispose of the waste streams to rivers and seas.

When our used water and the waste it carries can be reclaimed on farms to our fiscal and environmental profit, it is hard to reconcile the practice of closing farms for water that will be discarded after a single use. Reason stands squarely in support of agriculture and municipalities working together for their mutual benefit: water for the town should only be borrowed from the farm, then returned with valuable, growth-stimulating nutrients (which also came from the farm via the food chain).

The circular concept, creating what we call farm-city loops, can elicit a new, much-needed spirit of urban-rural cooperation that is now unattainable in many regions because of the long-standing conflict over rights to water. It is common for state laws to give municipal needs legal precedence over rural needs for water, so that when the chips are down the town can buy farms for their water through legal condemnation if negotiation fails. The linear approach to the resource ensures that no one wins with such settlements. Some townspeople have their water, but nature and society are losers. The rural water ends up as municipal wastewater and helps contaminate other potential sources in its disposal. The defunct farm represents loss of jobs and diminished supplies of food and fiber. Finally, the water reservoir, above or below the earth, can be jeopardized with man drawing on it faster than nature can restore it. The farm-city loop goes to the core of the problem. The townspeople still have their water, the ruralists keep their farms and jobs, and both parties enjoy new fiscal benefits from the saving in disposal costs and the earnings from the reclaimed resources.

The water crisis of the newly developing areas is definitely a candidate for circular solutions. As with Tucson, the future of many of these regions is precarious because their water is limited, increasingly expensive and mismanaged through linear systems. Californians who worry and fight over water transported hundreds of miles from the Owens and Colorado rivers blithely dump most of what they receive into the Pacific after a single pass-through. The irrigators of the Great Plains are often indicted for squandering the vast Ogallala Aquifer—which may be true—however, the blame has to be shared (but seldom is) by linear water and wastewater systems in municipalities on the plains. At least a portion of the farmers' irrigant gets back to the aquifer, but once-used community supplies are generally dumped into rivers. Still usable water from the hard-pressed Ogallala is thereby siphoned off by the trillions of gallons to the Gulf of Mexico. It could be returned to the municipalities or the aquifer via land treatment systems, with newfound profits en route. Of all the nation's areas of water crisis, the sun belt is probably in the greatest peril from the linear management of its tenuous supplies. At the same time the region undoubtedly has the greatest opportunity of all to trade in its straight-line trip to depletion for circular management of the resource that determines the future.

In discussing how such change could occur, we are inclined to emphasize the ways it can be done technically, but the most formidable barriers are not technical—not land availability, pipes, pumps, health, odors or whatever. The real problems are attitudes. Technical problems can invariably be overcome with technical solutions, if those in charge are of a mind to find them. But attitudes are something else, for in the linear world of water they are locked in patterns like fossils and held by an establishment that appears unwilling to change. This establishment is the "they" that most people and their elected officials expect to provide clean, safe water. It consists of the consulting engineers for water and sewage, the equipment manufacturers who make the treatment plants and other paraphernalia of our linear systems, the contractors who construct the systems and the suppliers of chlorine and other ingredients for traditional works.

In a world where water has been cheap and sewage unspeakable, this establishment often flourishes in a virtual vacuum, relatively unnoticed. Great projects are proposed and approved with hardly anyone except the immediate participants involved. For example, at Fort Worth, Texas, not long ago a public hearing mandated by law was held on a proposed treatment project that would cost about $200 million. It was scheduled on a night before the start of a long weekend. About a dozen people showed up, and of those, only one could be rightfully described as a citizen. Most of the others were from the consulting firm that had proposed the project. In such vacuums the players frequently lose sight of their original objective of clean water, and they often measure effectiveness by how many systems built and administrative criteria met, never mind that the effort falls short of really providing clean water.

This little-publicized monolith is a weighty persuader at the centers of power, from the nation's capital to country town halls. In Washington its combined lobbying is on the scale of the National Rifle Association and other such special interests. The water and wastewater lobbyists are represented by such organizations as the Water Pollution Control Federation. Their members are committed to the crusty precept of disposal by dilution at the end of linear systems. The defenders of the commitment, now with multibillion-dollar expenditures at stake, are understandably opposed to circular systems. The new methods threaten drastic change for professions secure and comfortable with concepts (and accompanying paraphernalia) that have remained essentially static for three quarters of a century. The fear of such change surfaced at a public workshop in Dallas not long ago, when participants were considering the relative merits of a land treatment system and a conventional activated sludge works. As if making a telling point against the land alternative, a representative from one of the nation's leading sanitary engineering firms suddenly pronounced, "We have a profession to back up and we got the whole profession that we're really standing for here; then if we're wrong then a whole lot of other people are wrong."

This professional rigidity, which has long had a hammerlock on the state of our water, leaves us far short of the cleanliness we were supposed to enjoy by the mid-1980s under the amendments of 1972. At the top of the law's first page, its number one national goal was "that the discharge of pollutants into the navigable waters [defined as virtually all surface waters] be eliminated by 1985." After the amendments were passed this goal was sometimes described as "zero discharge," but the slogan was soon shot down by the proponents of traditional systems, complaining it was unrealistic for their conventional means of purification. If they made an exception, advanced wastewater treatment of the Lake Tahoe variety was it, but the costly failures of such systems in the 1970s removed even the hope that traditional linear systems could discharge pure water. So the people we should expect to lead us to clean water redefined the ends to fit the means. The traditional means of wastewater treatment that separates out some but not all the waste ingredients have been used to determine the diminished goal for the discharge of pollutants. The nation's sights are well below the dream of the 1970s for zero discharge.

But as those inquisitive visitors to Muskegon County must admit, that laudable goal is not unrealistic. There in Michigan, and at other projects that we will discuss, the idea of zero discharge proves to be a practical route to solutions for our water problems. What was admittedly unrealistic was the naïve assumption that the goal endorsed overwhelmingly by the Ninety-second Congress when it overrode President Nixon's veto in October, 1972, would be reached because there was a law to motivate the relevant professions to fulfill the mandate. Muskegon and the few other circular models that point the way to solving the water crisis are successes *despite* some of the professionals who should be leading us to solutions. Those who unrealistically thought otherwise are now convinced that the goal of clean water will be reached only by going around the establishment and the government agencies it influences. As discussed earlier, the way can be found through bankable enterprises, supported by new coalitions of private interests. Their contributions to alleviating the water crisis can be motivated, not by grants for conventional water and sewage works, but by conventional economics.

The remaining chapters will elaborate on how circular systems can solve the impending water crisis and finally how the Congress of the United States can stimulate, at little or no cost to the treasury, the kind of private efforts that will, in fact, accomplish what the Ninety-second Congress tried to do.

IX

The World's Greatest Water Filter

If there's a secret to solving the impending water crisis with circular systems, it lies in what a Penn State information officer aptly named the living filter, the vital combination of soil and plants acting as a water purifier. But the living filter is hardly a secret—yes, it is overlooked and forgotten, but certainly not hidden. It is a main component in the endless cycle of life that governs our natural world. The cycle begins when the energy of the sun, beating down on the seas, lakes and rivers, evaporates the uppermost water. The vapor rises and condenses to form clouds. Meanwhile, salt particles cast loose from the seas by breaking waves are lifted by the wind and deposited in the clouds to become the nuclei for ice crystals. They later fall as snowflakes or raindrops on the land, hundreds or thousands of miles away. The snowmelt and rainwater either percolate into the soil or run off into rivers to be carried back to the oceans. The water returned to the earth dissolves human and other animal wastes excreted onto the land, but they are soon filtered out and decomposed by bacteria resident in the soil. The waste ingredients are worked into the earth, and the cycle of life thereby incorporates plants and animals, humans included. The water goes on its way, cleaned by the living filter.

But in our hurry to be rid of human wastes, western civilization abandoned the cycle of life and its fundamental law of return. With flush toilets and sewerage we short-circuit the natural system, bypassing the living filter to hurry our wastes into the nearest water out of range of our eyes and noses. When the penalty was obnoxious pollution and diminished water supplies, we decided in our technological cunning to outdo the living filter by designing a more compact, faster-working model. From the Lawrence Experiment Station three quarters of a century ago to South Lake Tahoe in recent years, scientists and engineers tried but failed to perfect a filter that could return our expanding flow of wastewater to potability and reuse. Despite the ongoing failure we continue, lemminglike, to do more of the same, and the most serious water crisis of all will come up ahead.The incongruity of what has happened was stated another way by Senator Mark Hatfield of Oregon as he discussed how we handle human waste:

"We have been making technological choices," he said, "that have been displacing products and processes which fit in with the cycles of nature. Then to rescue nature, we have been applying 'environmental technology' which substitutes for natural processes, and therefore duplicates the work available from the ecological sector. This displacement and duplication is a crippling economic handicap."

While we talk about such sin and the penance it imposes, the opportunity for absolution surrounds us. It is found in the sun and wind, in green plants and in the soil and resident organisms. The combination, and even the separate components, offers the ultimate in water filtration. Where they have not been destroyed by concrete and asphalt, these components remain at work in the natural scheme of things. Given our genius for innovation, their creative use can convert water purification from a losing technological battle to one assured of success by enlisting the living filter. We have barely made a beginning, but proof that the possibilities exist comes from considerable research and many examples.

One of the most remarkable cases of natural elements being employed creatively—indeed, not even with their full potential—to purify and reuse municipal wastewater is found at Santee, California. Since the 1960s the community northeast of San Diego has enjoyed a series of man-made lakes that were approved by the state for boating, fishing and swimming—despite nearly every drop of the water being provided by the municipality's sewage.

With only ten inches of rain a year, Santee was always troubled by the tenuous availability of water. Before the 1940s it was a small agricultural community dependent on irrigation. Water for crops was pumped by windmills from an aquifer beneath the San Diego River basin, where Santee is located. But that source (which had been replenished by the natural infiltration from the river) was quickly depleted when a new upstream water-supply impoundment dried up the San Diego below the dam. Santee's irrigated farms soon vanished. The town eventually became a post–World War II bedroom community for the expanding city of San Diego. For municipal water Santee joined the Metropolitan Water District of Southern California and received a supply transported more than 300 miles through the Colorado River Aqueduct system.

In the usual pattern, the town's growing population consumed more and more water, which increased the sewage flow until, in the late 1950s, the discharge of an overloaded treatment plant to a local creek failed to meet state effluent requirements. Santee was urged to tie into a large sewerage system being built around San Diego. The system would collect the region's wastewater and dispose of it into the Pacific. But the young manager of the newly formed Santee County Water District, Ray Stoyer, felt the scheme was fundamentally wrong. His district was purchasing Colorado River water at a high price that was certain to increase. After a single use it would be dumped into the ocean at a service fee also expected to escalate. Moreover, the town's wastewater would offer no possible good to the Pacific. Stoyer convinced his district board not to join the big sewerage system and to give him a chance to find a way of reusing Santee's water.

For a solution he turned to nature, and arid Santee was rewarded with a treasure of seven freshwater lakes made from reclaimed wastewater. They were constructed in an unsightly gravel-mining area at the edge of town, and when completed, they formed a line of interconnected lakes surrounded by grass, trees and shrubs. By reclaiming its wastewater the community realized triple use of its Colorado River water (whose cost did, in fact, increase tremendously over the years). First, it served the routine municipal needs. In its second use, the water was enjoyed by tens of thousands of people for recreation. And on the third round, the supply was pumped from the lakes to irrigate their parklike surroundings, as well as the fairways and greens of a nearby golf course and crops on a local farm. Uses two and three would have been lost had Santee made the usual, nonreturnable investment in sewage disposal. Instead its unusual investment was returnable in recreation, in irrigation for beautification and crops and in making the community a more attractive place to live and work. Furthermore, the town did not contribute to pollution of the Pacific.

In developing the Santee project, Stoyer came up with two main components for reclaiming the wastewater. First the discharge from the town's beset treatment plant was led into a 16-acre man-made lagoon, really a simple pond, technically called an oxidation pond or waste stabilization pond. Here, during a retention period of about 30 days, the water quality was improved by biological action. For example, the growth of bacteria beneficial to water purity was stimulated by the natural oxidation of the water through the play of wind, sunshine and the growth of aquatic plants. In the process the water became clearer, deodorized and less contaminated by pathogens harmful to human health.

Stoyer's second and most important purification unit cost only $30,000, a pittance as sewage treatment expenditures go. It consisted of several soil percolation beds, each 50 by 100 feet. They were terraced into the gentle slope of a shallow canyon close to where the recreation lakes were being excavated. Water pumped from the oxidation pond was spread on the beds, with applications alternated from one bed to another as the water took its time to seep down through the soil. At the canyon's base the filtered water was collected by a channel leading to the first of the interconnected lakes.

Extensive tests of the final, soil-filtered effluent revealed it was practically as clean as Santee's domestic water. The most important scientific work was an exhaustive search for viral organisms. When done, the scientists reported it was nearly impossible for viruses to get through the soil beds. State health officials, who remained rightly skeptical until the final tests were complete, approved the Santee lakes for full recreational use, swimming included.

Not long after the pioneering project was finished, Santee was selected for federal assistance to build and demonstrate an advanced wastewater treatment plant similar to South Tahoe's Proponents of the technological system assumed the percolation beds would be short-lived and that the tertiary plant would be needed to take over their job. The move came while the Tahoe kind of technology was still considered the panacea for clean water problems. A plant was built, but like its prototype, it was unreliable. The system was eventually closed down, leaving another monument to the inadequacies of advanced treatment technology. Stoyer's lagoon and soil filtration system continue to maintain Santee's lakes, and nature is expected to serve long into the future.

Travelers came to the California town from all over the world to learn what magic formula made possible the return of sewage water to safe usage. But as Stoyer was the first to point out, he had discovered nothing new. The two components that completed his wastewater purification process had been around for ages.

Ponds had been used for centuries to store and stabilize animal wastes on farms. Then, earlier in this century, two communities in the United States accidentally discovered that municipal sewage could be treated to the secondary level of purification by a simple pond. In 1924 the sewage of Santa Rosa, California, was badly polluting the Santa Rosa Creek, but the community was unable to afford a treatment plant. To do something, sanitation officials discharged the town's raw sewage into a gravel pit, hoping the mess would disappear into the earth. However, solids sealed the pit's bottom, making a pond. An odoriferous calamity was anticipated, but it did not materialize. Natural forces worked on the wastewater, and the quality of the pond's overflow was comparable to the secondary effluent that had been expected from the trickling filter plant Santa Rosa could not afford. Practically the same story was repeated four years later at Fessenden, North Dakota, and its accidental pond served as a secondary treatment system for decades.

Many communities then built oxidation ponds, and military installations adopted them during World War II. But the scientific understanding of their functions and design came after the war. When Santee's lagoon was built, considerable engineering know-how was available, and over 1,600 oxidation ponds were successfully operating in the United States.

Their designers learned that effective treatment meant selecting the best-size pond to hold a given amount of wastewater for an ideal "detention time" in a specific climate. Essentially, enough holding time had to be allowed for the water to take up sufficient oxygen to stimulate the biological action responsible for purification. Ordinarily wind and sunshine would provide adequate oxygenation, but if necessary the process could be speeded up by floating churns aerating the water. Later, more efficient systems blew air in from the bottoms of ponds. When well designed, such lagoons could substantially (but not completely) reduce the contaminants between the inflow and outflow. For example, every sample from Santee's influent contained 1 or more of 13 different viruses, but 75 percent of its lagoon effluent samples contained no viruses at all.

The second component of Stoyer's system, the percolation beds, was also adapted from a time-worn idea. The filtration powers of the earth had been known even in aboriginal times. Natives of Australia and Africa avoided drinking directly from stagnant pools or sluggish streams. Instead they scooped out pockets in the earth adjacent to the questionable sources, allowed the liquid to seep through the soil into the holes and then drank the filtered water.

On a grander scale the Netherlands adopted a similar technique to provide drinking water for Amsterdam (beginning in 1853) and The Hague (1874). Water along the Dutch coast was filtered through sand dunes and then drawn up from wells to supply the domestic needs of the two cities. Even today the Netherlands' "dune water" provides some of the best public supplies in Europe. Early in this century, water from the lower Rhine in Germany was filtered through the soil of the riverbanks and then used directly for the drinking supply. For half the century the bank-filtered water had no additional treatment, but after World War II pollution of the Rhine increased greatly, and water treatment plants were built to augment the soil purification process. Bank filtration continues on the Rhine, along with technological treatment systems, but the purification plants carry less of a burden than they would without natural cleansing by the earth.

Certainly the nineteenth-century proponents of circular land treatment for sewage recognized the purification capabilities of soil; still, they lacked the sound scientific foundations needed for the successful design of land systems. But with the turn of the century, the relatively new art of microscopy provided the intimate view required to describe the natural processes at work in the earth's top layers. In 1906 a fellow of the Royal Institute of British Architects, J. Donkin, wrote, "Science has taught us that the upper layers of the soil are teeming with forms of life whose hunger is inexhaustible and whose power of absorption is so active that anything that is even thrown on the surface of the ground speedily disappears, and, whether animal or vegetable, become humified and so incorporated with the soil as to become actually indistinguishable from it."

As investigations of soil continued, they confirmed that common dirt houses a virtual factory of activities prepared to deal with practically anything contacting the earth. In its role as a water filter—whether the liquid arrives carrying the wastes of forests and fields with their plants, insects and animals, or the discards of modern society—three processes are involved.

The first is physical. Soil consists mostly of an insoluble skeleton with pores of many sizes, some large enough to allow the earth to drain after heavy rains, others sized for holding enough moisture to water the roots of plants and nourish them with nutrients held in aqueous solution (such as those in wastewater). The structure acts as a strainer, removing extraneous matter from water to incorporate it into the soil skeleton or to feed it to plants. Different soils, of course, have different porosities, which influence their filtration qualities, and the differences have to be considered when the earth is called upon to clean wastewater and do it well.

The second process is chemical—for that matter, a whole series of processes are at work, including chemical alteration, ion exchange and adsorption and precipitation. In this division of the soil factory, the ingredients carried by water may be changed chemically (and rendered harmless in many cases of toxic substances), taken up and held by the soil or converted to gas for release to the atmosphere.

Third, soil acts as a biological filter, employing a variety of countless microbes in the top few inches of the earth. Their main job, for which their population increases and changes according to demand, is decomposing organic material and adding it as humus to the soil. This material then helps the physical and chemical processes. Some of the microbes can also degrade toxic materials and undesirable compounds,which, for example, may come from industrial discharges, detergents and pesticides. And certain microorganisms have a key function in the removal of nitrogen from water and, where possible, in putting it back to work in plant growth. Their numbers also include the forces manning the soil bastions to prevent the passage of pathogens, so that the living filter becomes a dead end for disease germs, bacteria and viruses.

When engineers attempt to replicate this three-part filter, they may succeed briefly, but then their creations often suffer from both design and operational problems (called O & M, for operation and maintenance). The South Lake Tahoe plant was a particular victim, but the failure is common in all kinds of treatment plants. Nature's soil system, however, is far more resilient in sustaining the kinds of knockout blows that come with the changing, difficult filtrates of modern life. Nature's O & M has been perfected over the eons, so the living filter's durability is difficult to match.

For two important reasons the natural system is self-buffering. First it can, in a sense, roll with the punches by adapting quickly to a wide range of waterborne ingredients, from the wastes of animals and insects to chemical discharges from modern industry. For its rapid adaptability the soil often changes help, hastily raising new forces of microbes with skills relevant to a new purification problem. Sewage treatment plant managers often hope for the same to happen when their systems falter, but the environment of frothing solutions in steel tanks, compared to that of soil, is not always conducive to a fast, adaptive change of microbes.

Second, the living filter, in a properly designed land treatment system, has size and time on its side. The wastewater at Muskegon, for example, literally has a 5,300-acre filter, whereas filtration in a conventional treatment plant for a comparable amount of wastewater might be tightly packed into a city block. Any specific area—any square foot, yard or mile—of the living filter, lightly and intermittently spray-irrigated with wastewater, receives in any given period a minuscule portion of the total waste delivered to the site. The natural systems are therefore not hard pressed and have time to adapt to new waterborne substances, like toxic industrial chemicals, that demand new microbic forces. So even in the worst of cases, when wastewater might carry devastating "slugs" of contaminants, the living filter is unlikely to be knocked out of commission. On the other hand the biological components of highly confined treatment plants are forever being put out of service by such slugs, and partially treated sewage passes to the receiving waters until the toxicity subsides and replacement populations of bacteria are cultivated. The Muskegon system really cannot be knocked out to the point that raw wastes reach the effluent flowing from the farm's underdrains. Even if the manager decides that the contamination is severe enough to damage the living filter, the system's immense storage lagoons can be used to withhold the substance, dilute it, confine it to a slow application on one area of land or whatever is required to avert the potential disaster. The conventional treatment plant manager seldom enjoys this option of time, for his system may be spoiled almost instantaneously, and unless his plant is one of relatively few with emergency storage ponds, raw potent pollutants will flow from the system.

Another remarkable feature of the living filter is its capacity to function either in part (for a long time) or in full (for a much longer time). Santee's filtration depends on soil alone with no plants. Similar settling basins have been designed to purify wastewater so it will be returned for reuse in groundwater serving drinking supplies. For example, since 1962 secondary effluent from Los Angeles sewage, mixed with natural runoff and

Colorado River water, has been filtered through spreading basins at the Whittier Narrows Water Reclamation Plant. The seepage then enters groundwater that provides drinking water for a large area of Los Angeles County. Such systems, properly sited, designed, operated and maintained, can serve as limited forms of circular systems, but obviously they lose an important potential of the living filter. While soil alone may last a long time as a filter, its effective life is certain to be shorter than that of soil with the vital removal forces of harvested plants. Effective nitrogen removal, for example, relies heavily on nitrogen's being taken up by growing and harvesting plants. Systems built without consideration of the weaknesses as well as the capabilities of soil filtration naturally run the risk of early failure or even becoming disasters.

The risk is evident with nearly 20 million individual housing units in the United States that depend on subsurface soil to filter wastewater through leaching fields after partial purification in septic tanks and cesspools. The discharge to the fields is usually through patterns of perforated or loosely jointed pipes buried deep enough so they will not be clogged by the root systems of large plants, like trees. In theory the leaching fields are part of an effective circular system, cleaning and returning wastewater to underground supplies for reuse via wells. But in practice they are often failures, poorly sited, designed and operated.

The problems were demonstrated by research at the Connecticut Agricultural Experiment Station on wastewater filtered through columns of soil in a laboratory. The results substantiated the power of soil alone as a filter, but also revealed there are hazards when root systems are not involved. A report on the research stated: "The results of our studies also tell us about the fate of nitrate and phosphate from septic tank systems which utilize only the subsoil to purify effluent. . . . Phosphate, passing through the septic system, is effectively removed. But nitrate is not removed and its discharge in the soil is generally below the depth of feeding root systems. Some may be converted to harmless nitrogen gas by anaerobic bacteria in water-logged soil but much of the nitrate leaches to ground-water supplies. Usually it is dilute enough to be harmless but great numbers of septic systems in sandy areas may create intolerable concentrations in ground water."

Because of such problems, areas of the nation that rely heavily on septic systems, like California and the Northeast, suffer considerable groundwater contamination. Thus the unknowing homeowner often fouls his and his neighbors' wells. Many owners exacerbate the damage when they use commercial septic-tank cleaning fluids to unclog leaching fields. The fluids may open up the fields, but they may also deliver carcinogens, such as trichloroethylene, to groundwater used for drinking supplies. In 1979 an estimated 400,000 gallons of such cleaners were used by homeowners on Long Island, New York, and the result was widespread contamination that forced the closing of many private and public wells.

But even when made to work efficiently, leaching fields and settling basins are truncated uses of the living filter and, as such, are more susceptible to problems and shortened lives. In full dress, incorporating green growth, the living filter is a dynamic system that can go on and on taking up and benefiting from the wastes that come with the water. As a full system the concept really offers more than just a filter. We might enlarge the description from Penn State, saying it is a living filter/factory that can offer investors economic benefits. Besides cleaning water, it can produce salable goods, including food, fiber and (as we shall see) even energy. Benefits in the truncated soil-only system are limited to water cleaning.

The potential life-span of the full dynamic system of soil and plants is difficult to assess. In theory a properly sited, planned and operated land treatment system—especially if designed to deliver only minuscule traces of contaminants per square inch per wastewater application, as at Muskegon—could remain effective for centuries. In practice we know from one remarkable case that a system can last most of a century, and there are indications it can continue for a long time beyond that. The evidence is in Australia. Since 1893, Melbourne, a large industrial metropolis, has irrigated a huge farm at nearby Werribee with the metropolitan area's wastewater. About half the flow is treated in a series of lagoons before irrigation, but the remainder is applied to the land raw, as was true of all the wastewater until the 1950s. The farm, with a total area of approximately 27,000 acres, receives the wastewater from some 2 million people, and most is applied to forage crops on land that has been continuously under pasture since 1914. The irrigated pastures are grazed throughout the year by up to 22,000 head of cattle, and up to 50,000 sheep are fattened on the land during the spring and summer. In a country acclaimed for good beef, the Melbourne and Metropolitan Board of Works Farm—which sells 7,000 cattle a year—is known for some of the best beef in Australia. In 1978 the board of works chairman, A. H. Croxford, told a Chicago meeting of the American Society of Agricultural Engineers, "Livestock thrive on the Farm and require only the same care and attention as livestock elsewhere." Going on to discuss the farm employees, Croxford pointed out, "There has never been an epidemic or outbreak of disease amongst Farm employees or residents, although no precautions other than normal hygiene practices have been taken. The general health of Farm employees or residents is no different to the community in general, in fact a recent survey showed that Farm people had a health status better than average." Of 328 people employed at the farm, the chairman explained, most live in a nearby township surrounded by land irrigated with wastewater, but 40 workers live on the farm itself. The board's full staff, over 9,000 people, uses the farm extensively for recreation and social events. Barbecue facilities and playing fields are located within the land filtration areas. Intraboard sporting events are held there, including cricket, football and tennis competitions. And when the board needs a place for public relations functions, or to entertain visitors, the Werribee farm is often the chosen site. All the while, the productive, attractive area thoroughly cleans the wastewater from the metropolis, releasing potable effluent to a popular fishing ground in Port Phillip Bay. And studies of the farm soil in recent years indicate the site is far from exhausted as a land treatment system.

The capacity of the living filter used in land treatment has been confirmed by increasing research over the years, so that a growing body of scientific and technical literature is available on how water can be purified while stimulating the growth of crops. In addition to describing the filtration characteristics of various soils, the material provides information on the selection and preparation of sites, and on crops, irrigation equipment and other design considerations for using the living filter and making it as fully self-supporting as possible.

Despite evidence such as that from Melbourne and other successful wastewater irrigation systems, opponents to land treatment still ignore the positive and focus on what they contend are the negative consequences it might have for human health. However, even as they dwell on the argument, their own stance on the question is often flawed. While they warn that applying wastewater to the land is a way of exposing human populations to disease and toxic substances, they themselves usually condone discharging the same wastes to rivers and lakes. This alternative definitely spreads the health hazards of wastewater—often from community to community, and frequently into the drinking water supplies of hundreds of thousands of people. When taken to the land, the same hazards are not only minimized by the soil but they can be observed and dealt with if necessary.

The industrial disposal of mercury—which in any case should be reclaimed, not thrown away—is an example. For years people have been warned that fish having consumed mercury are a potential hazard to health if eaten by humans. The metallic chemical discharged to a stream can definitely become a hazard, for it is picked up and spread by fine particulate matter normally suspended in the liquid. In the migrations of the particles, aquatic life may ingest the metal, and from there it has a possible route to the human food chain. However, when the same mercury is applied to the soil of a land treatment system, its travels end. Having become a meaningless fraction of a vast filter, its threat to human health is practically nonexistent because the substance is confined to the soil, and the plants, which offer its one route to the food chain, decline to take up the chemical.

The same difference applies to the harmful microbes of wastewater when delivered to natural bodies of water, as opposed to the land. Discharged to a river, a disease germ finds itself in a relatively friendly environment. And as is true of mercury, the germ and its progeny can travel by water, thus enlarging upon the organism's opportunities to do harm to humans. Its aquatic avenues to people are several, including water recreation, fish food and drinking water. However, the disease germ in spray-irrigated wastewater may expire even before it arrives on the ground (by desiccation when it is exposed to the air as its aqueous environment suddenly evaporates). But if it lands on the earth, the germ is promptly strained from the water and devoured by hostile microorganisms (which are harmless to humans). Finally the germ's remains become part of the living filter, even improving its functions. But again, should such a pathogen survive in a land treatment system with others of its own kind, the contamination would be confined to an identifiable location and the problem could be dealt with. Land, unlike water, tends to stay put, especially if soil erosion is controlled.

The contrast between the effects of land and water on pathogens is pronounced with the most dread organisms of all, viruses. A list of 32 known diseases caused by viruses commonly found in sewage was published by *Oceanus,* a journal from the Woods Hole (Massachusetts) Oceanographic Institution. The maladies ranged from the common cold and infant diarrhea to infectious hepatitis and sudden infant death syndrome. The accompanying article stated, "One of the most unpredictable aspects of sewage-borne viruses is their survival capabilities on leaving sewage treatment plants, especially when they enter marine waters." The author, J. M. Vaughn, pointed out that "despite massive dilution and adverse environmental conditions posed by coastal marine waters, there is growing concern that viruses will be capable of surviving for a period of days to weeks following discharge"—and possibly infect people through recreation, water-related work and consumption of filter-feeding shellfish. In contrast, research (such as that at Santee) shows that waterborne viruses are eliminated by soil filtration. A related report in *Science* came from Phoenix, Arizona, where investigators at the Flushing Meadows Project had been studying the purification of secondary sewage effluent by soil. "Our results," the scientists wrote, "indicate that human viral pathogens do not move through soil into the groundwater, which is significant, especially since the Flushing Meadows Project had renovated wastewater continually for 7 years at infiltration rates of about 100 m [328 feet] per year." Comparable results came in 1978 from a test site for wastewater irrigation at Roswell, New Mexico. The investigators, whose project was sponsored by the Environmental Protection Agency, reported that "the experience in this study confirmed that of other investigations in that recovery of viruses is rare from groundwater even near the surface or at sites of wastewater application and wherever the soil contains sufficient clay particles and the application is intermittent." The scientists also reported that neither the surface nor tissues of corn grown with wastewater had been contaminated with viruses. "These results," the researchers stated, "corroborated previous observations that crops rarely incorporate human viruses in their tissues and if allowed to be exposed to drying and sunlight, rarely exhibit viruses on their surface."

Nature's facility for neutralizing even the most serious contamination of soil and plants was pointed out years ago by two unusual studies. During the Korean War the U.S. Army Quartermaster Corps was concerned about troops in the Orient eating vegetables fertilized with "night soil" (untreated human waste). Rutgers University agreed to investigate the possible hazard, using test plots of vegetables, like lettuce, tomatoes and spinach. They were fertilized with raw sewage intentionally contaminated with a variety of hazardous pathogens. Test results showed the organisms were rendered harmless in short order by the power of soil, air and sunshine. Concentrations of bacteria on plants grown with raw sewage were no greater than on vegetables raised with conventional fertilizers. The scientists concluded that even when thoroughly sprayed with untreated wastewater, the crops were safe to eat if harvested one month after the last irrigation.

A few years earlier the effects on public health from exposure to sewage were studied from a very different but relevant perspective. Since the coming of railways to America, the tracks had been continually doused with raw sewage released from the toilets of passenger cars carrying millions of people. Through city and countryside alike the trains crisscrossed the United States and their discharges landed everywhere except (if the usual rule was obeyed) in railroad stations. What was the impact on public health? The question was reviewed in 1946 by a prominent epidemiologist, Professor Kenneth Maxcy. He focused on three classes of people whose health could have been jeopardized:

(1) those living close to tracks and terminals, (2) railway employees, and (3) consumers of water supplies located near the railroads. Looking for associations between illnesses and the railway sewage practice, Maxcy surveyed typhoid fever cases from 1900 to 1920 (when the disease was rampant and spread by human waste) and of gastroenteric diseases from 1920 to 1945. In neither case could the epidemiologist find evidence that the nationwide broadcasting of railway sewage had affected the health of the three classes of people.

Extensive research on the living filter has been going on at Penn State since 1962. When the work began, the rapidly growing university at State College, Pennsylvania, faced serious problems with water and sewage. The institution's wastewater was polluting Spring Creek, one of the state's finest trout streams. At the same time, trouble was predicted for the local water supply, which came from an aquifer that was being drawn down faster than nature could replenish it. A Waste Water Renovation and Conservation Project was initiated by the university to study and alleviate the problems. The project was run by a team of civil and agricultural engineers, foresters, geologists, microbiologists, biochemists and zoologists. Their studies led to a land treatment system that used croplands (raising feed corn, wheat, oats, alfalfa, red clover and reed canary grass) and woodlands (mixed hardwoods, red pine and white spruce). The spray irrigation of partially treated and disinfected sewage effluent alternated from the croplands in the growing season to woodlands for the remainder of the year. The seasonal shift answered the fact that in cold seasons heavy frost blocked infiltration of the water on open croplands, while the porous forest duff remained open to seepage. The system was operated both as a research project and to clean up the university's wastewater, return it for reuse to the groundwater supply and alleviate the pollution of Spring Creek.

Since its inception the work at Penn State has added considerably to the scientific and technical literature on the living filter. Comparative studies of irrigated and unirrigated crops revealed that the former produced far more than the latter. Yields of corn grain on irrigated plots increased by 8 to 346 percent, and corn silage by 79 to 136 percent. The growth of sugar maples increased 300 percent when irrigated with an inch (as rainfall is measured) of wastewater weekly.

Meanwhile studies of how the irrigation affected the health of wildlife showed positive results. Cottontail rabbits, for example, were better off on the irrigated than unirrigated sites, as revealed by higher body weights and increased population densities. Songbirds liked the irrigated lands, especially in late summer, when the moist soil had more worms and other food than did unirrigated areas. As the scientists looked for animal health problems related to the wastewater, they found no significant differences between sprayed and unsprayed areas.

Finally the Penn Staters concluded that their original goal of recharging the local groundwater supplies with safe, renovated water was succeeding. They ascertained that about 90 percent of the wastewater applied to the living filter was finding its way back to the underground drinking water reservoir. This result showed how a community can have its water and drink it too, even over and over again, while enjoying the amenities that can come from stimulating green growth in fields, forests and practically anyplace else where water and plants are desirable.

While research at Penn State and elsewhere confirms that the living filter is a capable, dependable tool for purifying and reclaiming wastewater—as well as the other resources it contains—these remarkable qualities still must be put to work intelligently if the living filter is to serve our pressing needs for clean water. Each adaptation of the filter must be custom-designed to harmonize with nature, which may demand diverse skills seldom available among conventional sanitary-engineering consultants. The needed talents range from those of agricultural engineers, who know soils, crops and drainage techniques, to those of meteorologists, who can make certain that a system will function compatibly with local temperatures, wind and precipitation. Whatever arrangement is worked out with nature it must, of course, stand ready to accommodate the anticipated waste stream. Today's wastewater, reflecting the goods and services of modern society, can include exotic materials that in some instances may determine the basic design of the living filter.

The most controversial of these ingredients are the elements known as heavy metals. In the tiny (trace) amounts usually associated with domestic sewage, they can benefit plant growth. But sometimes when industrial waste is present they show up in larger, toxic quantities. One dozen are involved: cadmium, chromium, cobalt, copper, iron, lead, manganese, mercury, molybdenum, nickel, tin and zinc. Relatively large quantities of iron and manganese are already present in soil, so adding small amounts is meaningless. All but four of the remaining ten metals are filtered from waste streams by the soil and trapped there to do no harm. The four exceptions are zinc, copper, nickel and cadmium. They, too, are removed from water by the soil, but then they may be taken up by plants. Too much zinc, copper and nickel may damage growth in some plants. Cadmium does not damage plants; however, too much of the element may be harmful to their consumers.

If these metals in amounts damaging to plants or other living beings threaten a land treatment system, they must be either kept out of the irrigation water in the first place, or compensated for in the selection of the system's plants. If, for example, cadmium was a problem, crops might be limited to trees or shrubs in which the metal take-up would make no difference. Or if a food crop was desired, it could be one of those (like feed corn) with edible grain that excludes cadmium, even though the metal has entered the stalks and leaves.

The first comprehensive book on the subject was published in 1978 by Geoffrey W. Leeper, emeritus professor of chemistry at the University of Melbourne, Australia. The volume, *Managing the Heavy Metals on the Land,* explores the interaction of these elements with soil and plants, discussing how they can be dealt with in the design and operation of land treatment systems. Leeper's work reveals that heavy metals need not be the formidable barrier to land treatment that some of its opponents maintain. In the conclusion of a summary for lay readers, Leeper states, "It is no light matter to decide to multiply the naturally occurring burdens of heavy metals in soils. . . . Yet most soils can carry such burdens without incurring any more serious penalty than the need for occasionally liming the soil to near the neutral point."

While plants and soil as used in agriculture and silviculture hold the greatest potential for the living filter, the possibilities for cleaning water while producing valuable crops may be increased if aquaculture is also considered. In this case the harvest may be fish or aquatic plants.

To raise fish, an aquaculture system can be a simple pond where algae is intentionally cultivated by nutrients introduced with partially treated wastewater. The body of water is stocked with fish that feed and thrive on the algae. When properly fattened, the fish are harvested for food or for protein supplement, usually after they are moved to freshwater for a period of time. This combination of aquaculture and advanced wastewater treatment has not been practiced to any extent in the United States, but it has been used in Europe for a long time. The most notable example has been in operation at Munich, West Germany, for decades. Treated wastewater has been diluted and channeled through a series of ponds from 10 to 12 acres apiece. Each pond has been reported to contain about 5,000 carp, which are fattened and harvested to produce nearly a quarter ton of fish flesh per acre per year. Other such systems at Berlin and Kielce, Poland, have reported even higher yields, with the latter's annual production attaining more than a half ton of fish flesh per acre.

In aquaculture systems where nutrient-removing plants are cultivated and harvested instead of fish, the plants can serve as "biomass" from which energy can be produced as "biogas" (methane and carbon dioxide). The gas can be burned for heat or used to fuel an engine-generator that makes electricity. The idea of employing aquaculture as a combination of advanced wastewater treatment and a producer of crops for energy is still in the experimental, pilot-plant stages of development. Considerable research is in progress around the country. For example, an experimental "seaweed farm" is found at the Marine Sciences Research Center at Stony Brook, Long Island, New York. The seaweed, whose growth will clean water, will be harvested to produce biogas.

Unquestionably the technical know-how can be developed to make use of the resources in wastewater as raw materials, but the most perplexing difficulties are often social in nature. Land treatment can, of course, be vulnerable to public fears—and the lingering histories of disastrous sewage farms still contribute.

Moreover, the opponents of land treatment—the forces of orthodoxy discussed earlier—often play on these fears to undermine support for such systems, from both citizens and public officials. The assumption that people will not tolerate land treatment often becomes the official reason for not considering the option at all.

But experience, and, in fact, opinion research, confirms that an informed public is likely to react the opposite way from the assumption. When people learn how nature's recycling abilities can work for us, common sense becomes a powerful persuader to take advantage of them. Santee is the best case in point. When Ray Stoyer developed the project, he continually explained to townspeople how his idea would be workable, safe and beneficial. Eventually public pressure built in favor of, not against, the idea. The citizenry became convinced, along with Stoyer, that the reclaimed sewage effluent would be safe and nuisance free for the much-desired lakes. Then, when the project was completed but still lacked state approval for recreation, people became frustrated, for they could see the enticing freshwater but were forbidden to use it. Their impatience turned to intolerance over the time health officials were taking to give approval. The resulting public pressure was, of course, an important ingredient in the project's eventually being okayed for recreation.

Two more case histories further support the argument that public intolerance for land treatment is often more shadow than substance. The first comes from Colorado Springs. The city's streets and other public areas are dressed up with a great deal of green that would be brown if not for irrigation by partially purified sewage effluent from the municipal treatment system. The treated, disinfected wastewater irrigates and fertilizes median strips of some of the nicest boulevards in the city. The same is true for parks, golf courses and even a large cemetery. The savings are measured in the conservation of potable water at the public supply and in savings of fertilizer that would have to be purchased with public funds. Even the entire campus of the city's most famous school, Colorado College, receives a share of the water-fertilizer combination. The remarkable in-town irrigation program came into being with a careful public information program. It started with a highway beautification effort at the edge of town and gradually expanded to the irrigated areas of the inner city.

Perhaps more surprising than the case of Colorado Springs is that of San Francisco's Golden Gate Park, which has millions of visitors. For a half century, partially purified sewage effluent was used to irrigate the park. Golden Gate, one of the world's largest, most beautiful inner-city parks, was built on what nineteenth-century opponents to buying the land called "the great sand waste," a 1,000-acre parcel consisting largely of windswept dunes inhospitable to vegetation. The soil was first built up with street sweepings containing a good portion of horse manure. In 1932 one of the city's sewage treatment plants was built in the middle of the park, and thenceforth it contributed both nutrient-rich effluent for irrigation of grass and shrubs, and sewage sludge for soil conditioner. The practice continues. Sterilized, treated sewage effluent is pumped to a storage pond on a hill where time, air and sunlight further stabilize the wastewater, thereby upgrading its quality. From there it flows as needed to several ornamental lakes and irrigation systems for lawns, playing fields and a large number of exotic flowers, shrubs and trees imported from various parts of the world. A share of the water in Stow Lake, on which park visitors go rowing in rented boats, consists of the wastewater effluent. And beautiful Huntington Falls, one of the park's prize ornaments, is sometimes all sewage effluent. In a half century of such applications in the midst of millions of visitors, no problems have arisen to indicate the system is a public nuisance or health hazard. When San Franciscans learn of how their lovely park is beautified with their own waste, they usually praise those responsible.

Not long after Santee's unique experience had undermined the crusty assumption that people would not reuse their own wastewater, James J. Johnson at the University of Chicago made an opinion survey of the reuse question and confirmed much that Stoyer had learned firsthand. Johnson's study, conducted in five major American cities, indicated the majority of people had no qualms about water reuse when it was responsibly carried out. And the more knowledge they had on how it was done, the more likely they were to accept reuse. Perhaps most significant for the impending water crisis of the 1980s was Johnson's finding that threats of shortages made people more willing to accept wastewater reclamation. The researcher confirmed that most of the negativism toward reclamation came, not from the lay citizen, but from the public official who dismissed the idea out of hand, falsely assuming his constituents would reject reclaimed water. And as Stoyer sensed the need for public education on his project, Johnson concluded it had to be part of any attempt at reuse, and the first students ought to be the public officials who would be involved.

Less than 100 years ago, passengers on European trains could often tell when they were close to a major city, for their cars would pass through belts of unusually fertile fields where the growth was more verdant than elsewhere. The trains were passing through the land treatment sites of those days, when wastewater was taken out of urban areas, used to raise crops for the cities and returned as purified water. In today's America, afflicted with too much gray concrete and black, bituminous pavement, stimulating air pollution and encroaching on the nation's farmlands, we need a great deal more of the vibrant greenery seen from the European trains. We need it both as aesthetic relief from our paved urban scene and as sinks for the air pollution rising from the pavement. Because of the water crisis we also should have those verdant areas created as a means of abiding by nature's law of return and to enjoy all the water we need. With today's scientific knowledge of the living filter and the makeup of our wastewaters, we have the opportunity to move away from the losing battle of linear systems with their unattractive treatment works and unrelieved water pollution, toward the promise of circular systems with their potential public amenities of decorative lakes, open space with green growth and the return of freshwater in the bargain.

X

Resources out of Place

In the introduction to his satirical but serious book *The Toilet Papers,* Sim Van der Ryn, California's state architect and professor of architecture at the University of California, Berkeley, asks readers to imagine some future archaeologist trying to figure out the artifacts of America's linear water and sewage systems. The future scientist, says Van der Ryn, "would need to be a genius to guess at the destructiveness and irrationality of present-day 'sanitary engineering.' " So it would be understandable if the archaeologist came up with a reversed image of what had happened on the wastewater end of the line with "the curiously shaped ceramic bowl in each house, hooked up through miles of pipe to a central factory of tanks, stirrers, cookers and ponds. . . ." He could assume, says Van der Ryn, that "by early in the twentieth century urban earthlings had devised a highly ingenious food production system whereby algae were cultivated in large centralized farms and piped directly into a ceramic food receptacle in each home."

The California architect is one of a growing number of people who recognize the loss we sustain in fertilizing resources and the damage we inflict upon increasingly precious water supplies with our disposal-dilution philosophy of wastewater. In his book, Van der Ryn makes the point with an aerial photograph of Los Angeles's huge Hyperion Sewage Treatment Plant, sandwiched between the ocean and a thickly settled urban area. The plant, he reveals, discharges some 335 million gallons of effluent a day, most of which is treated only to the primary level (simply allowing solids to settle from the water). The outflow is carried 5 miles out under the ocean through a 12-foot pipe and discharged into a 197-foot depth. Another big pipe carries the plant's sludge (the settled solids) 7 miles out to the brink of a marine canyon where the ocean is 300 feet deep. Van der Ryn estimated that each day the pipes dispose of fertilizing nutrients that could "grow 5,000 tons of vegetables, enough to provide everyone in Los Angeles with a pound or two of fresh produce daily." Subsequently he learned that the nutrients had cultivated an overpopulation of sea urchins that were devouring giant kelp and robbing valuable marine life of its food and habitat. The loss was so serious that the Los Angeles County Department of Parks and Recreation called for volunteer divers to kill the sea urchins.

Unlike this book with the memorable title, most discussions of the impending water crisis neglect the sewage side of our linear systems. But anyone willing to put queasiness aside and look at the ingredients of wastewater will see why the nation's huge flows offer a choice of continual degradation of good water or the opportunity for the most important solution to the water crisis.

First of all, our burgeoning sewage flow squanders a great deal of the water we so badly need. With the traditional "water carriage" method of removing our wastes, the flow ends up as all water except for a relatively minute percentage of waste. Sewage is far, far more pure than dirty. A "Citizen Handbook," *Municipal Wastewater Processes: Overview,* prepared by the Institute of State and Regional Affairs of Pennsylvania State University, explains, "Sewage is more than 99.9 percent pure water. This amounts to about two drops of waste in a quart of water."

As the typical American flushes and washes, little water is spared. The most profligate converter of pure water to sewage in the home is the flush toilet. Five gallons is the general use per flush, according to the *Journal of the American Water Works Association.* So a cup of urine, itself nearly all water, is swept away by 85 times its volume in pure water. Next in profligacy comes bathing and showering, which accounts for 30 percent of home consumption as gallons of good water carry off the hardly measurable grime of daily life. Water has been cheap, so the same imbalance between waste and pure water has been possible for all sources of sewage, homes, businesses and industry.

We have calculated that the barely tainted flow issuing from the waste end of the nation's linear systems amounts to some 40 billion gallons a day (not including the large quantities of cooling water from electric generation plants). So if all but a minor fraction of this immense, once-used gallonage is pure water, we lose a huge potential supply through our questionable disposal practices. In a 1980 report the Congressional Research Service of the Library of Congress showed that freshwater consumed in the conterminous United States was 96 billion gallons a day (which would include considerable amounts lost to evaporation, retention in products and disposal through means other than municipal sewerage systems). Thus in our 40 billion gallons of sewage daily, we are throwing away a potential supply equal to some 42 percent of the national freshwater withdrawal. But actually we are talking about more than 42 percent, because disposal of the waste riding the water carriage renders unusable more potential supplies than can be calculated, including both surface waters and groundwater sources contaminated by induced infiltration from sewage-burdened rivers.

The less than 0.1 percent of materials that convert pure water to sewage contains the ingredients that can be the key to releasing the good water in wastewater—if we will recognize and invest in them as raw materials to be put back to work, rather than useless, superfluous waste to be rid of whatever the cost.

The major raw materials in wastewater are three fertilizing nutrients: nitrogen, phosphorus and potassium, known as NPK. These three letters are on a colorful chart displayed in many American classrooms. Entitled "The Nutrient Cycle," the chart shows a wheel that illustrates the circular course followed by NPK, from the earth through crops and animals to a family at a dining table, then on around the circle, back to the earth. Avoiding scatology, the chart does not indicate how the three nutrients return from the people to the soil. And perhaps just as well, for in much of modern civilization NPK does not go back to the soil. A diagram of what really happens would complicate the chart. The circle would have to be broken, showing a great deal of NPK going off on a tangent to a nearby river. A caption would have to explain that we violate the nutrient cycle by disposing of considerable NPK through sewerage works to natural bodies of water. Moreover, the river in the revised chart would have to be colored green, representing algae and other aquatic plants cultivated by the off-course NPK.

The point is that the nation's 40 billion gallons of wastewater per day carries off billions of pounds of NPK, which, if we practiced the classroom lesson, would remain in the nutrient cycle. Moreover, most of these dissolved nutrients pass unharmed through conventional treatment plants on the way to disposal (secondary treatment leaves about 80 percent of the N, 70 percent of the P and 90 percent of the K). So if all the nation's wastewater received secondary treatment (which it does not), the effluent each year would carry away some 2.4 billion pounds of nitrogen, 1.2 billion pounds of phosphorus and 1.2 billion pounds of potassium.

The loss of fertilizer—to say nothing of the damage inflicted on receiving waters—is accentuated if a price tag is attached to the nutrients, and inflation is worked into the figure over half a decade. In 1976 the lost nutrients (if they were part of a typical mixed fertilizer used by farmers) would have cost some $375 million, but by 1981 they would have sold for about $525 million. According to the United States Department of Agriculture, prices for mixed fertilizer rose nearly 150 percent from 1967 to 1980 (and they continue going up). In the same 13 years, demand for the nutrients increased greatly, with N up some 80 percent; P, 70 percent; and K, 25 percent. While demand contributed to the rising cost, the inflation was also tied to the upward surge of oil prices. Today's chemical fertilizers are petroleum intensive, for large amounts of oil and natural gas are consumed in the mining, manufacture and transportation of the crucial nutrients. So we can say that the nutrients wasted in the nation's wastewater require 2.25 billion gallons (or over 53 million barrels) of crude oil annually to replace them. This represents 5 percent, or 18 days' supply, of our imported oil, and (at $34 a barrel) $1.8 billion.

The amount of NPK in secondary effluent has been substantiated by the years of research at Pennsylvania State University. The scientists have found that in spray-irrigating their experimental croplands with two inches of effluent per week during the growing season, they simultaneously deliver approximately 200 pounds of nitrogen, 90 pounds of phosphorus and 190 pounds of potassium per acre. The season's application, the researchers noted, would be equal to applying 2,000 pounds of 10-10-11 fertilizer. As previously revealed, the fertilizer-laden irrigant has produced remarkable yields while effectively cleaning the water.

But such use of wastewater as fertilizer is minimal in the United States, although the misplaced resource is one that we cannot afford to throw away. In 1981 John Douglas of the Tennessee Valley Authority's National Fertilizer Development Center told a reporter that "demand for all nitrogen products is the most intense in recent memory." And to emphasize the importance of the key fertilizing component, Douglas said, ". . . we have an old rule of thumb in this business—one ton of nitrogen equals ten tons of grain." Applying his rule to the nitrogen we waste with secondary effluent discharged to the detriment of receiving waters, the lost potential in production is 12 million tons of grain.

The success of the Muskegon land treatment system was related to the NPK and water applied to otherwise unproductive land. In 1975 the county's wastewater delivered 500,000 pounds of nitrogen, 200,000 of phosphorus and 550,000 of potassium. The value as fertilizer was figured at $112,000—a price that has escalated since then and continues to do so.

With values like these at stake, as well as a potential solution to the impending water crisis, environmentalists who lobby assiduously for bottle bills might be even more productive in pushing nutrient bills to recycle used fertilizer. One of their earliest leaders, ecologist Barry Commoner, was working at the idea in 1971 when he testified before the Illinois Pollution Control Board. "I'm proposing a very simple thing," he said. "Lend the nitrogen to the city folks—but get it back!"

Two more resources in sewage are worth getting back. Though they are not so easily tagged with a dollar figure, they are priceless to anyone close to the soil. First, soil-enriching organic matter comes with the solids in domestic and industrial wastewater. Second, various trace elements (micronutrients) are found in wastewater, and they too can be priceless for good crops.

One of the main jobs for conventional sewage treatment is removal of organic matter, which can become a leading cause of water pollution. When dumped in a river or lake, organic matter feeds aerobic bacteria and their proliferation literally chokes the water to death. The bacterial population explosion consumes dissolved oxygen needed by other organisms and plants that help keep water fresh. When the sanitary engineer tries to reduce organic matter in treated effluent, he is holding down what is called BOD, biochemical oxygen demand. Too high a BOD contributes to the most obnoxious, publicly irritating kind of water pollution.

The greatest percentage of organic matter removed by treatment works ends up in sludge that—as any newspaper reader should know—has become a national disposal problem. Sludge, like the wastewater from which it comes, is also primarily water, 95 to 98 percent. The first task in getting rid of it is called dewatering, and an array of techniques are used. One is commonly called decanting, where the solids are allowed to settle and the water is drawn off the top. Other methods involve vacuum filters, belt presses and chemical additives, all of which concentrate the solids and, in a sense, squeeze out the water. Whatever the process, the sludge, which probably remains as much as 80 percent water, still has to be disposed of. Where to put it plagues many of the nation's communities. Some dump it in landfills, where it leaches into groundwater and surface water resources, again diminishing sources of clean supplies. Cities on the oceans are piping or barging the mess out to sea, hoping it will vanish in the briny deep (but it does not, as the instigators of the practice often hear from swimmers). Some communities attempt to burn sludge. They thereby consume ever more expensive oil for incinerators and pollute the air with materials that might have polluted water. Even then the incinerators end up with residuals that must be disposed of. The nation's sludge handlers, who are always trying to be completely rid of the stuff, are forever confronted with the simple axiom that "everything must be someplace."

But while organic matter may be the bane of the traditional sewage works man, it is the boon of anyone concerned about healthy soil and green growth. It is a crucial binding agent for fine particles of clay and silt. Organic matter keeps soil soft, easier to work and less likely to be washed away by rain. In a sense the material gives elbow room to the earth, so microbes can breathe and carry out their essential work of helping to supply nutrients for plants.

When sludge is recognized as a valuable source of organic matter rather than something to be dumped, the rewards are often amazing. The dividends have been realized, for instance, where sludge has revitalized strip-mine spoils. The spoils (surface mining of coal has disturbed about 4 million acres of land in the United States) can become a deathly, impoverished environment. It is inhospitable to the germination of seeds, and runoff from the desolate territories causes water pollution. Since the 1960s numerous research and demonstration projects have shown how sewage sludge can restore and revitalize these spoils. Dr. William Sopper, professor of forest hydrology at Penn State, says, "The results of these studies indicate that properly treated municipal sludge is a valuable resource. This waste product can be used beneficially to revegetate bituminous strip mine spoils and anthracite refuse banks throughout the Appalachian region. This ultimately restores them to an aesthetically acceptable and productive state without adverse environmental impact." As an example, Sopper cites how sludge from the Scranton-Dunmore (Pennsylvania) treatment works was applied to an anthracite refuse bank. The application was started in May, 1974, and by September the treated area had a thick vegetative cover, which continued to improve in the ensuing growing seasons.

One of the most remarkable cases of land restoration with sludge occurred at Ottawa, Illinois, where wastes from grinding and polishing glass at the Libbey-Owens-Ford Company had covered and destroyed many acres of land. Traffic on a nearby highway sometimes had to be stopped because of wind-driven storms of the glass waste. In a three-month period, however, the desolate area became a beautiful field of green grass after being covered with sludge from Chicago's sewage treatment works.

Once more, in discussing the organic matter of wastewater, we are talking about another potential raw material that can either go on destroying good water or be put to productive use in soil. On a land treatment site, maintaining a relatively high level of organic matter in the irrigation water—so much that it could cause pollution in stream disposal—can be beneficial to the earth and crops. Moreover, the lesser amounts of sludge that collect in the treatment units can be occasionally removed and injected into the land as additional soil conditioner. At the Muskegon site, for example, sludge settling in the treatment and storage lagoons is occasionally dredged and applied to the land. On such a land treatment site, where industrial effluent may include undue amounts of heavy metals, maintaining organic matter in the soil has the additional advantage of helping the earth contain and retain the metals, rendering them harmless to the reclaimed water and the crops.

The second potential resource besides NPK in wastewater is the trace elements (including soluble materials), such as heavy metals and nonmetalic materials like sulfur, boron, iodine, arsenic and selenium. In trace amounts distributed through the soil, these elements can make the difference between healthy and sickly plants, between marginal and bumper crops.

Geoffrey Leeper, of the University of Melbourne, once told of how the gardeners of London learned about the importance of the trace element sulfur. When the city stopped burning coal back in the 1950s, it ended the famous London fog (really smog), but also left its garden plots in trouble. Gardeners soon discovered their soil was missing trace amounts of sulfur previously supplied by the polluted air (through acid rain), and the element had to be replaced to restore the bountiful harvests of the past.

These micronutrients, if properly managed, can be part of the raw materials of wastewater. Even the heavy metals that are loosely characterized by some people as the undoing of land treatment can be beneficial as trace elements essential to healthy plant life. The intelligent use of these elements, as opposed to unthinking disposal, can include them as potential raw materials of wastewater that in turn can contribute to solving the water crisis.

In thinking about the waste ingredients of sewage as raw materials, one might assume that increasing our flows of wastewater would even be advisable, but actually it would not. To the contrary, water conservation can become all the more important, in terms of both the water resource and the waste resources. To begin with the obvious, "water saved is water gained." But water saved does not diminish the waste ingredients carried by sewage. The valuable nutrients (NPK), organic matter and trace elements remain the same; thus with water being conserved they are simply transported in more concentrated form. When they arrive at a land treatment site, the more concentrated the waste the better. To the system manager it means handling and storing less water, while enjoying the same growth-stimulating resources. Efficient use of the living filter, therefore, provides another reason for conserving water.

The scientific management of all the resources in wastewater, from the preponderance of pure water down to the minute trace elements, is the key to turning the distress of sewage into a blessing. We now have the knowledge and a growing wealth of experience to show us how the unholy freight of the water carriage can be the payload, even for privately funding our way out of the linear debacle behind the water crisis.

In 1976 Senator Muskie summed it up when he wrote:

> In the greatest food-producing country the world has ever seen, we continue to consider nutrients as pollutants. Phosphorus, nitrogen and potassium have been the targets for water pollution clean-up efforts for years, and then viewed as a sludge disposal problem, while the cost of fertilizer has escalated to unacceptable levels.
>
> I am especially interested in those treatment systems which produce financial, as well as environmental benefits, benefits which recover valuable resources.
>
> Systems which cooperate with nature are cheaper in the short run, and in the long run use less of our valuable resources because they are renewable.

XI

The Water Self-sufficient Community

Three miles west of Chicago's O'Hare International Airport, in Itasca, Illinois, an innovative new development has significance for solving the water crisis faced by American cities, young and old. The Itasca complex, when fully constructed, will contain 6 million square feet of hotel and office floor space on 274 acres, and, in population density, it will be comparable to the downtowns of our older cities. In fact, one might envision the development, partially completed and opened in 1980, as a section carved from an American city. The project is called Hamilton Lakes. Its namesake, Allan Hamilton, was chiefly responsible for the development. The endeavor would probably still be only plans on paper if Hamilton had not found and taken a new direction in water and wastewater management. The project came to life as a water self-sufficient community that immediately attained the nationally elusive wastewater goal of zero discharge. Moreover, Hamilton found that the new direction was worthy of private investment, so that Hamilton Lakes was built around a circular system that required none of the usual state and federal grants raised from taxes. The project, which in one stroke avoided the water crisis faced by many urban areas, points a way that others might follow in dealing with their intensifying problems of water and wastewater.

Back in the mid-1970s Hamilton, managing partner of the Trammell Crow Company of Chicago, had the Hamilton Lakes plans, but construction was stymied. The gordian knot was in the project's ties to Itasca for municipal water and sewerage services, and that small city's difficulties were holding everything up. Itasca was experiencing explosive growth, with its 1970 population of 4,638 on the way to becoming 8,000 in 1980. Typically, its water and sewerage systems were unable to keep up with the growth, and the large Trammell Crow development could not be accommodated for many years.

In search of ways to untie the knot, Hamilton contacted the then new firm of Sheaffer & Roland, whose president was one of the present authors (Sheaffer). The member-owned company had formed around a nucleus of scientists and engineers who had worked on the Muskegon project. They included Fred Roland (the new firm's vice-president), Wayne A. Cowlishaw, William Eyring and Fred Neal. Unlike most consulting firms (which are organized primarily to provide technical services for pay), this one's primary focus was a commitment to a philosophy. The members had decided to limit their services to the development of ecologically sound urban centers, recognizing three principles: (1) that everything about land, water and air is interconnected and what affects one is likely to affect all three, (2) that we are bound by nature's closed systems, from which nothing disappears and in which everything has its rightful place, and (3) that so-called pollutants are really resources out of place.

Hamilton's dilemma seemed to be solvable by Sheaffer & Roland's ideas. Not only did they point the way to an ecologically sound development, but they indicated that a circular system for water and wastewater could free the project of its problematical ties with Itasca. As it turned out, the results were applicable to the perplexing problems that many municipalities suffer with their linear systems tormented by growth, old age, a welter of changing regulations and on and on.

Sheaffer & Roland was retained in December, 1977, to prepare a "Comprehensive Resource Management Plan" for the 274-acre site. One year later the state of Illinois agreed to a concept that included the first land treatment system within its borders. Unlike the Muskegon plan of nearly a decade earlier, the system would not grow food; in keeping with the landscaping of a luxury hotel and modern office complex, the plants would be grass, shrubs and trees. In conjunction with the land treatment area there would be a series of attractive lakes, playing a role in the circular management of the water as well as being amenities for the hotel guests and office employees. When the state approved the plan, it untied the gordian knot binding the Trammell Crow project to Itasca's conventional problems of water and sewerage. While the town's difficulties continued (and still do), construction proceeded at Hamilton Lakes, and occupancy of the first buildings began in December, 1980.

Today's guests at the Hamilton, a dramatic 12-story hotel with a massive 200-foot atrium under a glass dome, may find the outdoors as attractive as the interior. And the same is true for employees in an adjacent 15-story office building. Guests and office workers alike can enjoy attractive walks around the lawns, trees, shrubs and five freshwater lakes with small connecting waterfalls. The lakes range from about 3.5 to 6 acres, with a total surface of 24.5 acres. Their average depth is seven feet, but they include especially shallow areas where common reeds and cattails grow. The lakes are connected with two pumping stations that can supply the project's fire hydrants and standpipes with 3,000 gallons of water per minute for eight hours. The uninformed visitor strolling around the lakes has no reason to suspect that their setting and the contrasting buildings with their paved parking areas are all integral parts of Hamilton Lakes' self-contained water and wastewater system.

The project's water supply is designed to integrate two sources, groundwater from below and precipitation from above. Both sources are involved in the total circular concept at Hamilton Lakes..

The groundwater supply comes from an aquifer beneath the site. Two wells provide about 1,000 gallons a minute for the hotel and offices. Both buildings are equipped with water-conserving plumbing designed to hold water usage to the minimum possible without affecting lifestyle or comfort. The planned flow is about a quarter-million gallons a day, a low figure for a 440-room hotel, several restaurants and office, commercial and industrial space that can accommodate 18,000 employees.

Sewage from the complex is collected and pumped to either of two treatment lagoons in one corner of the site. The lagoons, which are 19 feet deep and cover just over an acre and a half, are engineered so any given amount of wastewater remains there for 39 days. Forced air from tubes in their bottoms oxygenates the wastewater as bubbles rise to the surface. The oxygenation, along with the play of air and sunshine on the surface, prevents the lagoons from becoming odorous, and it stimulates aerobic bacteria that metabolize and consume most of the organic pollutants. There is also a small lake that provides storage for the treated wastewater for 120 days in the cold months when irrigation is impractical. During the remaining 245 days of the year, the treated effluent is distributed at night through 316 sprinklers to the project's lawns and other green growth. Meanwhile, the workaday treatment and storage ponds are attractive bodies of water—especially to the area's waterfowl.

The living filter—which here at Itasca is the rich, verdant landscape—acts as an advanced wastewater treatment system, completing the purification so water can be returned to the natural supply for reuse. Initially the land treatment area was 32.5 acres, but as the project grows, the irrigated landscape will be expanded to 83 acres. During treatment some of the water percolates down through the soil, back to the aquifer where it started. A larger portion is cleaned as it moves horizontally through the soil into ten sedimentation basins. In the basins the water receives one last filtering, seeping down through sand to underdrains that discharge into the lakes. At this point more of the purified water gets into the aquifer, by infiltration through the bottoms of the lakes.

In addition, stormwater is carefully managed at Hamilton Lakes, both to make use of natural precipitation and to control flooding in heavy rains. The design is such that rainwater and the melt of snow and ice run off slowly through the soil and vegetation in the same manner as the project's wastewater. The design also ensures that stormwater runoff from roofs and parking lots is guided from building drains and paved surfaces out to the combination landscape–land treatment areas. This drainage, as is true of all stormwater runoff from such surfaces, can be polluted, so it is treated by the living filter as the liquid percolates into the earth or moves horizontally to the sediment basins and the lakes. Thus the full complement of stormwater landing on the project helps replenish its groundwater supply and its lakes.

At the same time the entire site was designed with flood control in mind, specifically to control runoff from what is technically called the 100-year storm. This is the heaviest rainstorm with a 1 percent chance of occurring in a given region in a given year. The 100-year storm for the Chicago region is generally taken as six inches of rain in 24 hours. The Hamilton Lakes site and buildings were designed to receive the water from a storm of this magnitude and gradually release it without hazardous flooding. Thus the utilitarian site also provides a flood control system that towns and cities generally do not enjoy.

Indeed, outside of Hamilton Lakes, hardly any other community in the nation can look favorably upon urban stormwater as an added, valuable source of water supply. In most other municipalities stormwater caught by impervious surfaces remains an insidious source of trouble. Besides causing floods, it is a leading contributor to water pollution, and thus a cause for diminishment of potential water supplies. It gathers up potent ingredients, from spilled antifreeze to pet droppings, and often delivers them directly to streams and lakes—or through combined sewers to conventional treatment plants. The plants are frequently hit by sudden, storm-induced slugs of the potent mixture, their purification systems are knocked out and inadequately treated sewage from all sources escapes to receiving waters. But if stormwater could be taken as a resource out of place, rather than something simply to be rid of, the disposal cost be damned, it could in fact become an important alternative source for many a city's troubled water supply.

With its privately funded circular water and wastewater system, Hamilton Lakes enjoys a degree of independence whose value is impossible to tag with a price. Of course the development is not locked into Itasca's water supply and therefore subject to the municipality's growth pains, financial headaches, shortages, political squabbles, purification problems and other common difficulties over which the new project would have little or no control. But probably a more important element of Hamilton Lakes' independence comes from its truly providing zero discharge, the concept that was withered by ridicule in the 1970s. As the Itasca project was planned and engineered, government regulatory agencies became convinced that the zero-discharge goal was attainable by the design, and they agreed to exempt Hamilton Lakes from the usual permit requirement of the National Pollution Discharge Elimination System. (The NPDES permit system was set up to diminish sewage pollutants systematically and eliminate their discharge by 1985 through more and more stringent permit requirements; but the system has failed simply because heavily relied upon conventional treatment plants cannot eliminate pollutants.) No pollutants were to be discharged from the new development to public waters, so in the eyes of the NPDES no permit was needed. This independence from the permit system relieved the new development of many headaches common to conventional systems. If, for example, the project were subject to the federal discharge permits, it could be whiplashed by NPDES changes made in Washington, even though they might be locally irrelevant.

Hamilton Lakes' financial independence also avoided the nightmare of frustrations, delays and inevitable disappointments that are suffered when federal funds are depended upon for planning, engineering and constructing wastewater systems. While federal law provides sizable grants to reimburse communities for building water pollution control systems, actually getting the money is anything but quick and simple. The average time from start to finish of a conventional wastewater project has stretched out to nine years.

But the most significant point was this: through private investment Hamilton Lakes benefited far more than it would have by following the public grants route to a traditional linear system that could be more cause than cure for our water problems. In breaking away from the orthodox technology, Allan Hamilton was able to move directly to a circular system with a renewable water supply and a wastewater treatment system that, in using the waste as raw materials, makes a return on the private investment.

The contrast between the development and its county neighbors was pointed up by Casey Bukro, environmental editor of the *Chicago Tribune:* "Du Page County is famous for towns haunted by the specter of running dry. The threat is so real that 27 county communities have banded together to build a $300 million pipeline to tap Chicago's water system. In this scramble for fresh water [Hamilton Lakes is] an oasis in Du Page County where there are no water shortages."

Going around the establishment is an avenue that can lead to solutions for the water crises plaguing American communities. Hamilton Lakes stands as a model proving it can be done.

XII

The Problems and Possibilities of Scale

In the 1970s the U.S. Army Corps of Engineers, which had been deeply involved in building (and widely criticized for overdoing) flood control and water supply dams, began concerning itself with alternative methods for cleaning up the nation's waters. The move pleasantly surprised some of the corps's severest critics, who recognized the organization had immense capabilities applicable to the nation's difficult water pollution control problems. In their new role, the corps's engineers began a Pilot Wastewater Management Program, which involved five major metropolitan areas, and in March, 1972, they completed a comprehensive study of alternatives for the massive wastewater management job in "Chicagoland," which covered 2,500 square miles with more than 80 townships and over 7 million people in 4 Illinois and 3 Indiana counties. It also had 13,500 industries, including the huge, water-demanding steel mills along Lake Michigan, the area's primary source of water. The region's incredible volume of wastewater was mostly diverted away from the lake via watercourses leading to the Mississippi. Chicagoland's discharges were so immense that in times of low flow, receiving streams consisted largely of sewage effluent.

"Virtually all the wastewater is given secondary treatment before discharge," the corps's report explained. "Nevertheless, the water quality of the area watercourses is affected by phytoplankton and filamentous algae, as well as duck weed and clay turbidity. Many of the area's rivers and potential water impoundments are affected by in-place or accumulated pollution sources. . . ."

At the time, the Metropolitan Sanitary District of Greater Chicago operated ten sewage treatment plants, including the largest in the world, at Stickney. Together they treated 1.38 billion gallons of sewage a day and produced about 1,000 tons of sludge daily, posing a tremendous disposal problem. The corps found the Chicago district had plans to consolidate area sewage collection and treatment systems into eight centralized regions. Three would use and expand upon existing secondary treatment plants. The other five would require new treatment plants. It was acknowledged that all eight plants would also need some form of advanced treatment if water pollution was to be eliminated. The corps's study considered three advanced alternatives. Two were technological, one comparable to the South Lake Tahoe system then being hailed as the panacea for water pollution control, the other a physical-chemical appendage to a conventional secondary treatment plant. The third alternative was a big land treatment system, similar to, but far larger than, the Muskegon project, then under construction.

The corps's financial projections showed the two technological alternatives would cost substantially more than land treatment. Going the technological route, the estimated capital outlay for constructing each million gallons of treatment capacity was $1,260,000, but only $843,000 for land treatment. The operations and maintenance costs per million gallons for the treatment plants were estimated as more than double those for land treatment: $170 against $75. As to the systems' effectiveness, the investigators simply assumed that the three alternatives could remove all pollutants equally well (an assumption that experience at Lake Tahoe and Muskegon was to prove false).

Despite the study's conclusion, the least expensive, most effective alternative, land treatment, had no chance whatsoever. Its greatest problem was obviously one of scale, for the corps's proposal was that Chicago make a massive, mind-boggling change, both of philosophy and of method, one that would virtually unhinge the barons of water and wastewater with their mind-sets fixed on traditional systems. Instead of eight super treatment plants using the conventional method of partly separating pollutants from water, there could be, according to the corps, a single land treatment system, immense in size, about 30 miles south of Lake Michigan. To prove their suggestion was feasible the Army engineers worked out a system on paper that could have treated all of Chicagoland's wastewater.

The plan used the existing collection network, but sewage flows would all be led to one deep tunnel, 25 feet in diameter, extending out to the land treatment system. The site—most of it in Indiana, but overlapping an edge of Illinois—would cover about 700 square miles, or 448,000 acres. The land here was "glacial outwash sands," poorly suited to conventional agriculture, but good for land treatment. The corps ascertained that the acreage was enough to handle an estimated wastewater flow for 1990 averaging more than 2.3 billion gallons daily from a projected population of over 9 million, plus industrial discharges and stormwater runoff.

The vast amounts of wastewater would be treated in lagoons with floating aerators and mixers, like those being installed at Muskegon. After three days of treatment, the effluent would be piped to eight storage lagoons, each covering nine square miles. During the coldest, nonirrigation months, they would hold a 155-day accumulation, or 369 billion gallons of the treated wastewater. In the year's remaining 210 days, the effluent would be released to a network of open channels surrounding four large irrigation sites. The water would then be pumped to thousands of center-pivot irrigation rigs that would sprinkle interlocking circles, each 4,000 feet in diameter. The corps proposed that income-producing crops, like corn and reed canary grass, could serve as part of the living filter. The plant-and-soil-filtered water would be collected by agricultural underdrains, led to another tunnel and sent on to the Calumet River, then back to its origin, Lake Michigan. Thus Chicagoland would only be borrowing and returning portions from its legal share of Lake Michigan—as opposed to shunting all its once-used water off to the Mississippi. (Today, when the amount the metropolis can draw from the lake is approaching the limit allowed by international treaty, Chicago could have been in a much more secure position had it decided to follow nature's law of return.)

The Corps of Engineers also proposed how Chicago could

finally be relieved of its increasingly onerous burden of sewage sludge. Under their plan, sludge would be carried in the wastewater flow to the massive treatment farm, and there the organic materials would settle to the bottoms of the various lagoons. In due time the accumulation would be dredged and applied to the land as soil conditioner. The engineers figured the site could "profitably accept" the sludge for at least the half-century term being considered for all three alternatives.

The corps estimated that the land treatment alternative would require relocating 20,000 people in about 5,400 households—which the engineers felt was not unreasonable given that 103,417 housing units had recently been moved by the federal highway program in only a four-year period. Against the disadvantage of moving people, the corps cited other possible benefits, like the creation of new jobs, using wastewater flows to generate hydroelectric power and employing the land area itself for the site of a nuclear generating station that would borrow the stored irrigant for cooling water.

This scale of thinking was nothing new in the Chicago sewage world, but the thoughts themselves were seen as either treason or folly—unacceptable no matter how they were perceived. The conventional plans and creations of the sanitary-engineering establishment were too monumental and firmly in place to move aside for a new alternative, despite its indicated advantages. The corps's report, a fascinating aberration in the wastewater annals of the Windy City, was filed, and the Metropolitan Sanitary District proceeded on the tried, though less than true, disposal-dilution route.

In fact, at the time the district had barely begun a long-term demonstration of how firmly committed the traditionalists were to the treatment plant alternative. The project, called TARP (Tunnel and Reservoir Plan), is still far from finished, and it is literally and figuratively a big hole. TARP was designed to deal only with the effects of the area's stormwater, but it is expected to cost between three and four times the corps's capital estimate for the big land treatment system—which would have handled all wastewater, stormwater included. When the TARP project is finished, if it ever is, the city will own 131 miles of tunnels far below its streets. The conduits are being carved from gray dolomite by machines called moles, and mountains of the mole carvings deposited on the surface have become part of the city's skyscape. When completed, the tunnels, 9 to 35 feet in diameter, will be able to catch, store and convey millions of gallons of stormwater runoff. The deluge has continually flooded streets and basements and swamped Chicago's combined sewerage system, which collects both sewage and stormwater. Massive gushes of the dirty mix, often unleashed by brief summer thunderstorms, have had to be bypassed around treatment plants to prevent their being put out of commission. The roundabout flow, inadequately treated sewage included, has then run directly into the area's watercourses. The tunnels will absorb such gluts and feed them to three large storage reservoirs, including an open quarry 2.5 miles long, 1,000 feet wide and 200 feet deep. When a storm has subsided, the polluted residue stored by TARP will be pumped into metropolitan treatment plants at such a rate that they can partially purify it and discharge it to watercourses.

When TARP was first planned back in the 1960s, its estimated cost was $3 billion. A subsequent report from the comptroller general of the United States estimated the price would have risen by 1983 to $11 billion—and even so the completion date was said to be 1990 at the earliest. The comptroller general noted, "Funding for the total project is uncertain." TARP was described in 1982 by *Technology Illustrated* as "what may be the largest public works project ever tried in this country . . . compared to the building of the Great Wall of China." The magazine pointed out that in 1981 "Senator Charles Percy of Illinois, a former TARP backer, subjected the project to a blistering attack as a potential boondoggle."

Whether TARP is a boondoggle or not, the pity is that Chicago spends billions of dollars underground to throw away a huge water resource that could be employed beneficially on the surface—as we have seen at Hamilton Lakes. But TARP represents the kind of thinking wherein the goal of clean water has been lost to a traditional goal of building big, dramatic projects that often do not improve our water to the degree their costs would indicate. The comptroller general recognized this failing when his investigators looked at stormwater problems in dozens of American cities. His report said that many projects "tend to be structurally intensive, multimillion dollar efforts"—which were described as "projects that primarily involve extensive construction activity, i.e., tunnels, new sewers, treatment facilities, etc." The report also claimed the problem solvers were biased toward bigness. "Big projects are built because that is the way things have traditionally been accomplished," the federal document stated. "Some biases show up in the reluctance to turn to less costly alternative approaches."

The worship of big, costly, traditional structures, ostensibly to solve our clean water problems, is a religion not to be easily changed or displaced. In Chicago and other cities it amounts to an impregnable barrier against innovative solutions that could be applied to our most serious water problems. Trying to make converts from such devout worshipers is a discouraging mission. As missionaries, the Corps of Engineers, no strangers to the cult of bigness, were met with derision and hostility when they revealed their land treatment alternative. If they could not cultivate change, the chances are slim, indeed, for others to do so.

For a time many who believed in the need to change from linear to circular water and wastewater systems—thus fulfilling the intent of the 1972 clean water law—felt it had to happen by big replacing big. It worked that way at Muskegon, thanks to a unique group of local leaders, but elsewhere innovative bigness seldom budges traditional bigness. This stalemate led proponents of circular systems for large cities to think of a new strategy. Instead of pursuing big, publicly funded projects, the kind exemplified by Muskegon, some believe success may be found in enterprises on a scale comparable to Hamilton Lakes. With this approach a city's linear system would become circular a piece at a time, perhaps through private, bankable projects. While making wastes unavailable for the pollution of water, the circular projects could begin meeting a number of urban needs with the potential bonuses we cited earlier, like new sources of jobs and wealth, new supplies of food, fiber and energy, decreased government deficits and reduced inflationary spending. The public revenues added from such new economic sources and from savings in the old traditional expenditures for waste disposal could help rebuild our deteriorating urban infrastructures.

Another Chicago study, completed a decade after the Corps

of Engineers effort, demonstrated the feasibility of an in-city project designed on a small scale. It was one that could be developed either privately or publicly and, it was hoped, would act as a bellwether for other such projects in the Chicago region. Instead of taking the Army's approach of tackling the entire metropolitan area, the new effort would deal with a single piece of Chicagoland. The study, whose funding came from private foundations including the Rockefeller Brothers Fund of New York, was sponsored by a Chicago nonprofit technical assistance organization, the Center for Neighborhood Technology. The center was headed by Scott Bernstein, who had been aware for a long time of "how waste and water in a region like Chicago are inextricably intertwined." The engineering feasibility study was prepared by the Sheaffer & Roland group, which upon completing its project at Hamilton Lakes wanted to explore how that new development's concept and scale might be applied to an urban area's old problems. While the wastewater at Hamilton Lakes had economic value for irrigating and fertilizing the landscape, it was impractical to think that Chicago's sewage, with its huge volumes carrying a great deal of industrial waste, could be easily used on a cityscape encased in concrete and steel with a minimum of green growth. The urban point of attack had to be different than that used at the Itasca development.

The investigation soon recognized that an opportunity might be found in a knotty problem common to many of America's older cities, suffering from a diminishing industrial base with the loss of jobs and the municipal income needed to restore their deteriorating urban infrastructures. A main factor in this complex of difficulties is the rising costs of treating industrial wastes, tied to the old disposal patterns of aging cities. Getting rid of the wastes depends on municipal sewage treatment works' being able to handle the materials while trying to attain and maintain the quality of effluent demanded by state and federal laws. To defray the costs of added municipal treatment caused by an industry's waste, the company usually has to pay public surcharges, or, in the case of certain potent disposables, the firm has to pretreat (remove the worst ingredients) before sewerage authorities will accept the waste (and even then probably with surcharges). In any case, the costs, which often become serious economic burdens for the businesses involved, are a reason for the exodus of industries from older cities. This is also a factor in the inability of the aging urban areas to attract new industries.

The study sponsored by the Center for Neighborhood Technology revealed that many of Chicago's industrial wastes, presently being thrown away at a high cost to the waste producers, could be turned into raw materials for the production of valuable food, energy and fertilizer. Thus these so-called pollutants—which in their disposal were hurting the industries, the city as a place to do business and the streams receiving the partially purified residue—might be converted from a bane to a blessing. But it was soon clear that if the full value of these wastes was to be realized in a small-scale urban project, they had to be used before, not after, they had been turned into sewage and lost in the voluminous water carriage (with that ratio of less than 1 percent waste to more than 99 percent water). Obviously a method had to be found for capitalizing upon the wastes themselves while offering a technically sound, economically attractive alternative to the municipal sewerage system.

To develop such an alternative, the members of the new Chicago study group selected what they called a "high-class waste," one with great potential value as a raw material, as well as one whose disposal is a major expense for the producers. The waste chosen, which comes from Chicago's extensive food-processing industries, is high in organic matter. While the organics make the wastes potentially valuable for the production of salable products, they are presently a financial liability because of the surcharges imposed to compensate for the impact the materials have on the city's sewage treatment plants. With this waste in mind, the study's planners and engineers developed a profitable alternative to the unprofitable sewer line, calling it a biomass utility. A planning-level feasibility study was completed for the utility. Its potential site is the Chicago Center for Industry, a community-owned industrial park (once used by International Harvester) in the westside Chicago community of Lawndale. The design of the biomass utility calls for it to occupy 18 acres of the park. The system will handle 120 tons of waste per day—a figure arrived at after a survey of food-processing companies in the Chicago area. The utility is designed to produce and sell electricity, ethyl alcohol, steam for industrial use, vegetables, ornamentals for homes and landscaping and potting soil.

As planned, the biomass utility will be built around an anaerobic digestion system using six airtight tanks, 70 feet in diameter and 25 feet high. Food-processing wastes will be trucked to the utility, either as solid waste or as sludge. Large streams of liquid waste from a single source, such as a wet corn mill, may be pipelined to the utility. From 10 to 30 truckloads of this feedstock will be mixed with water recycled from the system itself and pumped into the digesters. There its temperature will be held at about 95 degrees Fahrenheit to stimulate the growth and action of anaerobic bacteria. The digesters are designed to generate 2.2 million cubic feet of biogas from the daily waste load. The methane–carbon dioxide mixture will have a heating value roughly one half that of common pipeline-quality natural gas.

A relatively small part of the biogas will be recycled and used to heat the digesters, but the bulk of it will fuel an on-site cogeneration system to produce both electricity and low-pressure steam. The heart of the system will consist of seven engine-generators fueled with the biogas and capable of producing 87,600 kilowatt hours of electricity a day (enough to supply over 3,000 homes with families of four and using electric hot-water heating). The seven generators will be fitted with heat recovery systems, which will produce the steam. Portions of both the electricity and the steam will be used in other parts of the utility, and the remainder will be sold. The other components include a fermentation alcohol plant, a greenhouse complex and a compost facility.

The alcohol plant's raw material will be sugar-based wastes that were identified as a disposal problem in the Chicago area. Both steam and electricity from the biogas system will be used in the three steps of alcohol production: fermentation, distillation and drying. The stillage (residue after fermentation) will be added to the anaerobic digesters' feedstock and will contribute to the biogas production. The alcohol plant is designed to produce 1 million gallons per year of 198-proof ethyl alcohol (also known as anhydrous ethanol). The product may be used as fuel by blending it with gasoline. It is also valuable as a chemical for making solvents, dyes, pharmaceuticals and other products.

The plan for the Chicago Center for Industry also calls for construction of nearly six and a half acres of greenhouses, with some possibly using hydroponics (growing plants in nutrient-rich liquids rather than soil). Energy from the complex that might ordinarily be wasted will serve some of the venture's important needs. Hot water from the alcohol plant and the effluent from the digesters called supernatant will yield approximately 53 million BTUs daily to heat and cool the greenhouses, which will also rely on solar systems and energy conservation techniques. The supernatant may provide fertilizing nutrients to stimulate plant growth and, in turn, the growth can serve as a living filter to upgrade the quality of water discharged from the system. Finally, the cogeneration system is a valuable source of carbon dioxide (ordinarily wasted to the air), which can be used to enhance productivity in the greenhouses. The carbon dioxide is released from the biogas when it is burned to make electricity in the engine-generators. Projections of earnings from the greenhouses are difficult to make because productivity will depend on management methods that can adapt crops to seasonal markets, but the designers of the system concluded from a review of technical literature and interviews with experts that the net economic return per square foot of greenhouse will range from $5 to $16 per year.

The last component of the biomass utility design is a compost facility. The operation's main feedstock will consist of solid materials separated from the digesters' supernatant. It will be mixed with woodchips to keep it from packing too tightly and to allow for its forced ventilation by large blowers powered with the utility's own electricity. The chips, which can be reused in as many as five batches of compost, will come from a common municipal waste that presents a disposal problem: trimmings from trees in parks and the borders of streets and roadways. During composting, the mixture will break down into a rich, dark humus. The product is valuable as a soil mulch for increasing the water-holding capacity of sandy soil and for loosening clay soils so roots can develop more easily. The compost facility, which will cover a third of the 18-acre site, will produce about 38 tons of soil mulch per day. Some of it may be used in the utility's greenhouses and the remainder will be sold, possibly in bags for home gardeners.

The conclusion of the biomass utility study consisted of a financial analysis for the system. The projected capital costs, for purchasing the land and constructing the facilities, was $12.7 million. The annual operating costs were set at $3.2 million, and the yearly sales of electricity, alcohol, greenhouse crops and compost were estimated at $7.3 million. Thus the projected revenue (before taxes and interest payments) was $4.1 million. Given a ten-year financing period, the return on investment would be 30 percent. If available investment and energy tax credits were taken advantage of by private entrepreneurs, the return could be considerably higher.

This kind of investment potential is what it takes to attract private investors, who would understandably look upon such a utility as a novel, high-risk venture. But in these difficult days for big-city finances, the biomass utility could also be attractive for public investment through revenue bonds. The system, publicly owned and operated, could have at least two major advantages for the community. It could be built and operated without increasing taxes or incurring user fees, while generating income for the city treasury. And by lowering the waste load on sewage treatment plants, the utility would reduce inflationary, deficit-creating expenditures for disposal services.

Such a venture, whether public or private, stands to improve the economic health of the city. It can create new wealth from wastes whose traditional disposal eats into old wealth. It can create new jobs. The biomass utility planned for the Chicago Center for Industry would require up to 100 employees. And such a system would help the area retain businesses now beset with waste problems, while new businesses might find the area an advantageous place in which to locate. These benefits would contribute directly or indirectly to local treasuries, and the funds could be used to address other urban problems.

But in a sense, these demonstrable advantages of the biomass utility may be only bonuses added to the biggest, most important benefit of all. The concept can make a start at changing large urban areas from linear to circular water systems, thus dealing a blow to the growing water crisis by turning wastes to raw materials and making them unavailable for pollution. Of course, the Corps of Engineers had the same aim in the 1970s when it drew up the dramatic plan for land treatment of all Chicago wastewater, but this was like trying to swallow an elephant whole. The later plan sponsored by the Center for Neighborhood Technology aims to start nibbling away at the elephant. When completed, the biomass utility will show how water, now afflicted sewerage, can be freed of extra-strength urban waste by using it beneficially in the city itself. It is hoped the demonstration will educate people to the fact that there is a beneficial alternative to the damage we do to our water resources by using them to carry off wastes that in themselves are resources worth exploiting. If this concept can be understood by enough people, it may lead to the attitudinal change needed to move from linear to circular systems.

Meanwhile, the nibbling at the elephant of a problem should continue—Chicago, incidentally, has enough industrial wastes for a half-dozen biomass utilities—and who knows? In another decade the common sense of the circular solution to water may even be well enough understood and accepted that corps-scale plans for cities like Chicago will finally be sent out for bids.

XIII

The Oasis on the Troubled Ogallala

As crisis journalism was wearing out the oil crisis of the 1970s and discovering the water crisis of the 1980s, assignment editors sometimes had their tongues twisted around the Native American name Ogallala. They had learned that the unfamiliar title stood for the aquifer stretching under the Great Plains from Gaines County, Texas, to the South Dakota border. In the national water crisis, the Ogallala had a big role. Its troubles were not only American, but, indeed, global, for the Ogallala is responsible in part for the United States' ability to help feed the world. The newsworthy problem: the aquifer was going dry.

Reporters from big-city dailies, the wire services and national newsmagazines were dispatched to learn about the disaster. The Texas High Plains, the southern extension of the Great Plains, were most seriously threatened, so that was the place to go, specifically to Lubbock and the High Plains Underground Water Conservation District Number One. There officials explained that the Ogallala was being drawn down by irrigation pumps faster than nature could replenish it. Some areas were already depleted and others were on the way. The loss of water jeopardized one of the nation's most important agricultural areas.

When the day's reporting was done and their stories were on the wires, some of the journalists may have stayed to see Lubbock. In this semi-arid part of America, where the annual rainfall is less than 20 inches and the natural color is generally light brown or tan, the visitors might have been surprised to see green throughout the city. They might then have discovered that Lubbock enjoyed one of the largest urban parks in America, a 6-mile greenbelt running through the community—1,450 acres, 610 more than Central Park in New York City. At the center of the liberally irrigated area, the journalists would have found four lovely lakes. In this city beset by a water disaster, it would have to seem strange to find so much water so freely used to green up an unusually big park for a city of 174,000 people. The reason, if the journalists found it out, generally went unreported—even though it might have been a clue to what could be done to help preserve the Ogallala.

The water for the lakes and irrigated parkland comes from southeast of town, from underneath an unusual farm owned and managed from the 1930s to 1982 by Frank Gray. Unlike his neighbors on the High Plains, Gray farmed atop a growing volume of groundwater. The reason: Since 1932 his croplands were irrigated with secondary effluent from Lubbock's sewage treatment plant. As the effluent percolated into the earth, it literally formed a great dome of groundwater below the farm. Now, in the 1980s, groundwater pumped up through 23 wells from Gray's huge accumulation is returned to town to irrigate the greenbelt and fill the four lakes.

The story of Frank Gray's farm seems to escape many of those who come to learn about the crisis of the Ogallala. Perhaps it is the common aversion to talking about sewage—whatever the reason, the fact is missed that a small piece, some 4,000 acres, of the afflicted Ogallala is an underground oasis. While the High Plains' water table was dropping at a worrisome rate, it was rising under Gray's farm. In fact, between the 1930s and 1980s his groundwater rose more than 50 feet.

A lesson in contrast was waiting in this subsurface oasis when attention was drawn to it because of the Ogallala's intensifying troubles. Lubbock, unlike scores of other municipalities on the Great Plains, worked with a circular system and ended up with water to be reclaimed. Other plains communities, which draw municipal water directly or indirectly from the Ogallala, employed traditional linear systems; thus a lot of precious water was, and continues to be, siphoned off to the Gulf of Mexico. Now the Lubbock story continues with another large, innovative land treatment system sharing the city's wastewater with the Gray farm. The new system is the centerpiece of the Lubbock Land Treatment Research and Demonstration Program, which includes a scientific look at how such circular systems can help address the problems of the great aquifer. Perhaps the program also signals a new turn of mind at the Environmental Protection Agency. EPA's funding for the program, $9.5 million, was the largest such research grant in the agency's history. This kind of attention is overdue for the threatened Ogallala.

In his book *Killing the Hidden Waters,* Charles Bowden portrays the cause of the Ogallala's problem when he tells of strangers driving on a summer's night through Crosby County, Texas, and puzzling over the little lights they see flitting about the countryside. "The curious travelers have stumbled upon an army directing water across the High Plains," Bowden reveals. "Pickups bounce down country roads so that this legion of people can move irrigation pipes at two, three, four in the morning. Flashlights bob in the summer night for men linking ditch to furrow so that crops can drink. This work goes on in a din of sound as pumps suck water to the surface of the plains. Man, his livestock, and his plants satisfy their biological appetites in an environment of machines, chemicals and pumps. . . ."

The author explains that in daylight the traveler can see the modern "substitute for the humans shifting pipes through the night," huge mechanical irrigators that lift water from the Ogallala to sprinkle it on the plains, returning some to the water table, but losing a lot to the air (evaporation) and plants (transpiration). The people with the bobbing lights and their mechanical substitutes have turned the semi-arid plains—the Llano Estacado that Spanish explorers decided was uninhabitable for lack of water—into one of the world's greatest producers of food and fiber. The Texas High Plains, with an agricultural economy at the billion-dollar level, produce about a quarter of the nation's cotton and grain sorghum and 15 percent of the feed cattle. But these accomplishments have come at the expense of a vast water table falling faster than nature can replenish it. The *Los Angeles Times* reported in 1981 that "about six million acre-feet is pumped out annually, with natural recharge replacing only about 185,000 acre-feet per year." (One acre-foot equals 326,000 gallons.)

Early in the century, when scatterings of windmills powered pumps on the Ogallala, farmers believed they were tapping an endless water supply. They assumed their farms were above a great underground river, a hidden Mississippi flowing from the Rockies, Canada, the Arctic—the Lord only knew where. Charles Bowden quotes from a 1914 publication in which Zenas E. Black, executive secretary of the Plainview (Texas) Commercial Club, explained the endless bounty of the Ogallala came from the "Underground River," which started from snowmelt in the Rockies, dropped below the surface and was propelled southeast by gravity. "For hundreds of years this water has been flowing under the plains on its way to the Gulf and mankind knew it not," Black wrote. "Now that this subterranean pipeline is being tapped, the plainsmen claim that they have the nearest ideal system of agriculture on earth. . . ."

When Black wrote this assessment of the Ogallala, the U.S. Geological Survey had already explained it was not true. Survey scientists recognized that the windmills were drawing from a mammoth underground storage reservoir containing the residue of rain and snow, some of it deposited there thousands and thousands of years ago. But the myth of an endless river persisted beyond the half-century mark despite repeated warnings that economic growth, so dependent on irrigation, could drain the water to the bottom of the supposedly bottomless wells.

The Texas-size economic growth was made possible by the farmers' improved capability for pumping water. The plains' picturesque windmills gave way to rust and different sources of pumping power, such as gasoline, diesel fuel, electricity and indigenous natural gas—all at costs moving up and away from the freedom of the wind. By the 1970s studies at the University of Nebraska revealed that 43 percent of the energy used in the state's agriculture went into irrigation pumps.

With the proliferation of efficient irrigation wells, the ancient waters of the Ogallala were "mined" ever more rapidly than their natural replenishment. In 1930 the lonely Llana Estacado had only 170 irrigation wells. As the Great Depression abated, the number had multiplied twelvefold; in the early post–World War II years the total was over 8,000; and by 1957 there were 42,225 wells.

"By the sixties," Bowden writes, "the High Plains had 5,500,000 acres under irrigation. Fossil water and fossil fuels had made a billion dollar economy.

"There was one hitch. The Ogallala was running out of water. . . ."

The most depletive force of all, not only for the Ogallala but for all other groundwater below the plains, was the behemoth of irrigated agriculture, the center-pivot irrigation rig. Like the hands of giant clocks, riding on tandem-wheeled towers in green circles up to a mile in diameter, the spray-carrying arms reduced the fossil waters and the life-span of the hyped agricultural economy. From out in space American astronauts used clusters of the circles as check points, and above the Great Plains thousands of passengers on transcontinental flights puzzled over the patchworks of perfect circles five or six miles below. After the machine was patented in 1952, the number of center-pivot rigs increased so fast that the totals were hard to keep track of. In the 1970s Professor William E. Splinter and colleagues at the University of Nebraska counted the rigs with an electronic device that scanned satellite images. During a four-year period the researchers saw an increase from 2,000 or 3,000 center-pivot rigs to nearly 10,000 in Nebraska alone.

Splinter pointed out that the average rig drew 900 gallons of water per minute from a depth of 180 feet, and one operating center-pivot system "consumes water enough for a city of 10,000 people." The Nebraskan's energy studies showed that in his state "a typical center-pivot system consumes about 50 gallons of diesel fuel per acre per year in applying roughly 22 inches of water . . . ten times the fuel needed to till, plant, cultivate and harvest a crop such as corn."

As plains farmers were forced to concede that they were mining the Ogallala as well as other prehistoric groundwater reserves, they began worrying over the threat of natural impoverishment encountered by the early Spanish explorers on the Llano Estacado. The irrigators had numerous ideas for slowing the descent of the water table to disaster. The solutions ranged from techniques to ration water applied to plants, to restricting the drilling of new wells (as some states have already done), and to the grandest of all the notions, diverting water from the Mississippi or even the Great Lakes to the Great Plains—a proposal with a slim chance when Chicago is denied all the water it desires from the big lake only a few skips and jumps off Lake Shore Drive. Moreover, importation could greatly narrow the gap between the price of wine and the price of water—as indicated by some tentative Texas plans to sweeten the plains from distant supplies: the imported acre-foot could cost $600 to $700, compared to $75 for the same amount of water pumped on the spot from the Ogallala.

Regardless of cost, moving water around the country, especially the west, is comparable to firing on Fort Sumter, triggering a war between the states—or, for that matter, intrastate conflicts. A High Plains cotton farmer and speaker of the house in the Texas legislature, Bill Clayton, inadvertently raised the possibility of such a war in 1981. Clayton authored a successful bill prompting a referendum on a Texas constitutional amendment for a water trust fund. It would mandate that surplus state funds be used to deal with Texas water problems, especially on the High Plains. The fund could have grown to billions of dollars, but the idea practically set water-sufficient east Texas against water-poor west Texas. An amendment opponent, political reporter Bo Byers of the *Houston Chronicle,* wrote, "One of the things I am not sure about is what will happen when a Water Rights Commission says: 'There is more water over here at X-marks-the-spot river basin in East Texas than that area is reasonably going to need in the next 50 years so we vote to approve this request from Y-marks-the-spot in West Texas to allow temporary diversion of surplus water from X-marks-the-spot in East Texas to Y-marks-the-spot in West Texas." Enough voters of the Lone Star State were disturbed by such prospects to defeat Clayton's amendment.

A potential and at least partial solution to these water worries was present for decades at Frank Gray's farm southeast of Lubbock. In territory marked by water conflicts between farms and cities, cooperation between Lubbock and the Gray farm commenced in the 1930s. At the time, the small Texas city installed a new sewage treatment plant, but officials recognized the secondary effluent could damage a precious recreational lake, of which there were few in this semi-arid countryside. They were also aware that the effluent could be valuable for irrigation and fertilizer, so they bought some land where the wastewater could be applied. Coincidentally an adjacent landowner, a local physician, Dr. Fred Standefer, offered to include his 126-acre horse farm in the treatment site and to be responsible for using the sewage effluent. The doctor eventually bought the city land and agreed to use all the effluent the town could pipe to his expanded farm. Subsequently he hired a manager, Frank Gray, who had just received a college degree in agriculture. Gray later became a partner and then the farm's owner.

As Lubbock grew, Gray purchased surrounding acreage to accommodate the increasing, day-in-day-out flow of effluent. By 1970 he was irrigating 2,600 acres and supplying excess effluent for a neighboring farm to irrigate another 1,600 acres. Over the years Gray raised cotton, sorghum, wheat, barley, oats and rye. He also pastured livestock and even dairy cows on the irrigated land. For several years he ran a Grade A dairy farm, which always passed the state's health inspections. But unlike his High Plains neighbors, Gray and his help spent an unusual amount of time irrigating the land—indeed, frequently having to overirrigate heavily because they lacked sufficient storage facilities to provide control over the never-ending flow of wastewater. The farmer was practicing land treatment, but more or less by happenstance, because he had to learn as he proceeded under constant pressure to deal with the expanding flows of wastewater. Nevertheless, his learn-as-you-go procedures served Gray and the city well. Meanwhile, the irrigation cultivated some of the richest soil on the High Plains, and the renovated water accumulated below the farm. Here rested the supply that Lubbock had once bought and paid for, some of it piped about 120 miles from Lake Meredith on the Canadian River to the north, and some pumped up from the Ogallala.

In the 1960s a group of innovative city planners at Lubbock recognized that Gray's immense accumulation of water could be the basis for an in-town rehabilitation project using the city's most interesting, but blighted, topographical feature, Yellowhouse Canyon. In 1909 the Santa Fe Railroad, built along the canyon's western rim, stimulated the area's industrial development, and by the 1960s Yellowhouse Canyon, like so many other watercourses in American cities, had become a dismal belt of dirty water and visual pollution. "It consisted of open areas scarred with high weeds, caliche mining, and open dumping," stated a report from the city planners. "Water in the intermittent stream bed was usually stagnate, odorous, and a breeding place for disease. Those areas in the canyon which were developed were primarily industrial uses such as asphalt plants, wrecking yards, grease rendering plants, and prefabricated home building companies, none of which added to the aesthetic appearance of the canyon. Most of the activities in the canyon were of industrial or commercial type. Only four residential units existed within the [proposed] project."

In 1970 Lubbock voters approved a $2.8 million bond issue to start converting the canyon from dumping ground to greenbelt including a series of small man-made lakes. Water to irrigate the parklands and fill the lakes would come from an estimated 12 billion gallons of renovated wastewater under Frank Gray's farm. Its reuse in the city was publicly accepted when the bond issue was approved following a well-developed public education program assuring people it would be safe to use reclaimed sewage water.

The canyon cleanup had an unexpected byproduct when excavations uncovered a trove of archaeological artifacts from the last 12,000 years of human existence on the High Plains. Many Lubbock citizens who had found Yellowhouse Canyon repulsive became interested and for the first time learned the derivation of the canyon's name: Spanish explorers discovering cliff dwellings in the yellowish canyon walls decided they looked like tall, yellow houses.

As federal grants augmented local funds, wells were drilled on the Gray farm, and they supplied some 4 million gallons of water daily. It was pure enough for limited recreation, including fishing, but one exception to its purity prevented the water from being labeled potable. As explained earlier, Gray had been forced to overirrigate, and the living filter, which has limits like any filter, had been overtaxed. As the water percolated through the soil, the natural systems couldn't remove all the nitrogen, and excessive amounts were converted by nature to nitrate, which built up in the groundwater to levels higher than those permitted by federal drinking water standards. If the farmer had been able to irrigate with a lesser, scientifically determined quantity of effluent, the nitrogen removal would have been complete, thus avoiding the problem. Regardless, the reclaimed water was superior to any other potential source for the canyon project.

By the 1960s the Yellowhouse Canyon Lakes, as the development had been named, consisted of four attractive bodies of water in a series. They were connected with groupings of native rocks to form waterfalls and pools as the reclaimed water flowed from one lake to the next. The lakes were equipped with boat-launching ramps, fishing piers, rest shelters and foot bridges that connected with the area's "hike and bike" trails. The greened-up, irrigated surroundings were tied in with previously established parks, so that Texans, surrounded by one of the most serious water crises in the nation, could understandably brag, ". . . Lubbock has become a national leader in the creation of large urban parks and use of reclaimed water for these spaces."

But in this big, flat corner of America, where the falling water table is a presage of a declining economy, one naturally asks why the reclaimed water fills recreational lakes and stimulates grass in city parks instead of crops in the farmers' fields. Of course it simply happened that way, before the decline of the Ogallala was generally recognized as a serious problem. Nevertheless Lubbock, with its circular system, was a pioneer and obvious candidate for the EPA-funded research and demonstration project. Out of this effort may emerge elements of farm-city cooperation that can help both the rural and urban water crises caused by falling water tables.

The opportunity for the new project came in 1977 when a wealthy businessman and benefactor of Lubbock Christian College, J. E. Hancock, bought a large farm 18 miles south of Lubbock. Hancock agreed that while he would retain ownership, the farm's earnings would serve as an annuity for the college. But improved earnings required expanding irrigation, which had been relatively minor in the past. Using the farm's groundwater was economically unfeasible, for here, as elsewhere, the Ogallala had dropped so far that pumping would be too costly. At the same time, the city of Lubbock was under pressure from the EPA to become less dependent on the Gray farm, which was overburdened with municipal wastewater. Out of these dual needs of city and farm emerged the Lubbock Land Treatment Research and Demonstration Program.

The 4,000-acre Hancock farm became the site for a scientifically designed land treatment system that would eventually take about 40 percent of the city's treated wastewater, leaving the rest for the Gray farm and for cooling water at a local power plant. The research and operational management for the new system was assigned to an organization associated with the college, the LCC Institute of Water Research, with Dr. Dennis George as director. The land and operations were divided among nine tenant farmers, who would be advised by the institute on land treatment procedures. And a quarter section (160 acres) of the farm was reserved strictly for research.

The Lubbock project covers three areas of study. Primarily it will explore cropping and wastewater irrigation problems. Unlike the Muskegon project or the Gray farm, the Hancock land treatment system, which was designed under the direction of Wayne Cowlishaw of the Sheaffer & Roland group, was not meant to return purified water, to either the Ogallala or the city. The Hancock share of treated effluent is piped to the farm and stored in three lagoons during all but a dozen or so weeks of the year. In those weeks (a few in the spring, but most in the summer), the stored effluent is applied to 2,900 acres by 22 center-pivot irrigation rigs. The researchers will try to establish how best to use all the wastewater and nutrients for revenue-producing crops, leaving little or none to percolate to the aquifer. Initially the crops under study include cotton, sunflowers, milo, soybeans, oats and wheat. Simultaneously the investigators are exploring how such an enterprise can work with private (tenant) farmers so they will make proper use of the municipal effluent and turn a profit.

The second phase of the research is a long-term epidemiological study of the farmers and their families on the Hancock farm, as well as people on neighboring lands. This study, according to George, is one of only two such investigations in the world.

The other is at a land treatment system on an Israeli kibbutz. They are unusual in that the health of subjects is longitudinally assessed, beginning before and then continuing during their association with the project. The institute director claims that other such studies have been limited to testing subjects during or after their association with wastewater irrigation systems.

Third, data is being developed at the project to assess the EPA's technical criteria for land treatment in general. The federal agency began issuing technical guidance on the subject during 1975 in response to requirements of the Federal Water Pollution Control Act Amendments of 1972. The material has been occasionally upgraded since then, and it is hoped the Lubbock research will help improve the literature.

Meanwhile the Gray farm was sold in 1982 to a Yugoslavian family of three brothers and a sister, with one of the brothers, Mike Vladi, in charge of the operation. The Vladis are also working with the LCC institute to improve upon land treatment methods by changes in cropping and wastewater application rates. While the farm will continue returning its reclaimed water to the Yellowhouse Canyon Lakes project, the new owners, who have installed center-pivot irrigation rigs, intend to reuse the groundwater for irrigation, augmenting the city's reduced contribution of treated effluent.

The Lubbock systems do not offer a full solution to the difficult problems of the great pumps and sprawling rigs mining the Ogallala, but undeniably the Texas city points to a neglected source of water that can help slow down the depletion of the massive aquifer—and, indeed, of other groundwater reservoirs all over the west. A point seldom made in discussions of the Ogallala's decline (but one we have already raised) is that towns and cities also contribute to the aquifer's depletion with their linear water and wastewater systems. A center-pivot rig ordinarily pumps from the aquifer about 2 months a year, but a community draws water all 12 months, and while a good portion from the rig percolates back to the water table, practically all from the town leaves the area in rivers that are polluted by the discharge. With circular systems the once-used, nutrient-rich water from towns can cultivate crops with a portion of the liquid being purified and recharging the aquifer.

This concept of water returns, in conjunction with other ideas, may begin to lighten the tribulations of the Ogallala. Farmers and their advisers are already looking to ways of husbanding the water they pump up and apply to crops. By its very nature, the amazing center-pivot rig leads to overirrigation, but means are being explored to minimize the machine's applications—for example, by ascertaining with special sensors when plants most need to drink, or can go dry, farmers can learn to irrigate more efficiently. Also, studies in Nebraska and discussions in Colorado are considering how the off-growing-season flow of rivers might be used to help nature recharge the Ogallala. In 1982 a consulting geologist, Truman Bennett, wrote in the journal *Ground Water:*

> . . . we can recharge the Ogallala. Flood waters cross these plains every year, with millions of gallons of water, ample to supply the region, lost eventually to the sea. Most of the streams flow through alluvial valleys. Shallow wells in the alluvium can [become conduits for] extremely large quantities of induced flood-water infiltration and recharge billions of gallons of filtered, good quality . . . ground water into the underlying Ogallala. In some areas pumping would be required [to force the water into the ground]. In other areas direct communication would be possible, recharge being by gravity. If necessary, the entire facility could be underground and automatic. Expensive? Yes, but nothing compared to the alternatives.

Meanwhile countless billions of gallons of wastewater leave the plains and the Ogallala year-round. It is a rich resource worthy of private, returnable investments, as opposed to public, nonreturnable expenditures. And, once more, the obstacle to sensible use is the conventional commitment to linear wastewater systems honoring the disposal-dilution theory. But in a land that cannot afford to lose water of any amount or description, this obstacle—as the EPA has signaled at Lubbock—may have to give way to the recognition that wastewater disposal is detrimental to economic growth.

This community swimming pool, adjacent to Santee Lakes, is also filled with water that has filtered through the percolation beds. The lakes are state approved for fishing, boating and other forms of water recreation.
(Courtesy Leonard Stevens)

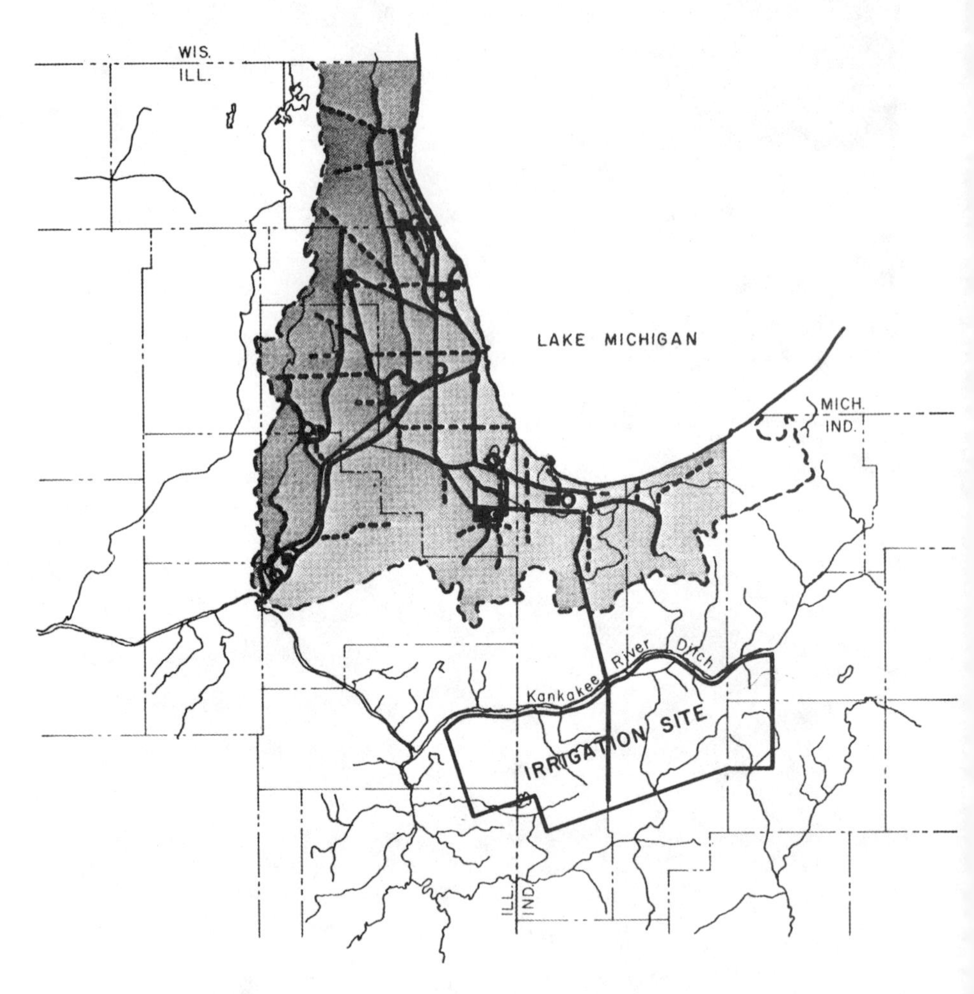

A Chicago land treatment proposal found in a 1972 U.S. Army Corps of Engineers study called for piping all the metropolitan region's wastewater to a mammoth irrigation site (indicated on this map) south and east of the city. Crops raised with the nutrient-rich water would bring a financial return to the system. Wastewater filtered through the crops and soil would be thoroughly cleaned, collected and sent back to Lake Michigan, from which it had originated as a water supply for the Windy City. The plan was not adopted.

Hamilton Lakes at Itasca, Illinois, is a water self-sufficient office and hotel complex, using a circular system to reclaim and reuse the development's wastewater (including stormwater runoff) and to capitalize on the fertilizing nutrients in the waterborne wastes. The wastewater is partially cleaned in a lagoon system, then sprayed on the verdant landscape as an irrigant and fertilizer. In the process it is purified before finding its way into the lakes. Hamilton Lakes demonstrates how we can better manage our water resources through relatively small-scale circular systems, even within busy city centers. *(Courtesy Trammell Crow Co.)*

Chicago's TARP (Tunnel and Reservoir Plan) includes the excavation of great tunnels beneath the city as part of a system to collect and temporarily store large gushes of stormwater runoff, so it can be treated later at a rate the metropolitan area's sewage plants can accommodate. One of the tunnels is shown here under construction. TARP, which has been in progress for many years and is far from finished, has become an extremely expensive venture with many critics who question its soundness. *(Courtesy The Metropolitan Sanitary District of Greater Chicago)*

Center-pivot irrigation rigs—in contrast to the all-but-gone farm windmills of earlier years—draw heavily upon the groundwater held in aquifers underlying the agricultural lands of our western states. Using powerful motorized pumps, the rigs force groundwater up through a center pivot and out along horizontal arms (sometimes a half mile or so) to be sprayed on crops. *(Courtesy Valmont Industries, Inc., Valley, Nebraska)*

The arms rotate around the pivots riding on motorized wheeled towers. They make huge verdant circles that are often seen from jetliners over the Great Plains, and form patterns visible from space vehicles. While such rigs have been a boon to America's food production, they are also having a serious impact on ancient stores of valuable groundwater. *(Courtesy Valmont Industries, Inc., Valley, Nebraska)*

The Canyon Lakes Project at Lubbock, Texas, is a large, inner-city park around a series of man-made lakes—all of which was possible because of the availability of water reclaimed from the community's sewage. For nearly a half century, effluent from Lubbock's secondary sewage treatment plant has been used to irrigate and fertilize a large farm on the city's outskirts. Billions of gallons of water purified by the soil and plants accumulated beneath the farmer's land. When Lubbock planners rehabilitated one of the most unsightly areas of town, Yellowhouse Canyon, and turned it into a park, they borrowed from the farm's huge accumulation of renovated wastewater to fill recreation lakes and revitalize the landscape. *(Courtesy Lubbock Parks & Recreation Department)*

At North Glenn, Colorado, these large lagoons treat and store municipal wastewater that will be used for irrigation at nearby farms. The water, which has always belonged to the farmers, is borrowed by North Glenn, used by the townspeople as their municipal supply and then sent as wastewater to the lagoons. Here it is partially purified and stored for use by the owner-farmers as they require irrigation. The city enjoys the farmers' water and, in its return, the farmers benefit from fertilizing nutrients that enhance the growth of their crops. North Glenn points the way to replacing the traditional and costly conflict between urban and rural water needs with a cooperative method, allowing both city and farm requirements to be satisfied with the same water. *(Courtesy City of North Glenn; photo by David C. Lutter)*

An anaerobic digester, shown here on a New England farm, can generate methane gas from organic wastes, such as those that cause serious disposal problems for food-processing industries. As methane is formed, the gas inflates the digester's long, plastic cover and is then used immediately as fuel in a nearby engine-generator that produces electricity. Such units can be used to take economic advantage of wastes that may otherwise pollute potential water supply sources. *(Courtesy Leonard Stevens)*

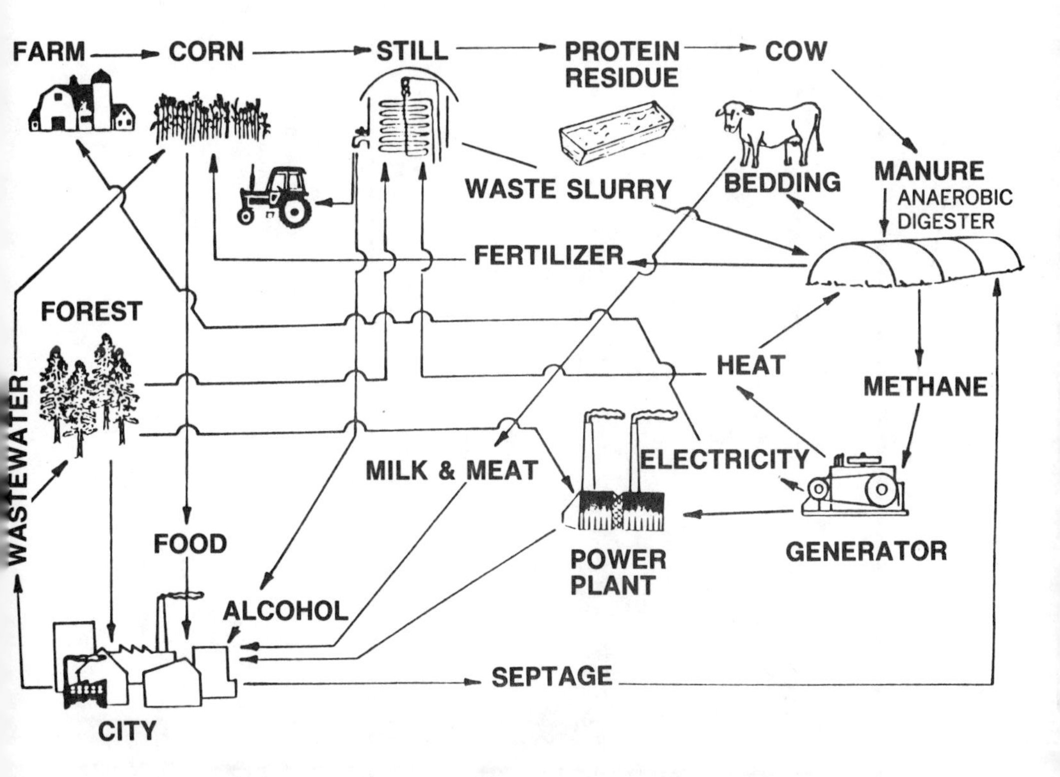

The farm-city loop illustrated here shows how wastes from a city—wastewater and "septage" (sewage sludge)—might be used as valuable resources in agriculture and silviculture, as opposed to their disposal by conventional means that contaminate water resources. In the loop, city wastewater goes to the farm to fertilize corn and forests. The septage goes to an anaerobic digester to be mixed with farm manure and methane gas. For these wastes, the city gains in the return of forest products, food, alcohol, fuel and electricity. In the farm-city loop the wastes are considered resources with economic value and thus become unavailable for the pollution of water. *(Courtesy Sheaffer and Roland Inc.)*

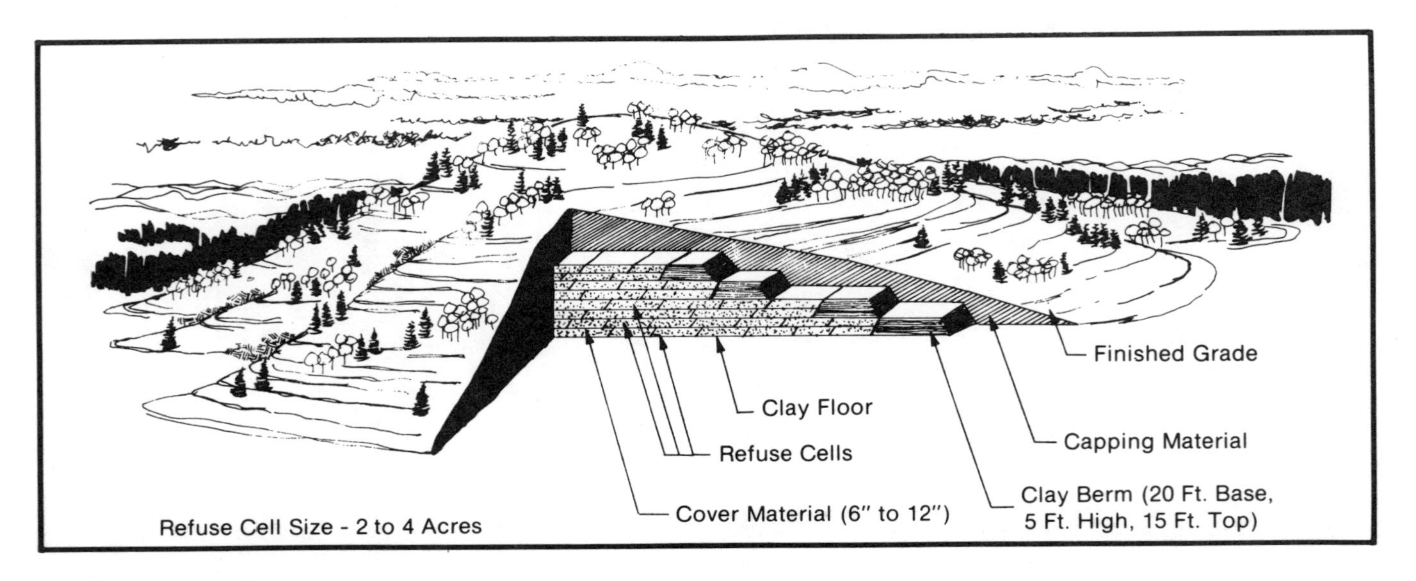

Mount Trashmore (now officially named Mount Hoy) in Du Page County, Illinois, is a mountain of solid waste collected from nearly 1 million people for most of a decade. The mountain (shown in the cutaway) was designed so the waste, with its potentially dangerous contaminants, would leach as little as possible into the underlying groundwater. Daily deliveries of trash were packed and encased in refuse cells, which formed the core of the mountain. The lower layer of cells was laid out on a clay floor to help isolate the mountain of waste from the groundwater underneath, and when completed, the great mound of cells was capped and graded so as to shed rainwater, keeping it out of the internal refuse as much as possible. Mount Trashmore, which became the centerpiece of a popular recreation area, has not contaminated the aquifer below its base. *(Courtesy Forest Preserve District of Du Page County, Illinois)*

XIV

Cooperation Instead of Conflict

When Jimmy Carter became President in 1977, one of his first acts was to recommend the abandonment of 18 dam projects in the south and west. The move plagued his administration for the next four years. On Capitol Hill it was virtually a domestic Pearl Harbor, tantamount to a sneak attack on one of Congress's holiest prerogatives, to determine how and where water resources are to be developed and financed. Proof that the President acted stealthily was evident to the lawmakers in his failure to warn the public works leaders of Congress of what he proposed to do. Carter and his advisers found themselves at war with the Hill as western senators and congressmen forgot political affiliations and joined to meet the dastardly attack. All he wanted, said the new Chief Executive, was to make sure that big dams funded by federal money were economically and environmentally sound. How presumptuous to think those criteria ruled in congressional deliberations on such matters! In the solons' eyes the man from Plains was dangerously misinformed on the subject of water. Nevertheless, the President kept pressing his case, and though he had backed off somewhat, he was still at it when defeated for reelection in 1980.

Representative Timothy E. Wirth, a Colorado Democrat, was one of those sorely put off by the President. In October, 1980, Wirth explained, "Mr. Carter seems never to have understood the emotional and substantive importance of water to the West. We cannot get through to him that the water conservation he keeps advocating means, in the West, storing it [behind big dams]. He's never begun to understand this region's water laws, which I'll concede are bewildering."

Whatever the validity of all else said in the water war between Carter and Congress, nothing could have been truer than Wirth's concession. No one, not even the highest-paid, best-informed water rights attorney west of the Mississippi, will deny that the subject is bewildering. It is a massive, perplexing contest of jackstraws (the game where players try to remove straws from a pile without moving any other straws). The straws (water rights) are piled all over the arid and semi-arid regions of America, and when one is moved, others are likely to be unsettled. Jimmy Carter might as well have come to play the game in an Army tank, for he threatened to upset the whole pile.

On America's drylands, surface water is the equivalent of property. In this case the property owner holds rights to shares of a given piece of water, whether it is flowing or quiescent. For example, a shareholder may have the right to take a given amount of water per year from a certain stream. Such water rights were often established decades ago and passed from one owner to the next down to the present. Understandably, water ownership in the west became a massive jumble in a highly fluid situation (literally and figuratively). Clearly the accumulated water rights on some streams have added up to more water than nature makes available—we have already discussed the most prominent example, the Colorado River. So it is evident, and a good thing, that some water rights remain uncalled, and those that are called are not demanded all at once. Should the total of these straws be pulled simultaneously, each rights holder would get short shrift, and we come up with the appalling image of western rivers sucked dry.

In the main, rights holders are farmers or municipalities. So there is farm water (for irrigation) and city water (for domestic and business use), and farms use a great deal more water than towns. In both cases, the waters follow the traditional pattern of linear flow, from sources to consumers for a single use. At first glance the two waters seem to flow on parallel courses that do not meet or mix. However, they do intertwine once the city water has been turned to sewage effluent. At this point ownership may change as rights to the effluent are sold by the municipality to farmers who use it for irrigation—really a form of land treatment, although not characterized as such. A great deal of western irrigation depends on sewage effluent dumped into rivers. Indeed, under certain circumstances in seasons of low flow, the percentage of effluent in a stream may be comparable to nature's contribution of water. However, if a community should stop its established discharge to a stream—say it adopted land treatment and thus changed where and how much water is returned to the natural system—it might face explosive problems from downstream farmers depending on the effluent for irrigation. In effect, such an act on the city's part would pull a jackstraw that could badly upset the pile.

Actually most states in the west have a built-in legal upset for the game. Urban needs generally take precedence over agricultural needs. So when a town's growth requires more water, it can legally force a farmer to sell his water rights by eminent domain. In the process the farm, with its essential water gone to town, has to close down. On the other hand, urbanization may overrun irrigated farms, converting them to subdivisions, and the former farmer, who has no more irrigation needs, continues to hold his rights to the water. He may sell them to another farmer or a municipality, or he may keep them as a sort of nest egg, waiting for the time when price increases for water will make a sale most worthwhile. In the meantime, his water may be sitting unused in an impoundment or flowing out of the west in a stream, perhaps to the Gulf of Mexico via the Mississippi River. Although the former farmer may be looking at the Pacific from a retirement home in La Jolla, California, he is likely to remain an avid player in the game of jackstraws back home.

This intricate tangle of water rights forms multiple patterns in the web of life throughout the west. It is evident in various ways on the South Platte River in and around Denver. In recent years, for example, the city's Greenway Foundation has been responsible for a remarkable restoration job along the little stream flowing north through the mile-high metropolis. The riverbanks have been graced with numerous parks and a magnificent downtown plaza. They are connected by a popular hike-bike trail along the banks the length of the South Platte from city line to city line. But the water, the focus of this development, does not belong to the city. The rights are held by downstream farmers. During the summer and fall, when streams are normally low, the Platte through Denver is largely dependent on water released from impoundments at the request of the farmers. Normally an irrigator who needs water calls the caretaker at one of the large dams upstream from the city and requests a share of the impounded water he has rights to. The caretaker releases the share, as long as he knows the stream has adequate flow to carry the water without a major loss. In the past such calls were made sporadically, so at any given time summer flows on the South Platte might not amount to much. They were seldom enough for canoeing or rafting. But when the river was upgraded and the desire for water recreation increased, the Greenway Foundation met the demand through a cooperative arrangement worked out with the farmers and state water officials. The irrigators now coordinate their calls for water, bunching them up so the Denver flow rises on summer weekends to make boating possible. This is a case of pulling jackstraws without upsetting the pile.

But in the 1960s Denver pulled a straw and the upset became a costly court battle lasting into the 1970s. The litigation was brought by several irrigation companies that served South Platte water to more than 1,000 farmers through a vast network of ditches extending hundreds of miles. The companies drew the water through a common headgate on the river at the downstream edge of Denver. For years the flow into the gate included inadequately purified sewage effluent discharged from a primary treatment plant within Denver city limits. But then the city formed the Metropolitan Sewage Disposal District with a dozen other area municipalities, and they built a large "Metro" treatment plant on the Platte below the irrigation companies' headgate. This meant the city sewage water, which the companies had depended upon for a long time, now bypassed the irrigation intake via a pipeline to the new treatment works. The irrigators went to court, complaining of their loss and maintaining the effluent should be returned to the headgate at public expense by pumping it back upstream through a pipeline. The court ruled in favor of the district, but to avoid more litigation the Metro agreed to install a pipeline and pump and send the effluent back to the ditches upstream. The jackstraws of water rights settled down, and farmers served by the far-flung ditches continued irrigating sugar beets, corn, barley and hay with the nutrient-rich sewage effluent.

All this is to make a point: anyone who proposes innovative solutions to the water crisis of the country's arid and semi-arid regions should be prepared for a serious game of jackstraws, because he is certain to jolt the snarled pile of water rights and the intense emotions associated with them. The water problems of the west are unlikely to be settled without altering the old linear patterns of water and wastewater, so the problem solvers can find themselves fighting on two fronts. On one there is the usual battle with the orthodoxy of consulting engineers wedded to linear systems. On the other front there is the bewildering pattern of water rights, where a hint of change sends shocks through the nervous systems of zealous holders of water rights. A major case in point is that of North Glenn, Colorado, a suburban community of 30,000 on Denver's north side.

In 1982 North Glenn began using an innovative water and wastewater system that met one of the key problems of the western water crisis. As the project was getting underway in the late 1970s, Colorado's Governor Richard D. Lamm said it represented "the most innovative, creative thinking I have seen in my ten years of politics." And President Carter, stopping in the area, praised the effort, saying, "This might be a vista of what we will see on a broad base in the future." On the water-impoverished shelf of the Rockies, the North Glenn project made good sense, and from the President and governor down to the man in the street it was widely praised. But despite the acclaim, the syndrome of resistance to fundamental change set in, and North Glenn had to complete the project while battling a variety of opposition that soon surfaced.

The problem addressed by the small city was that of the traditional conflict between rural and urban areas, the needs for drinking water in town versus irrigation in the country. But as we have seen, the legal rights pattern of the west separates water along a divide between the two needs, with the ultimate advantage falling to the urban areas, where the least water is needed, but where most of the votes are cast. The imbalance of the conflict may have favored the growth of large urban centers, like Denver, Tucson and other rapidly expanding metropolitan areas in the driest parts of America, but where there is not enough water to meet both needs, the denouement has also hurt the region's important agricultural economy. The North Glenn project was conceived on the theory that the city-farm conflict could be replaced by a cooperative plan for use of the same water by both parties. It was a conservationist's dream with a synergistic bonus, for in the cooperative solution to the old problem both parties stood to gain more than they could realize acting independently in the traditional manner.

North Glenn, which emerged as a group of subdivisions after World War II, remained an unincorporated area for several years. In the beginning a private utility company provided water and sewerage services, but then the utility was purchased by the adjoining city of Thornton. That left North Glenn citizens and businesses in the strange plight of finding their most vital municipal services and the arteries that went with them (water and sewer lines) owned and operated by the next-door neighbor.

In the mid-1970s North Glenn officials decided to sever this connection, for they felt the sewer and water pipes held them at the mercy of Thornton's decisions on the two fundamental needs. At the time North Glenn enjoyed a blend of leadership essential for any community to make progress with creative ideas —something the city would need to establish its independence. The group included Mayor Alvin Thomas, City Manager Stanley Bender, City Clerk Shirley Whitten and Public Works Manager Richard Lundahl. They understood that the severance from Thornton would not be easy, especially because water sources were rapidly dwindling and costs were rising dramatically. If there was a time for some fresh thinking on an old problem, this was it. To help them, Mayor Thomas and his colleagues called on an unusual group of experts, who agreed to join in a series of brainstorming sessions. The group consisted of two attorneys, John Musick, who was knowledgeable about the intricacies of Colorado water problems, and Joe Shoemaker, who was also an engineer with a public works background; the head of a bonding house, Walter Imhoff, with expertise on water; a water-oriented engineer, Kenneth Wright; the resource planner John Sheaffer (whose Muskegon project was then coming on line); and Sheaffer's Denver associate F. Robert McGregor.

The group was aware of the severe problems water seekers faced in the Denver metropolitan area. As we learned earlier, the outreach for new sources was bumping against its limits on both the eastern and western slopes of the Rockies. If North Glenn was to follow the traditional search route, it would be picking from the dregs of the century-long hunt for water in the region. The only possible new source would be a supply of local groundwater tapped by deep wells. Otherwise, the city might try to find and purchase shares in existing water rights within the South Platte basin. Neither alternative was very satisfactory. If the groundwater could be found, it would probably be limited and could not be depended upon as the main supply for a growing city. The purchase of surface water shares in the amounts needed would not only be costly, but could lead the community into the farm-city conflict, having to condemn water rights presently used for irrigation.

In their search for new approaches the brainstormers came upon the idea for a cooperative exchange of water between North Glenn and a firm known as FRICO (the Farmers Reservoir and Irrigation Company). After the idea was broached to FRICO, an agreement for the exchange was worked out, and plans for one of the most interesting water projects in the west were developed under John Musick and Robert McGregor's direction. They implemented an idea that might resolve the serious water problems faced by many communities around the region.

Instead of purchasing the farmers' water rights, by condemnation proceedings if necessary, North Glenn would borrow the water destined for irrigation (up to some 2.4 billion gallons a year) and return it as partially purified wastewater. The farmers' compensation would be receiving 10 percent more water than they had loaned. This fluid interest on their loan would come from three sources: (1) stormwater collected in the city, (2) the purchase of a comparatively few shares of water rights available from farms that had been overtaken by urbanization, and (3) wells in North Glenn used as a makeup supply for water lost by lawn sprinkling. In addition to the water bonus, FRICO's farms would also enjoy the fertilizing nutrients carried by the city wastewater to the irrigated fields.

Under the plan, the borrowed water would come from shares of FRICO's rights in the mountain stream Clear Creek, specifically from an impoundment called Standley Lake, a few miles west and uphill from the city. The supply would flow by gravity into North Glenn, be purified in a new water treatment plant and then be distributed to consumers. The borrowed water, plus the bonus amounts, would leave town as sewage. It would no longer follow the existing wastewater route—south via the Thornton collection system to the Denver Metro treatment plant for discharge to the South Platte—but would be piped eight miles north to four aerated treatment lagoons. Treated effluent from the lagoons would then be stored in a large, new reservoir for release as needed for irrigation by FRICO's farmers. When required it would flow into the Bull Canal, the irrigation ditch connecting the irrigators to the original water source, Standley Lake. In other words, the borrowed water would simply take a detour into North Glenn, serve its municipal needs, gather nutrients and 10 percent additional water and then flow back to the owners, the farmers.

Those were the plans so highly praised and eventually implemented, but they turned out to have some serious opponents, and the implementation came only after the antagonists had their day—indeed, many, many days—in court. Before the city's plan was completed, North Glenn had been the defendant in more than three dozen legal actions aimed at changing or bringing down the unusual project. The city suffered setbacks in only two of the cases, but the litigation was hamstringing, costly and nearly the cause of the entire project's destruction.

Some of the litigation might be characterized as normal for a nontraditional project like North Glenn's. Part reflected personal fears of citizens about being involved in something new, especially related to wastewater. Other legal actions were politically motivated, having to do with the city's striving for independence. But a great deal of the litigation was associated with our analogy of jackstraws and water rights. The North Glenn plan pulled a straw that jarred a pile of rights along the South Platte below Denver, especially the rights to North Glenn's wastewater.

As it became known that the small city's sewage flow would shift from south to north, the news racked the nerves of farmers using North Glenn's treated effluent (which they drew from the South Platte after it had been through the Denver Metro treatment plant and discharged to the river). It had become sort of a windfall of water shares, along with wastewater carried by the stream from other sources. The irrigators now saw their windfall of North Glenn's effluent heading north to a different set of farms, whose irrigation source had traditionally been Clear Creek, a tributary to the South Platte. Meanwhile, the city took the position that these farmers would continue receiving the shares to which they were entitled, but would lose the windfall shares derived from the community's wastewater. In this region, where water can be valued more than gold, the nervous shareholders began calling their lawyers and politicians, and a ruckus followed.

Needless to say there was extensive disagreement over how, or whether, the fundamental shift of water would work. Even though everyone was supposed to come out even, the disrupted jackstraws were not about to settle quietly into a new pile with an unfamiliar configuration. The resettling was an open sesame for farmers, lawyers, politicians and all comers who saw something to lose or gain in the fracas. Of course the legal melee had its hidden agendas, usually with the unspoken goal of simply killing the project—thus a lot of litigation addressed procedural matters, because the underlying issues would have had no chance in court. As praiseworthy as North Glenn's effort might have been in this land where water conservation can often be more words than deeds, the change it posed in the bewildering pattern of water ownership was a frightening prospect, like that raised by President Carter on a grander scale.

Nevertheless, the project survived. The reason lay in at least two important elements that must be present, as they were at North Glenn, for the success of almost any nontraditional solution to our water problems. First, such efforts require progressive, vigorous leadership willing to become committed to new ideas. North Glenn enjoyed that ingredient as the innovative water project was initiated. It was lost through political changes before the system was completed, but momentum and continuity from the original leadership helped carry the effort to fruition.

Second, such leadership must work with sound ideas. Many notions are offered for solving our water crises, but none can be declared sound until it has been translated into a workable plan of action. North Glenn's idea was turned into a plan solid enough to withstand the attacks that attended its implementation.

The validity and universality of the fundamental idea is now being demonstrated at North Glenn. The small Colorado city shows how municipalities and farms can cooperate to share the same water for the good of both. On first learning about the project and its history, some may ask why such a system is necessary when farmers are already using sewage effluent from the rivers to which it is discharged. The difference is efficient management of water resources, both of clean sources and of wastewater discharges. Under the North Glenn idea, one source can serve both urban and rural needs, and that confluence of use is certain to work generally toward more efficient management of the resource. And under the plan, the storage facilities for treated effluent ensure that nearly all the municipal wastewater and nutrients remain available for the benefit of the farms. Following the traditional method of using effluent after discharge to streams, great quantities of both the water and the nutrients (whose value is diminished by dilution in any event) are lost, a good part of them to the Gulf of Mexico. For example, during the many months when irrigation is not needed and North Glenn's undiluted effluent is being saved up in storage for maximum use in the growing season, the natural high flow of the South Platte is carrying off trillions of gallons of nutrient-rich wastewater—polluting watercourses en route, infiltrating and contaminating aquifers beneath the escape routes and doing no good at the final destination, the sea. In any event, North Glenn illustrates that both city and farm have much to gain through cooperation, as opposed to conflict leading to condemnation.

When this potential is perceived widely enough, and continuing crises provide the motivation, both urban and rural areas will learn how to play the game of jackstraws so water rights can be fairly adjusted as needed changes are made. The sorting out is practically certain to happen through the courts, legislatures, county seats and city halls of the region.

If cities and farms can be borrowers and lenders of common waters, there will be little need for the kind of actions taken in municipalities like Tucson, where, as we learned earlier, tens of thousands of acres of farms are being closed down for the sake of municipal water consumption in the forevermore-thirsty sun belt metropolis.

XV
The Farm-City Loop

If the most workable solutions for the nation's water crises lie in a move away from linear systems controlled by public agencies to circular systems run by private entrepreneurs, the best way of effecting change may be found in the further development of what we have called the farm-city loop. The loop is the basic circle that has already been well described. In its simplest form, nutrient-rich city water is carried to a farm as an irrigant and fertilizer for crops to be consumed in the city, while the water is simultaneously purified for reuse. Berlin, Germany, worked with four farm-city loops a century ago to return both food and reclaimed water to the city while solving its "sewage difficulty." Melbourne, Australia, with its huge farm at nearby Werribee, uses one of the world's oldest, most successful farm-city loops. For a half century, Lubbock, Texas, and a private farmer have used a loop with benefits both public and private. And at Muskegon, Michigan, some 30 million gallons of water per day flows around one of the most modern, successful farm-city loops.

But none of these circular systems captures all the potentials that could enhance their attractiveness to private entrepreneurs, who could accomplish what public officials restrained by the orthodoxy of consulting engineers fail to do—except where a few local leaders exercise the independence to go beyond the orthodox. One exception is at Vineland, New Jersey, which is in the construction stage of a plan that adds a major new dimension to the farm-city loop. The project shows that besides its usual benefits, the loop has a valuable energy component. In addition to returning food or fiber and clean water to the city, the land treatment system will also send back electricity and alcohol fuel.

Vineland is in Cumberland County, at the southern end of New Jersey. Philadelphia is about 40 miles to the north, and Atlantic City is not quite that far to the east. Cumberland County is one of the leading agricultural areas in the Garden State, noted for its truck farming. The county produces beans, tomatoes and other specialty crops that depend on irrigation. Food processing is the county's second-largest industry (the first is glass manufacturing, which uses the area's abundant, high-quality glass sand). Vineland's population of 53,000 makes it the county's largest city, and with 69 square miles it is New Jersey's biggest city by land area. The community lies in the basin of the Maurice River, which flows south into Delaware Bay. The tidal marshes near the river's mouth are rich with clams and contain the beds that are the center of the state's important oyster industry, a form of sea farming that has been severely curtailed by water pollution along other sections of the east coast.

Vineland obtains its public water supply from 12 wells located in and around the urban area. Between 1926 and 1971 the wells were driven into the underlying Cohansey-Kirkwood Aquifer at depths from 151 to 177 feet. The aquifer is a highly productive source of groundwater for both Vineland and nearby Millville. Vineland's dozen wells provide from 7 million to 12 million gallons of water per day; the larger amount is pumped during the growing season, when food-processing plants demand large supplies.

On the outflow side of the system, Vineland has relied on a truncated form of land treatment for many years. As late as the 1930s the city's wastewater was used to irrigate farmland, producing bountiful crops of corn that older residents still remember. But as happened elsewhere, neither the system nor its management was scientifically designed, and both failed; however, Vineland held to the idea of purifying wastewater by soil percolation. Since the 1930s sewage has been treated to the primary level in simple settling tanks and then spread on a number of rapid infiltration beds, from which the effluent seeps directly down through the soil to the groundwater.

By the 1970s Vineland's increasing wastewater flows became too much for these soil systems to handle. They had become overloaded with phosphorus, and their capacity for nitrogen removal was not adequate to meet water quality standards. Their failure threatened the underlying aquifer with an overdose of both elements and thus endangered the area's water supply. At the time two city agencies were responsible for wastewater treatment. One, serving 32,000 persons, was the Landis Sewerage Authority (named after the city's founder, Charles K. Landis). The other, the City of Vineland Water and Sewer Utility, served 9,000 people in the main business district (the "Old Borough"). Though their systems were separate, both agencies relied on primary treatment followed by soil infiltration—and by the 1970s both were in trouble from overloading. Then the New Jersey Department of Environmental Protection (DEP) and the federal EPA ordered the Landis authority to correct both its own and the Vineland utility's system. In the usual way, the Landis authority retained a firm of sanitary engineers, a study followed, a recommendation was made, and it was promptly endorsed by the New Jersey DEP. The engineers advised that Vineland turn to a new kind of sewage treatment plant, an import from Holland, with the trade name the Carrousel.

The machine, which was hardly a merry-go-round, was based on a design by a Dutch sanitary engineer, A. Pasveer. Prior to inventing the Carrousel, Pasveer had designed the oxidation ditch, which purified sewage to the secondary level. The system was an endless ditch, a few feet wide and a few feet deep, shaped like a racetrack. Horizontal rotors spanning the ditch pushed the wastewater around and around the racetrack, thus forcing oxygen into the sewage and stimulating biological action that partially purified the water. The capacity of Pasveer's ditch was limited, so the Dutch engineer developed what became the basis for the Carrousel to handle greater volumes. It was built in units, each essentially a large, oblong tank like a swimming pool. At one end a vertical rotor pushed the wastewater through the tank, around a series of channels, again to oxygenate the liquid and enhance biological activity. Still the machine discharged effluent hardly any better than that from the activated sludge plants widely used in America. If adopted at Vineland, as recommended, the system would discharge either to the Maurice River, or to the problem-prone infiltration beds and thus to the groundwater.

But the Carrousel did not play in Vineland, for serious questions were raised about it despite the consultants' $600,000 recommendation. The doubts, which led to a major change in direction, came from the Landis Sewerage Authority board. (During this time the board had a succession of three chairmen, William C. MacDade, Gaylord Evey and Leon Lowenstern.) First of all, the Carrousel clashed with the energy crisis, which was then becoming a major national concern. Undeniably, powering the machine's heavy rotors consumed a great deal of electricity. However, the board had a more fundamental question: how would the Dutch system help Vineland live up to the purposes of the Federal Water Pollution Control Act Amendments of 1972? Assuming the law's administrators were serious about it, they would soon have to demand more than secondary treatment to meet the zero-discharge goal of 1985. The Dutch system offered only secondary treatment, the level that the EPA had set as an interim goal for 1977. And here, practically on top of that date, Vineland was being advised to spend millions on a secondary treatment plant that probably would not even be completed until considerably after 1977. Such advice was especially perplexing to Lowenstern when he was chairman of the board. If the authority bought the Carrousel to meet only the lower standard, the rotors would hardly have given a turn when the EPA would be demanding that Vineland meet the law's ultimate 1985 goal. Then would Vinelanders, who had just sustained one multimillion-dollar wallop, suddenly get hit with another? Finding the answer took the questioners on a bureaucratic merry-go-round, on which the New Jersey DEP, the federal EPA and the consulting engineers went around without arriving at a satisfactory response.

Meanwhile a set of circumstances drew Lowenstern's attention to an idea the consultants seemed to have missed. Somehow they had glided over the possibility of land treatment, even though they were supposed to have assessed it as an alternative method. Furthermore, the EPA had allowed them to get away with the oversight, even though an agency regulation demanded that land treatment be thoroughly assessed in every study. Such regulatory laxity was common, as we have pointed out. Oddly enough, Lowenstern was introduced to the land method by an EPA branch located over 1,000 miles west of New Jersey, the Robert S. Kerr Environmental Research Laboratory at Ada, Oklahoma. Investigators from the Ground Water Research Branch at Ada had come east to assess the Vineland infiltration beds. Coincidentally they were studying the new Muskegon land treatment system and were finding that it was already close to meeting the 1985 zero-discharge goal of the federal clean water law. When Lowenstern came upon this revelation, he naturally wondered why Vineland could not do the same.

He and the Landis authority's engineer, William Goelzer, flew to Ada and spent a couple of days with Richard Thomas of the EPA reviewing the laboratory's research. They returned home believing they finally had the answer for Vineland. "I was convinced by Dr. Thomas and others out there," said Lowenstern, "that the future of sewage treatment was in land treatment. They also made me realize that if we were going to spend a lot of money, there was no sense in meeting a lower standard when we could go directly to the highest standard with a system that could be even more cost effective."

When the authority board revealed this thinking to the New Jersey DEP and regional EPA officials in New York City, the reception was hardly cordial. "We were actually summoned to New York, to the EPA office, and given an ultimatum," explained Lowenstern. "They told us we were doing nothing but stalling, that we didn't want to spend any money. Then they gave us just six weeks to produce a study that would prove land treatment was more cost effective than the Carrousel."

With the ultimatum, the Landis Sewerage Authority turned to two firms for help, Engineering Enterprises of Norman, Oklahoma, and Sheaffer & Roland of Chicago. A team from the Chicago firm led by John Marsh, William Rust and Fred Neal did the study, and the deadline was met. The team's report provided scientific proof supporting what Lowenstern and his colleagues believed.

"The study showed that even if we included the six hundred thousand dollars already spent for the Carrousel recommendation," the Landis chairman declared, "we would still save several millions of dollars if we changed to a land treatment system and went directly to the 1985 standard."

But the Vineland officials found, as did a few other like-minded communities, that they were bumping against a Himalayan bureaucracy interwoven with a private web of consulting engineers and equipment suppliers. Together they thought in primary, secondary and tertiary stages dominated by concrete and steel technology. In this private-public conglomerate, the goal of clean water had metamorphosed to a goal of adding sewage treatment plants *ad infinitum,* never mind that they could never fulfill the intent of the 1972 law or meet the zero-discharge goal of 1985. Still the Vineland officials continued pushing for a decision, and though it took two years to move the monolith, the state DEP and federal EPA finally bowed to the sense of the study that the latter agency had demanded in six weeks.

The persistent Landis Sewerage Authority had now earned the opportunity to explore in full the resources available in wastewater that would have otherwise been dumped at considerable expense—to federal, state and local treasuries and to the waters that would have suffered the contamination. As the Vineland agency proceeded with Sheaffer & Roland's assistance, it enlisted some powerful allies by forming a 32-member citizens' advisory committee. The committee, which met at least once a month during the planning stages, became an essential conduit to the general public. Without it, the project might very well have been wrecked on the shoals of public misunderstanding. The committee chairman, Robert Novak, was the manager of a large food-processing plant, the single largest contributor of wastewater to the community's treatment system. The other 31 members ranged from poultry processors to farmers, from nurserymen to various municipal officials, from builders and developers to environmentalists. The advisory committee brought information from the community to the planners, but perhaps more important, it returned information to the community. Robert Schwarz of the Landis Sewerage Authority served as public participation coordinator. While the new plan developed and the required public hearings were held, the two-way flow of information became a main force in gaining public acceptance for the sophisticated new system. When finished, the Vineland project is certain to become a bellwether solution for water crises across the country. It will not only demonstrate how we can clean and reclaim our water, but also how it can be done as a paying proposition worthy of private investment, development and management.

The central component of the Vineland plan is a land treatment system that preserves and makes use of the existing wastewater treatment works. Sewage will still be treated by the city's primary settling tanks, augmented by new ones. Primary effluent will continue going to the infiltration beds, but not to the underlying aquifer. Studies of the beds showed that the soil remains an effective filter for organic pollutants, those materials that become obnoxious nuisances when disposed of in rivers and lakes. The beds still fail to remove sufficient nitrogen and phosphorus; however, with the land treatment plan that failure will become a plus rather than a minus. The substances will, of course, be valuable nutrients when applied to croplands. So instead of continuing to seep directly down to the aquifer, the nutritive water in the new system will be diverted from below the infiltration beds via underdrains to the land treatment sites. The drainage will be equivalent to the secondary effluent that might have come from the Carrousel, but, of course, the capital and operational costs (especially for energy) will be relatively minor.

From the underdrains of the rapid infiltration beds the effluent will be pumped to a 100-acre storage lagoon formed with an earthen berm (an elongated mound of dirt). It will be built up on the surface of the ground, and then the insides and bottom will be sealed by an impervious clay lining. The lagoon will hold over 600 million gallons of the treated wastewater, enough to contain a 75-day flow at 8 million gallons a day (the rate anticipated for Vineland by the end of the design period, the year 2003). This capacity was chosen to allow for the storage of effluent during the two and a half nonirrigation months of the year.

When ready for use, the stored water will be drawn from the lagoon, disinfected if necessary and pumped to three irrigation areas for application to the land through center-pivot rigs and solid-set facilities (the common kind of spray devices that whirl around a fixed point). The system will irrigate and fertilize 1,030 acres of croplands to be developed for the project. Most of the production will be in corn and rye (double-cropped so that one crop of each is produced successively in the same soil per growing season). Other production may include hay, barley, soybeans and Christmas trees.

The drainage from the land treatment areas will be potable water, which could be returned to the Cohansey-Kirkwood Aquifer for drinking water supply, but this will not be necessary. The aquifer's problem, never one of insufficient water, has been the threat of contamination from Vineland's sewage, a threat removed by the new system. The purified water will end up in the Maurice River, to flow down to the Delaware Bay. Thus the system will preserve a distinction enjoyed by Vineland for decades. Of all the communities in the badly polluted Delaware River complex, the New Jersey municipality remains practically the only one along the 330-mile stream not following the practice of disposal by dilution.

While potable water and salable crops from land treatment would seem more than enough to expect of any wastewater system, the concept, as practiced to date, has still left another valuable resource unexploited. Sewage can also be a potential source of energy, and the Vineland plan takes advantage of it. The source is sludge, that unpalatable byproduct of any treatment system. As we have pointed out, sewage sludge, the black, gooey bane of city treatment works, can be plowed or injected into croplands as a soil conditioner—and that is how it has been used in land treatment so far. At Muskegon, the material is occasionally dredged from the lagoons and applied to the cornfields. But sludge also harbors energy—which is not a newly discovered fact, because the resource has sometimes been tapped for heat and power in conventional sewage treatment plants. However, more often than not, this potential resource is wasted by disposal in landfills or ocean dumping (frequently to the detriment of groundwater and with no benefits for the sea). At Vineland its potential as both a soil conditioner and a source of energy will be put to work in the unusual wastewater management system.

The settlings from the primary tanks will be the main source of sludge (an abundance of which they have always produced, but it has previously been dumped in a landfill). This sludge will now be pumped into two anaerobic digesters to generate up to 105,000 cubic feet of biogas daily. The gas will run 4 engine-generators that can make some 2,628,000 kilowatt hours of electricity per year (enough to furnish power for 438 typical residences). Thus the water-cleaning system becomes an energy producer rather than an energy drain. The power generation will not only make the Landis system energy self-sufficient, but will provide revenue from the sale of excess electricity to the local utility. About a quarter of the power will flow directly into part of the new project. The remaining three quarters will go to the utility, but a portion of this will flow back through existing circuits that will power the rest of the treatment system (this circuitous route will avoid extensive rewiring). However, when it is all worked out, the utility will buy more power from the project than it sells back, so the Landis authority will enjoy income from the arrangement.

This energy self-sufficiency will be a significant development because conventional wastewater treatment plants, with their pumps, aerators and mechanical filters, are among the leading contributors to municipal electric bills. Moreover, between 1968 and 1977, the national effort to improve water quality with short-measure secondary treatment plants raised the costs of energy for municipal sewage works an estimated five times, and the costs were expected to be double the 1977 figure by 1990. The Vineland system, while fully cleaning wastewater, will free the city from this inflationary burden.

But the new system will make more than electrical energy. The internal combustion engines will also produce a great deal of excess heat, which is ordinarily wasted. Some of the heat will be fed from the cooling system back to the anaerobic digesters to maintain their critical 95-degree temperature, but the remainder will be captured from the engines by a waste heat recovery system, which will produce steam. The steam will heat an alcohol production facility, specifically for the distillation and drying of 198-proof alcohol, which will either be blended with gasoline as an octane booster or used as a raw material in industry. The alcohol feedstock will be corn grown in the land treatment system. The project design anticipates an annual yield of 160,000 bushels of corn, which could produce 400,000 gallons of alcohol.

This production could be expected to bring nearly three quarters of a million dollars back to the community each year.

The planned complex of production systems feeding upon one another will continue wringing resources out of the wastewater ingredients. First, the sludge, after yielding its energy, will remain a valuable soil additive to be injected into the fields of the land treatment system. In fact, fermentation will have improved the material for use in the soil, having "stabilized" it, thus reducing both the odor and pathogenic contamination.

The corn in passing through the alcohol facility will also do triple duty. Besides serving as feedstock for the alcohol, it will break down into two valuable products. One, a slurry, ordinarily treated as a waste, will be fed to the anaerobic digesters to increase biogas production. The other, distillers' dry grain, which retains much of the corn's original protein, will be sold as a feed supplement for livestock and dairy cattle. The dry grain is especially valuable in New Jersey, where the Department of Agriculture claims that lack of readily accessible feed is a deterrent to expanding the Garden State's livestock and dairy industry. The Vineland plan targets annual production of distillers' dry grain at close to 2 million pounds, which could be sold for about $150,000.

When completed in 1985, the Landis Sewerage Authority Wastewater Management System will be the most sophisticated of all farm-city loops. The roundelay will virtually be an old MacDonald's farm of activities using sewage wastes as raw materials to produce goods and services, while eliminating a threat to the municipal water supply and the Maurice River basin with its precious fishery resources. In a letter to New Jersey's Governor Thomas Kean, Leon Lowenstern outlined the permanent economic benefits associated with the system. "The project," he wrote, "will create new jobs which, in turn, create new wealth in the County. There will be 17 new jobs to operate the various elements of the system. The products produced by the operation will have an annual value of $1,200,000. This revenue, along with the new jobs, will stimulate secondary impacts which will create 170 new permanent jobs in the County." Lowenstern went on to point out that the Landis authority's customer charges have been the lowest in the state, and he added, "By using the sewage as a raw material in our system, these low rates will continue. Thus, the economic stimulation that will result from the project will not be negated by dramatic increases in user charges to both residents and industries which could, in turn, fuel inflationary cost of living and business expense increases in the County. These low rates will help stimulate further economic expansion in South Jersey."

Vineland will provide one of the nation's most persuasive demonstrations of how economic rewards are available to investors from the misplaced resources now called water pollutants. The Landis Sewerage Authority's major contribution may be to show that wastewater has an energy as well as fertilizer potential. While the authority's energy will be available as electricity and alcohol, innovators elsewhere will certainly find other ways of capitalizing on the resource. One possibility is hydroponics, where plants are grown in nutritive solutions (that is, liquids instead of soil), and often in hothouses in cool climates. Hydroponic vegetables, like lettuce, cucumbers and tomatoes, are already being grown around the year where climates limit conventional growth to one summer crop. The hothouses' most costly requirements are electricity (for special growth-enhancing lights) and heat (for optimum growing temperature). The kind of farm-city loop under development at Vineland could fulfill both these requirements, thus adding to the products being returned to the city in exchange for the resources sent to the farm in wastewater.

Farm-city loops, large and small, simple and complex, offer the most useful of all tools to move away from the failures of linear systems under public agencies, toward circular systems privately run. Thus the farm-city loop may be our best hope for a general solution to the water crisis faced by the nation.

XVI
The Poison Plumes

On December 18, 1980, Neil Goldfine, a public official of Atlantic City, New Jersey, was perusing that day's *New York Times* when an article startled him. It was about an announcement made by Congressman Toby Moffett, chairman of the Environment, Energy and Natural Resources Subcommittee of the U.S. House of Representatives. Moffett had just released some disturbing information being developed by the EPA about an old landfill called Price's Pit. According to the congressman, EPA test wells indicated that chemicals leaching from the landfill were, as the *Times* pointed up, threatening Atlantic City's public water wells. Goldfine had reason to be startled, for recently he had become responsible for the purity of Atlantic City's drinking water, and the EPA had failed to inform him about the potential disaster.

The threat to the famous seaside resort made a dramatic news story at a time when many cases of contaminated wells were being reported across the nation. Congressman Moffett was often involved, for he was pushing the EPA to reveal what it was learning, but not publicizing, about the serious crisis faced by millions who depend on wells for drinking water. In September, 1980, his subcommittee had released an EPA list of over 2,100 dump sites located over "usable" groundwater sources "with no barrier reported between the waste and the ground water." Many of the sites were said to contain "potentially hazardous contaminants," and many were within a mile of a "potential water supply well." The report had pointed out, "This nation is highly dependent on ground water," and "ground water destruction will be one of the most serious environmental problems of the 1980's."

The prediction came true for Atlantic City. The threat from Price's Pit was, indeed, serious. The state had recently legalized gambling in the city, and old hotels were coming down to be replaced by lavish casino hotels, turning the fading resort into a glittering "Las Vegas of the East." By the early 1980s the casinos were taking in more than 1 billion dollars a year. But the good fortune could be spoiled by the toxic pollutants en route from Price's Pit, only a few miles from the city.

In the early 1970s the owner of the dump, Charles Price, had permitted the disposal of an estimated 8.3 million gallons of chemical wastes at the site. The practice was soon halted and the dump was closed, but not before the damage was done. The wastes found an open avenue through the sandy bottom of the landfill into the underlying Cohansey Aquifer, the largest underground reservoir of pure water east of the Mississippi. There in the all but motionless groundwater, the poisons formed a "plume," which might be compared to a plume of smoke from a chimney, except that its formation and flow in the groundwater would be timed in years compared to minutes for the smoke. Now, long after its start, the underground plume was apparently approaching Atlantic City's well fields. If this was true, Neil Goldfine had to act without delay.

He engaged a firm of groundwater specialists, who mapped the plume by drilling 35 test wells at various locations. The water samples allowed the investigators to define the outer edges of the contamination, its direction of flow and its speed. The data revealed the plume was headed for the municipal water supply carrying a deadly grog including benzene, chloroform, cadmium, lead, vinyl chloride and methylene chloride. The poison mix was only some 3,000 feet from the nearest city well, and should the worst come true, ten of Atlantic City's dozen wells could eventually be ruined. Developers of the gambling resort had been playing against a stacked deck.

The groundwater specialists, whose fee was some $350,000, recommended a dismayingly expensive solution: abandon the threatened wells and drill new ones at a safe distance from the endangered area of the aquifer—for an estimated $6.5 million.

Goldfine assumed that kind of money could come from the new federal "Superfund," established by Congress after the Love Canal tragedy in New York State. The $1.6 billion trust fund was supposed to help alleviate the kinds of burdens Price's Pit was forcing upon Atlantic City. But the fund's administrators in the EPA could not pay for the new wells without a study of their own. The agency took over at a slow bureaucratic pace, and the plume, traveling about seven inches a day, proceeded toward the well fields.

Not long before Price's Pit was forced to close in the 1970s, a landfill in Du Page County, Illinois, was closed according to plan and for a very different reason. Furthermore, while the New Jersey dump went on to threaten a major recreational resort, the one in Illinois actually became the center of a thriving recreational area. The activity developed around an unusual elevation on the otherwise level prairie west of Chicago. It continues to be called a mountain, although it is too low to qualify as one by Webster's definition. Nor does it appear on maps of Illinois. But over a quarter-million people a year find their way to the mountain, which is in the Roy C. Blackwell Recreational Forest Preserve. Some of the visitors ride on horseback and hike on the area's trails, and many climb to the summit of the small peak, from which, on a clear day, they can see the Chicago Loop. Glancing back down at the base of the mountain, they overlook three lakes. The largest, covering 70 acres, is used for boating and fishing. A second, 4-acre lake with a beach accommodates thousands of swimmers, up to 1,500 on many a summer day. The third lake, a reservoir, which augments the other two bodies of water, forms part of the verdant setting that includes numerous picnic and camping sites. In the winter the area is used for cross-country skiing, skating and ice fishing, but the most fun is had by hundreds of youngsters "tubing" on the mountain. They slide down the snowy slopes on inflated inner tubes rented at the forest preserve.

The mountain is officially called Mount Hoy, but it is commonly referred to as Mount Trashmore. Those who ascend to the summit, 150 feet above the surrounding prairie, are really climbing a huge pile of solid waste collected for the best part of a decade from nearly 1 million people in suburban Chicago.

Mount Trashmore was conceived and designed in the 1960s (by author Sheaffer) to accommodate the area's burgeoning waste. Moreover, it was developed to create something of benefit, other than a place to dump, for the county and, most of all, to protect its groundwater. Mount Trashmore was ahead of its time in addressing a problem that became a serious part of today's water crisis.

While many landfills, as the word implies, were traditionally started in holes in the ground, often in old gravel pits, Mount Trashmore was built on and above the earth's surface. The traditional dump in a pit posed two groundwater-related problems. The bottom of the trash pile, with its hazardous components, was close to, or even below, the water table. And the hole itself acted like a funnel, collecting rainwater that was contaminated by the waste as it moved on down to the groundwater. The Mount Trashmore design addressed both of these hazards. The mountain was built on a 40-acre, impermeable clay floor, which held the trash above, and sealed off from, the groundwater. As the waste arrived at the site, the material was encased in a relatively small clay cell, and as the cells multiplied to form the mountain, its sides were packed in more clay and topped with soil, which supported vegetation. When done, the structure formed a cone-like elevation that shed a large percentage of the natural precipitation, keeping it away from the internal waste. Excavation of the earthen materials used to pack the refuse into Mount Trashmore left large cavities near the base, and they became basins for the lakes. The same excavations also produced a great deal of gravel, which was sold to help pay for the project. When complete, the basins filled up with the groundwater that the entire affair was designed to protect.

Today, when citizens may even resort to violence to fight off a new landfill, Mount Trashmore remains a pioneering demonstration of how solid waste treated as a raw material, rather than a mess to be dumped, can be put to work beneficially instead of detrimentally. The thousands of recreationists attest to the social value of the idea. And water samples continually drawn form the lakes and 24 test wells reveal that the design continues to protect the area's groundwater. Mount Trashmore's success prompted Du Page County to construct two more such complexes, both taller, larger and more sophisticated than the original mountain (their completion is anticipated by 2000).

Du Page County's unusual kind of landfill ought to be more the rule than the exception, but the great majority of the nation's landfills are closer to Price's Pit than Trashmore. So the Atlantic City story is only one startling tale of hundreds across the country. Society committing suicide by poisoning its own well plays in the news media like a subplot to the nation's popular horror films. A *Newsweek* piece, asking, "How Safe Is Your Water?" replies with the warning that groundwater "has become the country's most urgent environmental problem," and then quotes the former EPA official Eckardt Beck as saying the "contamination of ground water is the 'environmental horror story of the 80s.' " A large share of the audience for this national drama, which features the closing of more than 2,000 wells, is understandably frightened, given that half of all United States residents depend on groundwater remaining potable. Their fears show up at testing laboratories where citizens with samples of their well-water come to see if they are players in the Gothic water tale of the decade.

For example, from the early 1970s to the 1980s, the small Ellis Tarlton Water Testing Laboratories of Danbury, Connecticut, quadrupled the average number of tests performed for private well owners. In 1982 Tarlton found one in four wells contaminated, compared to one in ten a decade earlier. Connecticut citizens, who depend on nearly a quarter-million private wells for drinking water, became especially aware of groundwater contamination because nearly half the state's 169 towns suffered from polluted wells between 1977 and 1982. The growing awareness is evident as more and more buyers of homes with private wells make their purchases contingent upon the water being pure. And no wonder there is caution when those learning about groundwater contamination are usually told that the problem, like the cancer it may cause, is virtually incurable. All in all, the average citizen might understandably decide that the last sanctuary for pure water, the dark, mysterious reservoirs in the earth, no longer provides a safe, dependable supply. With the potability of surface sources spoiled long ago, citizens are now taught that the country's aquifers are being either irretrievably ruined by contamination or depleted faster than they can be recharged by nature.

In truth the groundwater picture is not that bleak. Despite the drama, the problems afflict only a small portion of the nation's groundwater. Regardless of the growing belief that once contaminated an aquifer is forever doomed as a potable source, there are remedies. As Mount Trashmore proves, the means are also available for managing wastes to protect the vast amounts of groundwater that remain pure. And as for depletion, there are ways (as we have already indicated) of artificially recharging overdrawn aquifers.

Jay H. Lehr, one of the nation's leading authorities on groundwater, is, on the one hand, pleased that his favorite subject is finally receiving the public attention he had always hoped it would enjoy, but, on the other hand, he deplores the doomsday catalyst for the overdue attention. Since 1967, Lehr, a professor of hydrology at Ohio State University, has been executive director of the National Water Well Association. After arriving on the job he concluded "the public didn't know there was such a thing as ground water." However, by 1982 he feared that while people were learning about it, they were in danger of deciding, "What a shame we didn't discover ground water before it was all polluted."

"It is in the best interest of the public to better understand the situation," Lehr states, "specifically that ground-water pollution, while serious, is not quite the crisis some lead us to believe. We've got a problem and we want action: we want the press and the public to keep arguing for ground-water cleanup. But we don't need any Chicken Littles telling us that the sky is falling, because it most certainly is not."

To make his point Lehr compares what he claims is a highly conservative estimate of the nation's groundwater with an extremely liberal estimate of its contamination. He figures the conterminous United States has at least 100,000,000,000,000,000 (100 quadrillion) gallons of groundwater in the upper third of a mile of the earth's crust. Then, for the liberal number, Lehr totals up a possible (but improbable) 200,000 sources of pollution. Increasing the improbability, he allows that each source has been discharging for 40 years, and has formed a plume 1 mile long,

1,000 feet wide and 100 feet thick in aquiferous material 25 percent porous. This would leave some 200 trillion gallons of the nation's groundwater contaminated. Dividing his first estimate by the second, Lehr finds that only 0.2 percent of our subsurface supply is contaminated. In doing this exercise, he is not replacing Chicken Little with Pollyanna, but asking people to realize the nation's groundwater is far from a complete loss.

Lehr is among the first to agree that America, in fact, has a serious groundwater problem—and especially individuals whose private or municipal wells draw from those possible trillions of gallons that are contaminated or potentially so. Their numbers are greater than the minuscule percentage of pollution might indicate. Obviously, increased population density raises the potential for pollution; thus the fraction of contaminated groundwater is likely to be concentrated where its consumers are most thickly settled. Witness Atlantic City, where the drinking water for 36,000 residents and tens of thousands of tourists is jeopardized by a single dump. So nationally millions of people have reason to worry about such contamination. Their concerns have to be twofold: (1) remedying past sins by restoring the small, but crucial, part of groundwater that has been sullied, and (2) preventing future transgressions to preserve the big part that remains pure. Both should be high national priorities.

The restoration side of the priority was recognized by federal law when Congress was practically shoved into action two and a half years after the Love Canal tragedy of 1978. In December, 1980, the Comprehensive Environmental Response, Compensation and Liability Act was passed, establishing the so-called Superfund. The $1.6 billion fund was to be built up from taxes on oil and specified chemicals, from fines paid by certain polluters and from an appropriation of $44 million a year from 1981 to 1985. The Superfund was established to clean up "releases into the environment" when responsibility for them could not be established or when responsible parties were unwilling to clean up their contamination.

But as we have learned repeatedly, a law is no better than its administration. The EPA's administration of the Superfund was more characteristic of the act's long, laborious title than the fund's short, snappy name. After the agency's regional offices canvassed the nation to locate the worst sites for early action, their findings were assessed by a mathematical model to assign a "hazard-ranking score," which would help narrow the lists down to the most serious cases. The process of actually getting at the problems continued with the development of guidelines in volumes of "requisite promulgations" burdened with ifs, ands and buts concerning the involvement of states, responsible parties and so on and on, until the fund looked a lot less super than originally intended. Two years after the passage of the Superfund legislation, 115 priority sites had been selected; about half were under further study to determine what specifically to do, while action was being taken on only 3. The EPA's laxness led to congressional hearings that caused a supercrisis, for both the agency and President Ronald Reagan. The result was dismissal of the Superfund's administrator, followed by resignations of the top EPA administrator, Anne (Gorsuch) Burford, and several other high agency officials. The new administrator, William Ruckelshaus, finally seemed to recognize the kind of action intended by the Superfund legislation.

"What action?" a lay person might understandably ask, having learned from media reports that groundwater tainted is virtually groundwater doomed. But, as we have said, restoring potability is not always the impossibility or centuries-long act of God frequently indicated. Hopelessness is certainly not the mood of the Annual Symposium on Aquifer Restoration and Ground Water Monitoring started in 1981 under the auspices of the National Center for Ground Water Research, the National Water Well Association and the EPA. The symposium, which has attracted the largest groups of groundwater scientists ever assembled, has revealed various ways of restoring polluted aquifers, although the methods are not cheap, easy or always certain of success.

The remedies are likely to follow either of two courses. Action may be taken simply to confine the contamination to the smallest possible area of an aquifer and contain it there indefinitely. Or the polluted groundwater may be removed from the earth and, in a sense, laundered, allowing natural replenishment of the aquifer with freshwater or arranging the return of the original supply minus contaminants.

One way of confining the subsurface pollution is actually to imprison it in underground walls. To do so the shape and depth of the pollution are mapped, and an impermeable barrier is dropped down around it. One such barrier, which is installed in a deep, narrow trench, is called a slurry cutoff wall. As the trench is dug, the diggings are replaced with a slurry that includes bentonite (a clay of decomposed volcanic ash that absorbs water and swells greatly in the process). The trench, which the slurry keeps from collapsing, is cut down through the aquiferous material to the impermeable stratum that forms the aquifer's bottom. When the trenching is completed, the slurry forms a highly impermeable wall of "bentonite filter cake," capturing the contaminated groundwater within its perimeter. Such barriers, which have been extended down as much as 100 feet by using special excavating equipment, have been effective at imprisoning large areas of contamination.

Another technique involves the high-pressure pumping of cement mixtures down through carefully located holes into the pores of the aquiferous material, so as to fill vertical sections in the earth. When solidified, the injection forms an impermeable "grout curtain" enclosing the contamination. Of course, the installers of such curtains cannot see what they are doing, so ascertaining the completeness of the barrier is difficult. But a grout curtain can be installed relatively fast, and when successful, it can more or less stop the migration of contaminated water.

A third method, which has been used for a long time to prevent the underground movement of water, involves driving great, interlocking sheets of steel into the earth. The sheet piling, as it is called, forms a steel wall. But forcing it down through various geologic formations, while keeping the piling intact, is difficult—for the interlocked joints may come apart, and even if they do not, the seams may leak.

The horrendous expense of these subsurface retaining walls was illustrated in 1982 by what the EPA called the most expensive chemical cleanup in the agency's history. The supertab, $38.5 million all told, was reluctantly picked up by the Velsicol Chemical Company of Chicago. Its costly problem came with a notorious St. Louis, Michigan, plant that Velsicol had purchased from another chemical company. In the 1970s polybrominated biphenyls (PBBs) from the plant were responsible for the deaths of large numbers of cattle after the cancer-causing chemical had been accidentally mixed with animal feed. Velsicol was then sued by people who claimed the substance had damaged their health by way of the food chain. The PBBs and other hazardous chemicals were also implicated in the contamination of groundwater by the Gratiot County landfill, where company wastes had been dumped by the tons. The Michigan plant became Velsicol's bête noire, and the company began disposing of it. After the problematical plant was torn down, the 52-acre site was encircled by a relatively shallow slurry cutoff wall and then covered with an impermeable clay cap. The encapsulation was designed to prevent the property's residual contamination from migrating to a nearby river. At the Gratiot landfill, the state of Michigan began installing another slurry wall, this one 50 to 60 feet deep, enclosing some 40 acres. It was designed to prevent movement of the poison plume formed by seepage from the landfill. Once confined by the underground wall, contaminated water would be pumped out, piped some 5 miles and dumped down a 7,000-foot disposal well owned by Velsicol. The cost of all this was $13.5 million, to be paid by the company through the state, which in turn agreed to drop a $120 million lawsuit against the firm.

A different approach for preventing the spread of contamination in groundwater is called hydrodynamic control. To begin with, gravity keeps groundwater moving very slowly through an aquifer. As is true of water moving above ground, the surface of flowing subterranean water slopes in the direction of its movement—always toward some area of discharge, such as a river. Compared to surface water, the movement of groundwater is very slow, ordinarily a few inches a day. By pumping a "purge well" drilled into an aquifer, the slope of the water can be changed, causing it to tilt inward toward the sucking force of the pump and creating what is called a cone of depression. By pumping strategically located wells, the groundwater slope can be changed, altering its natural course and causing it to flow toward the wells. Using this principle, engineers can control the migration of a poison plume. By continuous pumping, the contamination can be virtually suspended in one place and slowly withdrawn for purification. If the groundwater is not far below the surface, the polluted plume can be intercepted by a trench dug perpendicular to its movement. As the water enters the trench, it can be pumped out and cleaned up. These processes may have to continue for several months or even years, depending on the extent of contamination and how fast the plume moves toward the wells or trench. While both methods may effectively remove the contamination, they can, of course, go on running up bills for a long time.

No matter how the problem is sliced, all the methods using subterranean walls or hydrodynamic controls are extremely expensive—definitely candidates for superfunds, whether public or private. And the costs can continue for a long time. As long as the contamination remains in the ground it is a potential threat, so continuing effectiveness requires perpetual monitoring and remedial action should the pollutants escape or bypass the control measures.

The more effective solution involves cleaning an aquifer of its pollutants, assuming they can be located, pumped to the surface and, in disposal, not simply moved to another source of water. At this point the same troublesome questions faced by water purification generally are encountered: what happens to the substances separated from the water? Are they simply to be dumped in other water sources, like a river, hoping they will vanish? One of the treatment methods frequently proposed is to absorb the organic pollutants with granular activated carbon, polymers or resins. The contaminated materials then must be gotten rid of, and their disposal may only move the problem from one place to another.

There are still better solutions to the groundwater treatment problem with more satisfactory conclusions. In some instances the organic pollutants can be volatilized and thus converted to harmless vapors. This may be done in simple aerated lagoons, which were described earlier. With more complex organic chemicals, the highly adaptive forces of land treatment can offer solutions. Contaminants may be removed by the living filter and held harmlessly in the soil, or decomposed by microorganisms that nature mobilizes for the specific problem at hand. The Muskegon land treatment system was successfully used for cleaning an aquifer of organic chemicals. Not long after the project was started up, it was given the job of purifying groundwater that had been contaminated by unsealed lagoons belonging to a Muskegon chemical company. Purge wells drilled into the aquifer were used to pump up the polluted groundwater, and it was sent to the large land treatment site. There the organic contaminants were removed by the living filter.

As is true for municipal wastewater management, the capabilities of land treatment for cleaning contaminated groundwater have yet to be fully explored and developed. Too often the potentials of soil filtration are dismissed out of hand by public officials and engineers who do not understand that the living filter must not be overloaded, any more than any other filter. Of course, overloading the soil in seepage pits, landfills and other forms of waste disposal leads to groundwater pollution—so it is easy for an uninformed person (or an opponent of land treatment) to say the soil was tried, and it failed. But persons knowledgeable about land treatment design realize that soil properly used can often work wonders in purifying contaminated water while safely taking care of the pollutants.

Whatever the solutions to the troubles besetting our subterranean water, none are better than prevention—and as Jay Lehr emphasizes, we have immense supplies to protect. Under normal circumstances, nature, relying on the fabulous capabilities of soil, is well prepared to protect the earth's aquifers, but humans interfere. In its 1981 report *Contamination of Ground Water by Toxic Organic Chemicals,* the federal Council on Environmental Quality stated, "Human activities in recharge areas—the siting of homes, roads, industry, and waste disposal facilities—significantly affect the quality of water recharging an aquifer. Policies and programs designed to protect ground-water quality, regardless of whether the efforts are public or private, national, state or local, will have to recognize the importance of activities in recharge areas."

But the recognition, in itself, is a momentous undertaking. It requires scanning the vast, complex hull of modern civilization, looking for a trillion leaks of chemical brews that people might ingest with drinking water to ruin the liver, damage the central nervous system, scramble the genes and decontrol the growth of cells. The insidious drippings seem to have broken out everywhere. Automobile service stations are prominent on the lists of infamous contributors to the devastation of groundwater. Industries produce enough liquid wastes annually to provide each American adult and child with 45,000 gallons. Much of it is disposed of in lagoons, ponds and pits whose loose bottoms dribble the stuff to the groundwater. The contaminators include well-meaning, public-minded citizens donating their time for the community good, as well as outright criminals whose crooked profits come from poisoning the community. Planning and zoning agencies often run by citizen volunteers frequently respond to growth pressures by permitting homes to be crowded above aquifers, on land ill suited for filtering out such contaminants as septic system effluent, lawn herbicides and fertilizers, drippings of automobile fuel, oil, antifreeze and cleaners—all to the detriment of the underlying water supply. Meanwhile a growing band of unscrupulous "midnight dumpers" service some producers of toxic waste by hauling it off for a fee and surreptitiously dumping it before dawn in pits, rivers, ponds, wells, storm sewers—somewhere tonight, somewhere else tomorrow night—the public waters be damned.

The size and complexity of the prevention job may be enough to deter tackling it, but the legal means are at hand for doing so. Both national and state laws to deal with the problem have been passed—they need only be enforced. Also, as we have indicated, techniques for keeping our wastes away from groundwater are available.

The key federal laws were passed in 1976, the Resource Conservation and Recovery Act and the Toxic Substance Control Act. The two measures were supposed to provide "cradle to grave" control of all hazardous substances. The births, active lives and final resting places of poisons were to be regulated to prevent undesirable migrations, especially into the country's drinking water. The laws, like the Federal Water Pollution Control Act Amendments of 1972, contain deadlines for action that have not been honored. Six years after passage of the control measures—which made it a felony to dump toxic wastes illegally —the EPA finally announced the formation of an investigative team to find the culprits. But what a team! It had only 25 members to cover the entire nation, a tiny force compared to the FBI's 7,600 agents.

The Resource Conservation and Recovery Act authorizes grants and technical assistance to enable states and local governments to deal with the country's immense waste problems, but again, six years after the law's passage, the funds and assistance amounted to feeble contributions. Supposedly the money and technical help were aimed at finding new directions for safe and sound waste management, but the traditional direction remains in place. As with sewage pollutants, the management of hazardous wastes is captive to our national penchant for disposal. The deleterious substances found in groundwater are frequently there because they were viewed as wastes to be rid of, when they could have become raw materials and been returned to productive use. Reuse, the vision of the 1976 law, has yet to become a reality. Instead of looking for places to throw away hazardous wastes, we should be concentrating on finding profitable reuses. This philosophy guides the planners of Chicago's biomass utility, discussed earlier, and a few other areas in the country—St. Louis is one—have developed "waste exchanges" to find out how one industry's poison can become another's raw material. But such innovations are too few and have yet to be drawn into the mainstream of the problem-solving effort. Meanwhile hazardous wastes that could be reclaimed and reused remain at large and available for the contamination of good water.

The idea of reclamation and reuse may seem facetious when one thinks of the typical landfill, the cluttered, sludge-laden site where rats thrive and sea gulls fly in from a distant seacoast to scavenge amid the trash. Our dumps are built on national habits that are the antithesis of our forefathers' admonition: waste not, want not. What's more, the behavior patterns that support the nation's proliferating dumps are firmly in place. Many Americans practically consider it a human right that their trash be collected (but not deposited within sight or smell). Every day the country disposes of enough waste to pack the Louisiana Superdome in New Orleans twice from top to bottom. In a year the collection heaps up into 150 million tons of cultch, from old mildewed jogging trunks to spoiled yogurt, joining such ingredients as the diseased residue from hospitals and medical laboratories. The combination, whether mushy or brittle, is called solid waste. Ten to 15 percent of the mix is said by the EPA to be hazardous to human health. Around 1970 the great hope for this mass of discards was to convert it to energy in "resource recovery plants" that would burn garbage to make steam for electric generation, but their great expense spoiled the economics, and the budding industry was, according to *Forbes* magazine, "plagued by technical problems, poor management and cost overruns." By 1981 only 27 plants were operating, 10 others had been built and closed, and the industry was processing but a "tiny fraction" of the nation's solid waste. The major receptacle for America's garbage remains the landfill. There the mess mixes with rainwater and snowmelt to form a potent liquor, called leachate because the concoction invariably leaches into the ground and on down to the water table. No one can say exactly what toxic solutions are seeping from the country's 200,000 operating landfills and "unauthorized" dumps, plus the countless abandoned sites still percolating yesterday's trash. Where could the patching possibly begin on such a mess?

Once an existing landfill starts leaking, the chances of sealing it are nil—unless someone has a Bunyanesque scheme for picking up the monstrous collection and putting it down on an impermeable bottom, known as a liner. Short of that improbability, corrective action seems limited to capping a dump so it sheds natural precipitation and reduces the formation of leachate. A badly leaking landfill in Windham, Connecticut, was capped when a plume of contaminated groundwater threatened the nearby Willimantic water supply reservoir. A few years later the state Department of Environmental Protection found that the plume was diminishing. But anyone who has tried to dry up a leaky basement will agree that keeping an entire landfill dry has to be a terribly frustrating endeavor unlikely to succeed. The most effective, but not very happy, solution to the leaky dump is to stop dumping and deal with the polluted water the best way possible.

While coping with the sins of our past solid-waste practices, it is important to make sure they do not continue and become sins of the future. The media's horror stories about poisoning our "hidden waters" has concentrated the minds of regulating bureaucrats on how such disasters can be prevented when new landfills are permitted. The most prevalent regulatory concern is that the bottoms of new dumps have liners.

Landfill liners are made of various substances, such as compacted clay, asphalt, bentonite mixes or synthetic membranes of plastic or rubber materials. Whatever the liner, the aim is to insulate the underlying groundwater from the dripping trash piled above. Of course, the process cannot stop with the lining, for the liquid, once collected, has to be removed and treated somehow. But when it comes to treatment, the problem solvers bump against all the old choices: dilution in a river; consignment to no-one-knows-where in the bowels of the earth via a deep disposal well; purification at the municipal sewage treatment works, in an aerated lagoon or by a land treatment system—or there may be other creative innovations. One idea involves spraying the leachate into the air so it falls back onto the trash, seeps down to the liner again, then repeats the aerial circuit—all in the hope that multiple round trips will result in some evaporative loss and the residuals will stabilize to the point where the leachate is no longer dangerous.

Even if the operator of a lined landfill finds a way of dealing with leachate, he still suffers the lingering worry that the liner may be leaking, because it usually is. At best, liners are only leak resistant. Clay, for example, is not totally waterproof after it has been excavated and repacked as a liner. Even synthetic liners, which consist of large sheets joined together, are vulnerable at the seams. And, of course, all liners are subjected to harsh chemicals that can break them down so they spring leaks.

While some states, like Pennsylvania, are depending heavily on liners in new landfills, others are not. Connecticut, for example, avoids them, feeling they cannot be relied upon. Instead, the state policy is to accept leakage into groundwater, but only where it is flowing directly toward and discharging to a vigorous "class B stream" (one already polluted so that the water has to be purified if used for drinking). In other words, a groundwater plume becomes, in effect, a dump's sewer line to a river. Of course, the policy relies on the disposal-by-dilution theory, which has been the rule for sewage discharges and the devastation of America's waterways. But under this policy only 0.3 percent of

Connecticut's land can qualify as sites for new landfills—and then only if all other siting problems are solvable.

Freeing our subterranean waters of leachates from landfills needs a more comprehensive solution to the problem than any ordinarily pursued. The Mount Trashmore concept, with design improvements developed since the original mountain was built, provides such comprehensiveness by doing something about every avenue that poisons may take from our solid waste to public supplies of groundwater. Here is how the most recent design for a mountain of trash works:

First, the site is carefully chosen so the mountain will go up over an area where test wells show the groundwater is flowing at a very slow rate toward a discharge point, usually a stream. This is done recognizing that, despite all efforts to prevent it, a landfill liner will leak and the leakage, even though a minor amount, needs to be managed. Thus the flow away from the mountain can be continually monitored, and if contaminants are detected, there will be time, because of the slow flow, to intercept them, pump them to the surface and treat them.

On this carefully selected site, the mountain building begins with a leak-resistant liner of the best available material, such as compacted clay. While the finished mountain will shed most of the precipitation falling upon it, some is certain to find its way inside and become the basis for hazardous leachate. The liner, designed to catch the leachate, is equal in area to the mountain's bottom and is put down on a slight tilt sloping toward a sump (a concrete pit) at the side. Once in place the liner is covered with a grid of perforated pipes, arranged so they will collect the leachate and drain it off to the sump. From there it can be piped away for treatment.

The mountain itself—as was true of Mount Trashmore—is assembled from thousands of soil-encased cells, each holding approximately one day's delivery of trash. This constant encapsulation during construction protects the waste from the elements so it will not be soaked in stormwater, keeps it free of rats and other scavengers, and holds down odors. When complete, the mountain in cross section is a honeycomb of solid waste cells.

As they pile up, the layers of cells are interlarded with more perforated pipes arranged in horizontal galleries, also with a slight tilt. The galleries, one above the other, are all connected together so as to form a whole network of pipes leading up to the mountaintop. The system is installed to collect biogas that is generated by anaerobic bacteria acting upon the trash. The flow starts soon after the mountain is enclosed and continues for several years. The gas, which is lighter than air, flows up through the galleries of pipes to the mountain's summit, from which it is removed and put to work—all of which makes the sophisticated heap of trash an energy producer. The biogas may be sold to a utility, thus providing funds to help pay for the project. Or it may be used on the site itself, for making electricity to supply the system's pumps, treatment aerators and other equipment, and/or to heat and light buildings used for recreational activities. (A gas collection system, though recommended, was not included in Mount Trashmore because of budgetary restraints; but after completion, the mountain had to be tapped to release rising gas pressure. The outflow is "flared off," burned and wasted. Du Page County's two trash mountains under construction contain biogas collection systems.)

The new, improved design described here provides for a treatment system to go with the mountain. Leachate fed to the sump from the liner and any intercepted after it unavoidably leaked through the liner are pumped to an aerated lagoon that can remove volatile components from the leachate, releasing them harmlessly to the atmosphere. Effluent from the lagoon goes to a relatively small land treatment system, where organic substances can be widely distributed and confined in the soil, or metabolized—in either case rendering them harmless. The irrigated land in this system may be kept as open space or even used to produce cash crops, like Christmas trees or nursery stock, again generating funds to help pay for the project.

Sculptured landscapes of the improved Mount Trashmore variety could safely, even beneficially, handle America's solid waste on a modest amount of land for a long time to come. In fact, less than 500 square miles, or .017 percent of the conterminous United States, would be required to locate molded mountains of trash (up to 130 feet high) generated by the nation for the next 50 years. The waste will end up somewhere, probably on that much or more land, so its last resting place might as well be properly prepared. In a molded mountain, the reactions that will take place within the waste, such as anaerobic digestion, will not cause pollution. Over time the waste fill will become stabilized, or dormant, and the formation will become just part of the landscape, its threat to the groundwater gone. Such landfills could take forms other than conical mountains and have purposes other than recreation. They might, for example, become visual and sound barriers if built as long, high berms parallel to and enclosing superhighways or railways.

By moving our trash from a disposal mode to a service mode free of poison plumes, we can reduce the crisis of our underground water.

XVII
Renewing and Resolving the Debate

Page 1 of the Federal Water Pollution Control Act Amendments of 1972 listed two national goals. As we have discussed, they were to be attained in the first half of the 1980s. One, which was to be reached by July 1, 1983—called the "fishable-swimmable" goal—was that "wherever attainable" we should enjoy "water quality which provides for the protection and propagation of fish, shellfish and wildlife and provides for recreation in and on the water. . . ." The other goal, the one that aspired to zero discharge, was contained in a simple declaration that the discharge of pollutants "be eliminated by 1985." The fishable-swimmable and zero-discharge goals remained intact after two amendments of the 1972 amendments (in 1977 and 1981); however, the chance of either goal ever being attained was probably less than when they were originally adopted by Congress. EPA officials explained away the delinquency by saying that these were only goals, not requirements of the law. However, the initial requirement of the 1972 legislation had not been carried out by 1983—the demand that by July 1, 1977, the quality of wastewater discharges be no less than effluent from a secondary treatment plant. Indeed, amendments to the original law had moved the requirement date forward to 1988. The secondary-treatment stipulation, as stated earlier, flouted the original intent of the law to move in a new direction. Shoving the unmet requirement 11 years into the future confirmed for the umpteenth time that clean water will not be restored to the nation by following the old direction.

This lesson that seems never to be learned was again taught at the dearest cost ever. In the ten years following passage of the 1972 legislation, the United States government spent $34 billion on construction grants authorized by the law. With state and local matching funds, the total came to some $50 billion. But the expenditure was only a starter if the country was to stay on the same course. Estimates reported by *The New York Times* in late 1982 indicated that "another $90 billion in subsidies would be needed by the year 2000 to meet all sewage treatment requirements. . . ."

With $50 billion already spent as we entered the year of the fishable-swimmable goal, it was obvious the taxpayer's money had not been well used. The Conservation Foundation, a Washington-based organization that worked for passage and implementation of the 1972 legislation, stated in 1982 that "there has been little change in water quality over the past seven years—at least in respect to conventional pollutants." The best that could be said for the costly program was that some water in some places had become clean enough for the return of certain fish and a few people unfussy enough to swim in a mixture of water and partially purified sewage effluent. The Delaware River was cited as evidence of how our expended billions were buying cleaner (but not clean) water. The river, whose stench in 1940 tarnished the brasswork on ships entering Philadelphia and offended the nostrils of airplane passengers in open cockpits a mile up, was less obnoxious by 1983, but certainly a long way from purity. In 1982, *Context,* the magazine of the Du Pont company, reported:

"Today, this money and effort [for sewage treatment] have resulted in a river that is, indeed, significantly cleaner. One can stand these days on the waterfront in Philadelphia, at Penn's Landing, and not be offended by what the nose can smell and the eye can see.

"Bacteria counts have been reduced. The load of oxygen-depleting pollutants discharged in the estuary daily is down to 399,000 pounds from a million pounds 20 years ago. The summertime low-oxygen 'pollution block' at Philadelphia no longer lasts as long nor extends as far up and down the river."

These may be laudable results given what can be expected from conventional wastewater treatment, but they are far short of providing clean water. The upgrading, according to the Du Pont report, was the fruit of about $1.5 billion in public and private funds expended on the Delaware, and, as the report was published, Philadelphia alone was spending $874 million for three new treatment plants that would still discharge only partially purified wastewater to the river.

The change in the Delaware, now cleaner but far from clean, less offensive to the senses but still an extension of municipal sewerage systems, is typical of what many public officials point to as progress from the billions spent on linear systems using technology that remains fundamentally unchanged after three quarters of a century. Such short-measure purification continues to rely on the disposal-by-dilution theory, and it is clung to at a startling cost, wasting potential resources while never really producing clean water. Meanwhile the new direction that the national lawmakers of 1972 hoped to promote with the billions that would be spent was represented by a scant few innovative projects (several of which we have discussed), and they had come into being in spite of the well-financed opposition of the linear-system proponents. More often than not, such projects were swiftly eliminated before they ever came close to the public bar for a fair appraisal. When one did make it to a public presentation, it often died in the birthing when the intense opposition of "water pollution control experts" smothered the "greenies" and their new ideas.

A series of events at Fort Worth, Texas, in the late 1970s and early 1980s provides an example of what happened when citizens raised the possibility of following the new direction encouraged by the federal clean water law. For three decades Fort Worth had followed the conventional route for treating its rapidly increasing flow of wastewater. In the 1950s the city built the Village Creek Wastewater Treatment Plant, originally designed to partially purify 5 million gallons of sewage per day. In the 1960s the plant was expanded twice, increasing its capacity to 45 million gallons daily, and in another ten years that capacity doubled. Future plans called for still more growth of the system until it would handle 135 million gallons of sewage per day.

By 1979 the Village Creek plant had become a vast complex of traditional primary and secondary treatment technology, occupying 150 acres. Its millions of gallons of less than clean effluent were discharged to the Trinity River, which flows through the Fort Worth area and continues through the Dallas area. Each day the sprawling plant also produced 800,000 gallons of sludge, which was held in lagoons covering another 325 acres of land. The growing complex of treatment technology and sludge lagoons was on Fort Worth's eastern edge, removed from the center of town; however, it was immediately on the border of Arlington, Texas. What was more, it was literally and figuratively under Arlington's nose, for the treatment works sat at the base of a bluff upon which hundreds of Arlington homes had been built.

As was the case nearly everywhere, the Village Creek system faltered when it came to the crucial business of O & M (operations and maintenance). The O & M problems meant that the percentage of pollutants discharged to the Trinity was continually higher than the plant design would have led one to believe. Worst of all, the faltering system with its outpouring of sludge created a terribly foul odor that ascended the bluff and plagued the innocent homesteaders. By 1979 the antagonistic aroma had irritated Arlingtonians enough that they formed a citizens group, People United to Save Our Homes (PUSH). PUSH's plan was to shove Fort Worth into doing something about the odor.

After sponsoring a preliminary study that confirmed the Village Creek Plant was truly to blame for the malodorous assault on their homes, the group assumed the leadership in finding an alternative for the treatment works. This soon led to the idea of land treatment, which had been perfunctorily considered and rejected by Fort Worth in the early 1970s. At the behest of PUSH, the city of Arlington commissioned a comprehensive feasibility study of what it would mean to substitute land treatment for the Village Creek plant. The study, completed in 1981, revealed that farmers on several ranches around the area would be willing to accept and were capable of using Fort Worth's wastewater, under a scientifically designed program to irrigate and fertilize crops while fully cleaning the water for reuse. It would follow the half-century lead of Lubbock, but on a much larger scale and under a more rigorously designed and controlled program. The investigation showed how both Fort Worth and the farmers would benefit if the city recognized its wastewater as a resource to be capitalized upon, rather than a pollutant to be dumped through a problematical disposal system that was a continual drain on tax-based funds, a troublemaker provoking a neighboring city and a permanent devastator of the Trinity's water quality. The Arlington report showed how the land treatment alternative could provide a full, advanced wastewater treatment system costing only 19 cents per 1,000 gallons treated, compared to 57 cents for the conventional Village Creek plant offering only secondary effluent, plus an unholy load of sludge. While eliminating the odors, the study claimed, land treatment could also increase the agricultural productivity of 18,160 acres of farmland near the Fort Worth metropolitan area. Most remarkable, the land system would return 100 million gallons of good water a day to the municipal supply, a bonus that would eliminate the necessity for a costly water-supply project that was being planned and would produce only 61 million gallons a day. Finally, the returned water would improve the quality and increase the flow of the Trinity, thus enhancing recreational opportunities on the river.

The Arlington proposal was rejected. It might have been a financial bonanza for city and farms, environmentally sound for the area's water and air, a wise use of resources with virtually a new source of water supply thrown in, a major saving of taxpayers' dollars, a blow to inflationary spending and budget deficits—still the Fort Worth decision makers were opposed, encouraged by their consulting engineers. When faced with such choices, a city father invariably goes down the traditional avenue of the experts on whom he has bet a king's ransom in fees, and he rejects, out of hand, the route prescribed by the outsider. Fort Worth's experts represented one of the country's largest sanitary-engineering firms, whose stock in trade was the kind of system exemplified by the Village Creek Wastewater Treatment Plant. There, indeed, stood one of America's many technological monuments funded by taxpayers for the sake of water pollution control. Arlington's intrusive land-treatment alternative challenged this and other such monuments, threatening to expose them as false idols fed on billions of dollars in the name of clean water, while the paying public was being warned that decreasing supplies of good water were symptomatic of what could become the nation's most serious resource crisis. As in other cases that we have discussed, the conventional advice followed by Fort Worth had come from an interpretation of the nation's clean water goal as one for expanding on the status quo. The point was illustrated at the workshop on land treatment at Dallas mentioned earlier. Actually it had been prompted by the Arlington proposal, and it was one of Fort Worth's consultants who inadvertently betrayed his concern, not for the merits of his traditional ideas, but for his profession and the possibility of its being proven wrong.

The Trinity at Fort Worth, the Delaware at Philadelphia and all of our other bountiful sources of water will, at best, remain in a purgatory of pollution, perhaps improving, but never making it to potability as long as we preserve orthodoxy with construction grants that perpetuate the use of our lakes and streams as end components in the water carriage system for sewage. In the horrendously expensive, century-long trial of this linear configuration for water and waste, marked by glossed-over requirements, unattained goals and a progressively more serious water crisis, the verdict is failure, and the matter should be labeled *res adjudicata*—finally settled and no longer worthy of argument. As long and as costly as the lesson may have been, we have to turn to a new direction, to a circular configuration, as intended by the Ninety-second Congress when it passed the Federal Water Pollution Control Act Amendments of 1972. If we do not make the move, it will eventually be forced upon us by the intensifying water crisis—but perhaps not until it is too late.

To summarize, five barriers block the change that could free the nation's water from its long and deepening state of crisis:

- the circular concept for reclaiming and reusing our immense wastewater flows has been declared anathema by the powerful barons of water and sewage, who self-servingly but effectively oppose the fundamental technological change it would require;
- a history of safe, inexpensive water, coupled with an out-

of-sight-out-of-mind attitude toward our own waste, lulls citizens, community leaders, the news media and public and business decision makers into complacency about what is causing the water crisis, so they fail to learn the real reasons for it and that there are alternative solutions to the problem;

- deleterious relationships between urban and rural water interests, ranging from mutual disregard to outright conflict, persist although cooperative action could benefit both parties in ways unavailable through their unilateral efforts;
- potential investors, public and private, disregard circular systems because of the false assumption that they are too unorthodox and extraordinarily risky, when in truth they are less exotic (relying on common agricultural practices) and far more predictable, dependable and effective than the conventional technology that attempts but fails to clean up our water;
- the public views waste negatively; wastes are abhorred. This misconception is kept alive by the widespread contamination and aesthetic insults associated with commonly practiced disposal operations of today.

While some advocates thought otherwise for a long time, few still believe that these barriers can be legislated away. The history of the clean water law from 1972 to the present has proven that a new direction is unlikely to emerge simply because the Congress of the United States commands that we take one. The lawmakers and those of us who cheered their efforts failed to understand, not the solution, but the problem itself. It was thought to be legal in nature, but a decade of failure has shown otherwise. In that period some of us realized the problem was really one of attitude, solidified and held firmly in place by a very common motive, the profit motive. The surest profits in wastewater purification were available from selling technology that had been familiar for most of the century. Veering off into unfamiliar concepts was a risky venture, never mind that the construction grants program urged such a course and, indeed, held out a carrot, a federal bonus for those who tried. The bonus turned out to be a peanut tossed to a pachyderm. The truly big profits came from acquiring federal grants made under the clean water law, using them for the old, linear technology and labeling the legislation's 1985 zero-discharge goal unrealistic.

But near the end of this decade of disappointment in the power of the law, an obvious answer to the circular-system proponent's dilemma emerged in a significant way. The confirmation came, not from a lawmaker, engineer, environmentalist, or anyone else one might associate with the problem, but from an internationally famous banker in New York City. After listening to an explanation of how the farm-city loop can produce food and energy from wastes while making them unavailable to pollute water, the financier said, "There's a bankable business there." Investigations had already indicated he was right. A 1980 estimate had revealed that if the waste fouling our national waters were used instead as raw materials to produce food, fiber and energy, the net value of the annual production would amount to over $18 billion, or more than a third of the annual domestic sales of the nation's automobile industry. The effort would also eliminate the need for conventional sewage treatment and thus save a nonproductive expenditure of $4 billion a year paid out of the public coffers. Finally, the venture could take us to that elusive goal of clean water and a solution to the water crisis.

The point is that we now have—as the previous chapters of this book have shown—the knowledge, experience and working models to demonstrate how both the nation's waters and the wastes they carry to everyone's detriment can be reclaimed and reused in profitable private enterprises. In other words, the profit motive can work in favor of a new direction for water and waste management, instead of against it. The enterprises can become the basis of a new era of cooperation between urban and rural interests. They can be built around the basic component that we have outlined as the farm-city loop, designed to capitalize on the wastes of wastewater and to return salable products and clean water. Such loops, as we have explained, can be small or large and adapted to the needs of their areas. While privately operated, they would of course be publicly regulated, as are other public utilities. Besides their return on private investments, they would have numerous public benefits, like improved regional economies, new sources of wealth that could be applied to mend our deteriorating infrastructure, new jobs, more recreational opportunities, pollution abatement and added energy self-sufficiency.

If it were not for what recent experience has taught us, we might say that more legislation is needed, this time to stimulate the private, profit-oriented approach to solving our water problems—and perhaps there are possibilities for such laws, but actually the necessary measures are practically all on the books for anyone who cares to use them. For example, there are numerous tax benefits available, like investment and energy credits, for such enterprises. But the most important need for establishing the new direction will not, as existing law proves, be enacted by Congress. It is hardly possible to legislate perspicacity—and that is what is required from many people, so they can discern the real cause of our impending water crisis and how we should cope with it.

Instead of more legislation, we have to work and hope for a new coalition of leaders who recognize the nation's clear need for the circular solution to its water problems—in other words, for a new establishment to counterbalance the traditional one that continues destroying our water by misusing it as the carriage for waste. The coalition needs to renew and resolve the turn-of-the-century debate between the linear- and circular-system proponents. The contest is no longer stacked against its early losers, for in recent years the linear position has been weakened and the circular strengthened. The traditional methods, relying on disposal by dilution, have not only failed, but in the process they have become a heavy economic burden that government can no longer carry in these times of tightened budgets and horrendous deficits. Meanwhile, the development of modern circular methods has proven they not only can succeed in restoring clean water, but can do so with a healthy return on private investments and with diminishing burdens on public treasuries.

As these disparate positions become known, the circular coalition will have the potential for attracting a broad base of supporters with a wide variety of complementary motivations, from the desire to make profitable returns on private investments to the public need to enjoy safe, dependable water supplies. The coalition can find strength in the renewal of old alliances and the discovery that old opponents can become bedfellows. By taking up the circular cause, the environmentalist can promote a truly effective alternative for water pollution control, knowing that it can also be good for business. In the same cause the businessman can find relief from the costly regulatory burdens that he suffers under traditional linear procedures for pollution control, and indeed he may find he can even add to his profits by participating in circular procedures. Farmers, consumer groups, political leaders, proponents of alternative energy and technology, journalists, bankers, agricultural equipment manufacturers and suppliers, educators and others can find reasons for becoming part of the circular coalition. While they may come with different motivations, their common purpose will be the building of an establishment to sponsor continued research on how the circular concept for water and waste can be adapted to a modern society and economy, to encourage projects that demonstrate how the concept works, to disseminate public information on the subject and to initiate educational programs necessary if we are to have future advocates and practitioners of this old but fundamental idea that harmonizes with nature to our mutual benefit.

In solving today's water problems by understanding that they arise from our misplacement of resources, the coalition will be acting on the wisdom expressed in Athens more than 2,000 years ago by the philosopher Zeno: "One of life's important challenges is to live in harmony with Nature."

References

PAPERS AND PUBLICATIONS

Chapter I

Adler, Jerry, William J. Cook, Stryker McGuire, Gerald C. Lubenow, Martin Kasindorf, Frank Maier and Holly Morriss. "Special Report: The Browning of America." *Newsweek* (February 23, 1981), pp. 26–37.

Banks, James T., Francis Dubrowski, John H. Chafee, Thomas C. Jorling and Thomas Whyatt. "Special Report—Clean Water: Act III." *The Amicus Journal,* 3:25–40 (Spring, 1982).

Boffey, Philip M. "Efforts to Gain 'Fishable-Swimmable' Waters Appear to Falter." *The New York Times,* October 12, 1982.

Canby, Thomas Y. "Our Most Precious Resource, Water." *National Geographic* (August, 1980), pp. 144–79.

Carr, D. E. *Death of the Sweet Waters.* New York: W. W. Norton, 1966.

Comptroller general of the United States. "Costly Wastewater Treatment Plants Fail to Perform As Expected." Washington, D.C.: U.S. General Accounting Office, 1980.

Hunt, C. A., and R. M. Garrels. *Water: The Web of Life.* New York: W. W. Norton, 1972.

Luoma, Jon R. "The $33 Billion Misunderstanding." *Audubon,* 83:6 (November, 1981).

Office of Inspector General. "EPA's Construction Grants Program: Increased Oversight or Increased Waste." OIG Report No. E1-W9-11-0018-10789. Washington, D.C.: U.S. Environmental Protection Agency, 1981.

Opie, John, Carol Polsgrove and John Buell. "Draining America Dry: What Will We Do When the Water Runs Out?" *The Progressive,* 45:20–23 (July, 1981).

Powledge, Fred. "The Next 'Energy Crisis': Water, Water Running Out." *The Nation,* 234:703, 714–16 (1982).

Reinhold, Robert, A. O. Sulzberger, Jr., William E. Schmidt, William K. Stevens and Philip Shabecoff. "Water in America: Solving the Quandry." Series of five articles. *The New York Times,* August 9–13, 1981.

Sheridan, Daniel. "The Desert Blooms—at a Price." *Environment,* 23:7–20 (April, 1981).

U. S. Congress. House of Representatives. Appropriations Committee. Survey and Investigations Staff. "A Report to the Committee on Appropriations, U.S. House of Representatives, on the Environmental Protection Agency Construction Grants Program." Washington, D.C.: 1979.

Chapter II

American Public Health Association. "Report of the Committee on the Pollution of Water Supplies." Read at the association's Annual Meeting, Milwaukee, November 22–23, 1888.

Arps, Louisa Ward. *Denver in Slices.* Denver: Sage Books, 1959.

Bell, Thomas J. *History of the Water Supply of the World.* Cincinnati: 1882.

Bigelow, Poultney. "The Pest at Our Gates." Reprinted from *The New Broadway Magazine.* New York: Merchants Association of New York Committee on Pollution of State Waters, circa 1908.

Blake, Nelson M. *Water for Cities.* Syracuse, N.Y.: Syracuse University Press, 1956.

Channing, Walter. "A Plea for Pure Water." Letter to Henry Williams, Esq. Boston: S. N. Dickson, 1844.

Chicago & Alton Railroad Company. "A Guide to the Chicago Drainage Canal." Booklet published for tourists visiting the canal construction via the railroad. Chicago: 1895.

Clendening, Logan. "John Snow: Cholera." *Source Book of Medical History.* New York: Dover, 1942.

Cooley, Lyman. *The Diversion of the Great Lakes.* Chicago: Sanitary District of Chicago, 1913.

Denver Board of Water Commissioners. "Denver's Water History" in "Annual Report to Consumers." Denver: 1968.

Denver Water Department. "Cheesman Dam, Turn of the Century Wonder." Brochure. Denver: circa 1966.

Denver Water Department. "1980 Annual Report." Denver: 1980.

Denver Water Department. "Water Reuse Demonstration Project." Brochure. Denver: 1981.

Hazen, Allen. *Clean Water and How to Get It.* 2nd ed. New York: John Wiley, 1914.

Kahrl, William F., et al. *The California Water Atlas.* Sacramento, Calif.: Governor's Office of Planning and Research, 1979.

Metropolitan Sanitary District of Greater Chicago. "Development of Sewage Treatment in Chicago Area." Chronological fact sheet. Chicago: circa 1971.

National Academy of Sciences and National Academy of Engineering. "Historical Note." *Drinking Water and Health: Summary Report.* Washington, D.C.: National Academy of Sciences, 1977.

Propst, Neil Brown. "Most Ugly of Rivers, Most Useless of Trees." *Forgotten People: A History of the South Platte Trail.* Boulder, Colo.: Pruett, 1979.

Sanitary District of Chicago. Chief engineer. *A Concise Report on Its Organization, Resources, Constructive Work, Methods and Progress.* Chicago: John F. Higgins, 1895.

Sherman, Steve. "How About Pumping the Connecticut River to Boston?" *Yankee Magazine* (February, 1979), p. 103.

Storrow, Charles. *A Treatise on Water-Works for Conveying and Distributing Supplies of Water.* Boston: 1835.

Whipple, George C. *The Microscopy of Drinking Water.* New York: John Wiley, 1927.

REFERENCES

Chapter III

Corfield, W. H. *The Treatment and Utilization of Sewage.* London: Macmillan, 1887.

Donkin, J. *Conservancy or Dry Sanitation Versus Water Carriage.* New York: Spon and Chamberlain, 1906.

Hugo, Victor. "The Intestine of the Leviathan." *Les Misérables,* Book Second. New York: Modern Library, 1931.

Latham, Baldwin. "A Lecture on the Sewage Difficulty." London: E. & F. N. Spon, 1867.

Rafter, George W. "Sewage Irrigation." *Water Supply and Irrigation Paper No. 3.* Washington, D.C.: U.S. Geological Survey, 1897.

Rafter, George W. "Sewage Irrigation, Part II." *Water Supply and Irrigation Paper No. 22.* Washington, D.C.: U.S. Geological Survey, 1897.

Roechling, Herman Alfred. "The Sewage Farms of Berlin." *Minutes of the Proceedings of the Institution of Civil Engineering,* 109:179–268 (1892).

Chapter IV

Committee on Federation History. *History of the Water Pollution Control Federation, 1928–1977.* Washington, D.C.: Water Pollution Control Federation, 1977.

Metcalf, Leonard, and Harrison P. Eddy. *Sewerage and Sewage Disposal.* New York: McGraw-Hill, 1922.

Montgomery, Austin H. "Water Pollution Control: A History." *Water and Sewage Works,* Vol. 119, No. 2:60–65 (1972).

Sawyer, Clair N. "Milestones in the Development of the Activated Sludge Process." *Journal Water Pollution Control Federation,* 37:151–62 (1965).

Vaughan, H. B., Jr. "The Need." Paper read at the Symposium on Water Pollution Abatement in the Delaware Basin, Philadelphia, October 24, 1941.

Wolman, Abel. "What Became of Sanitary Engineering?" *Journal of the American Water Works Association.* 69:515–18 (1977).

Chapter V

Bureau of Water Hygiene. *Community Water Supply Study: Analysis of National Survey Findings.* Washington, D.C.: U.S. Public Health Service, 1970.

McDermott, James H. *Community Water Supply Study: Significance of National Findings.* Washington, D.C.: Bureau of Water Hygiene, U.S. Public Health Service, 1970.

Maugh, Thomas H., II. "New Study Links Chlorination and Cancer." *Science,* 211:694 (1981).

NOVA. The Water Crisis. Boston: WGBH Transcripts, 1980.

Page, Talbot, Robert H. Harris and Samuel S. Epstein. "Drinking Water and Cancer Mortality in Louisiana." *Science,* 193:55–7 (1976).

U.S. Congress. House of Representatives Committee on Interstate and Foreign Commerce. Subcommittee on Public Health and Environment. "Safe Drinking Water." Hearings, 92nd Congress, 1st Session, Serial No. 92-24, May 24–26, 1971. Washington, D.C.: U.S. Government Printing Office, 1971.

U.S. Congress. Senate. Committee on Environment and Public Works. "The Safe Drinking Water Act." Committee print, 96th Congress, 2nd Session, Serial No. 96-20. Washington, D.C.: U.S. Government Printing Office, 1980.

Chapter VI

American Water Works Association. *Trihalomethanes in Drinking Water.* Denver: American Water Works Association, 1980.

Byars, Carlos. "Land in Western Harris Sinking as Water Withdrawn from Wells." *Houston Chronicle,* July 5, 1981.

Connecticut, State of. *Plan of Conservation and Development for Connecticut: Policies for Land and Water Resources.* Hartford: Department of Finance and Control, 1974.

Council on Environmental Quality. *Contamination of Ground Water by Toxic Organic Chemicals.* Washington D.C.: U.S. Government Printing Office, 1981.

Council on Environmental Quality. *Desertification of the United States.* Washington, D.C.: U.S. Government Printing Office, 1981.

Johnson, Rich. *The Central Arizona Project, 1918–1968.* Tucson: University of Arizona Press, 1977.

Jones, Lonnie L., and John P. Warren. "Land Subsidence Costs in the Houston-Baytown Area of Texas." *Journal of the American Water Works Association,* 68:597–99 (1976).

Miller, Mary John, J. Chester Johnson and George E. Peterson. *The Future of Boston's Capital Plant.* Washington, D.C.: The Urban Institute Press, 1981.

Milne, Lorus J., and Margery Milne. "Nor Any Drop to Drink." *The Country Journal,* August, 1980.

Public Law 92-500. "Federal Water Pollution Control Act Amendments of 1972." 92nd Congress, October 18, 1972.

Reinhold, Robert, et al. Op. cit. (Chapter I).

Schmidt, William E. "Phoenix, Despite Seemingly Limitless Supply of Water, Needs to Conserve." *The New York Times,* March 15, 1982.

Sheets, Kenneth. "Water: Will We Have Enough to Go Around?" *U.S. News and World Report* (June 29, 1981), pp. 34–38.

U.S. Congress. House of Representatives. Committee on Interstate and Foreign Commerce. Subcommittee on Public Health and Environment. "Quality of Drinking Water—1980." Hearings, 96th Congress, 2nd Session, Serial No. 96-188, June 6, 9 and August 18, 1980. Washington, D.C.: U.S. Government Printing Office, 1980.

U.S. Congress. Senate. Committee on Environment and Public Works. "The Clean Water Act Showing Changes Made by the 1977 Amendments." Federal Water Pollution Control Act (P.L. 92-500) as amended by the Clean Water Act of 1977 (P.L. 95-217). Committee print, 95th Congress, 1st Session, Serial No. 95-12. Washington, D.C.: U.S. Government Printing Office, 1977.

U.S. Congress. Senate. Committee on Environment and Public Works. "State and National Water Use Trends to the Year 2000." Report prepared by the Congressional Research Service, Library of Congress. Committee print, 96th Congress, 2nd Session, Serial No. 96-12. Washington, D.C.: U.S. Government Printing Office, 1980.

Vitullo-Martin, Julia. "Ending the Southwest's Water Binge." *Fortune* (February 23, 1981), pp. 93–104.

Wade, Nicholas. "Drinking Water: Health Hazards Still Not Resolved." *Science* 196:1421–22 (1977).
Warren, Jacqueline M. "Water, Water Everywhere." *The Amicus Journal,* 3: 15–21 (1981).

Chapter VII

American Water Works Association. Wastewater Reclamation Committee. R. L. Culp, chairman. "Report to the 1970 Washington, D.C. Conference." Denver: American Water Works Association, 1970.
Comptroller general of the United States. Op. cit. (Chapter I).
Consulting Panel on Wastewater Reclamation Plant Improvements. Harvey O. Banks, chairman. "Final Report: Evaluation of Wastewater Treatment System." South Lake Tahoe, Calif.: South Tahoe Public Utility District, 1978.
Cowlishaw, Wayne A. "Update on Muskegon County, Michigan, Land Treatment System." Paper presented at the Annual and National Environmental Engineering Convention of the American Society of Civil Engineers, Kansas City, Mo., October, 1974.
Culp, Russell L. "Nitrogen Removal by Air Stripping." Paper presented at the Second Annual University of California Sanitary Engineering Research Laboratory Workshop, Tahoe City, Calif., June 26, 1970.
Culp, Russell L., and Gordon L. Culp. *Advanced Wastewater Treatment.* New York: Van Nostrand Reinhold, 1971.
Culp/Wesner/Culp, Jones & Stoke Associates and Bartle Wells Associates. "Summary of Facility Plan for South Tahoe Public Utility District Wastewater Treatment System." South Lake Tahoe, Calif.: South Tahoe Public Utility District, 1978.
Demirjian, Y. A., R. R. Rediske and J. R. Westman. "The Fate of Organic Pollutants in a Wastewater Land Treatment System Using Lagoon Impoundment and Spray Irrigation." Report submitted to Robert S. Kerr Environmental Research Laboratory. Muskegon, Mich.: Muskegon County Wastewater Management System and Department of Public Works, 1982.
Hill, Gladwin. "Advances in Clean-Water Technology Proving Costly." *The New York Times,* November 6, 1978.
"Indian Creek Reservoir: A New Fishing and Recreational Lake from Reclaimed Waste Water." Illustrated brochure. Washington, D.C.: U.S. Environmental Protection Agency, circa 1973.
Luoma, Jon R. Op. cit. (Chapter I).
Muskegon, County of. "Comprehensive Annual Financial Report for the Year Ended December 31, 1981." Muskegon, Mich.: County of Muskegon Accounting Department, 1981.
Office of Inspector General. Op. cit. (Chapter I).
Robert S. Kerr Environmental Research Laboratory. Ground Water Research Branch. "Preliminary Survey of Toxic Pollutants at the Muskegon Wastewater Management System." Report prepared with Analytical Chemistry Branch, Athens Environmental Research Laboratory, Athens, Ga. Ada, Okla.: U.S. Environmental Protection Agency, 1977.
Sheaffer, John R. "Land Application of Waste: Important Alternative." *Ground Water,* 17:62–68 (January–February, 1979).
South Tahoe Public Utility District. "Annual Report: Water and Wastewater Systems Operation." South Lake Tahoe, Calif.: 1981.

Tyler, Patrick E. "Why the U.S. Failed to Clean Its Water." *San Francisco Chronicle,* August 8, 1981.
U.S. Congress. House of Representatives. Appropriations Committee. Survey and Investigations Staff. Op. cit. (Chapter I).
Walker, John M. *Wastewater: Is Muskegon County's Solution Your Solution?* 3rd printing. Prepared for the Office of Water Program Operations, U.S. Environmental Protection Agency. Washington, D.C.: U.S. Government Printing Office, 1979.

Chapter VIII

Adler, Jerry, et al. Op. cit. (Chapter I).
Diez, Roy L. "Growing National Crisis You've Probably Ignored." *Professional Builder* (June, 1982), pp. 7, 78–91.
Grossman, David A. *The Future of New York City's Capital Plant.* Washington, D.C.: The Urban Institute, 1979.
Herbers, John. "Alarm Rises over Decay in U.S. Public Works." *The New York Times,* July 18, 1982.
Humphrey, Nancy, George E. Peterson and Peter Wilson. *The Future of Cleveland's Capital Plant.* Washington, D.C.: The Urban Institute, 1979.
Miller, Mary John, et al. Op. cit. (Chapter VI).
Parizek, Richard R. "Site Selection Criteria for Wastewater Disposal: Soil and Hydrogeologic Considerations." William E. Sopper and Louis T. Kardos (eds.), *Recycling Treated Municipal Wastewater and Sludge Through Forest and Cropland.* University Park, Pa.: The Pennsylvania State University Press, 1973.
Sheaffer, John R. "Reusing Water: Making the Most of a Valuable Resource." Paper presented at the 1982 Woodlands Conference on Sustainable Societies, The Woodlands, Tex., November 7–10, 1982.
Sheaffer, John R., William M. Eyring, Ray I. Iehl and T. David Mullan. "A New Era in Water Resource Management." Chicago: Sheaffer & Roland, 1982.
Sheaffer, John R., Patricia A. Ledford, Bernard C. Nagelvoort, J. David Mullan and Lee T. Rozaklis. "A Synergistic View of Anaerobic Digestion." Paper prepared for the Corporation for Public/Private Ventures, Philadelphia, 1980.
Wilson, Peter. *The Future of Dallas's Capital Plant.* Washington, D.C.: The Urban Institute, 1980.

Chapter IX

Bardach, J. E., J. H. Ryther and W. O. McLarney. *Aquaculture: The Farming and Husbandry of Fresh Water and Marine Organisms.* New York: Wiley-Interscience, 1972.
Benham-Blair & Affiliates and Engineering Enterprises. "Long-Term Effects of Applying Domestic Wastewater to the Land: Roswell, New Mexico, Slow Rate Irrigation Site." Paper prepared for the Office of Research and Development, Robert S. Kerr Environmental Research Laboratory. Ada, Okla.: U.S. Environmental Protection Agency, 1978.
Croxford, A. H. "Melbourne, Australia, Wastewater System: Case Study." Paper presented at the Winter Meeting of the American Society of Agricultural Engineers, St. Joseph, Mich., 1978.

REFERENCES

Donkin, J. Op. cit. (Chapter III).

Ellis, Boyd G. "The Soil as a Chemical Filter." William E. Sopper and Louis T. Kardos (eds.), op. cit. (see Parizek, Richard R., Chapter VIII).

Gilbert, R. G., R. C. Rice, H. Bouwer, C. P. Gerba, C. Wallis and J. L. Melnick. "Wastewater Renovation and Reuse: Virus Removal by Soil Filtration." *Science,* 192:1004–5 (June 4, 1976).

Gloyna, Earnest F. *Waste Stabilization Ponds.* Geneva: World Health Organization, 1971.

Hill, David E. "The Purifying Power of Soil." *Frontiers of Plant Science* (New Haven, Conn.: Connecticut Agricultural Experiment Station), Fall, 1971.

Hyde, Charles Gilman. "The Beautification and Irrigation of Golden Gate Park with Activated Sludge Effluent." *Sewage Works Journal,* 9:929–41 (November, 1937).

Johnson, James F. "Renovated Waste Water." Research Paper 135, Department of Geography. Chicago: University of Chicago, 1971.

Leeper, G. W. *Managing the Heavy Metals on the Land.* New York: Marcel Dekker, 1978.

Leeper, G. W. "Reactions of Heavy Metals with Soil with Special Regard to Their Application in Sewage Wastes." Paper prepared for the Corps of Engineers, Department of the Army, Washington, D.C., 1972.

Martin, Benn. "Sewage Reclamation at Golden Gate Park." *Sewage and Industrial Wastes,* 23:319–20 (March, 1951).

Maxcy, Kenneth. "An Inquiry into the Public Health Hazard of Sewage Disposal from Railway Conveyances." Technical Report No. 2, Joint Commission on Railway Sanitation. New York: Association of American Railroads, 1946.

Miller, Robert H. "The Soil as a Biological Filter." William E. Sopper and Louis T. Kardos (eds.), op. cit. (see Parizek, Richard R., Chapter VIII).

Office of Water Program Operations. *Stabilization Ponds.* EPA-430/9-77-012. Washington, D.C.: U.S. Environmental Protection Agency, 1977.

Piet, G. J., and B.C.S. Zoeteman. "Organic Water Quality Changes During Bank and Dune Filtration of Surface Waters in the Netherlands." *Journal of the American Water Works Association,* 72:400–4 (July, 1980).

Riehenderfer, James L., and William E. Sopper. "Effect of Spray Irrigation of Treated Municipal Sewage Effluent on the Accumulation and Decomposition of the Forest Floor." Reprint Series No. 81, Institute for Research on Land and Water Resources. University Park, Pa.: The Pennsylvania State University, 1979.

Rudolfs, Willem, Lloyd L. Falk and Robert A. Ragotzkie. "Contamination of Vegetables Grown in Polluted Soil: I. Bacterial Contamination." *Sewage and Industrial Wastes,* 23:253–68 (1951).

Rudolfs, Willem, Lloyd L. Falk and Robert A. Ragotzkie. "Contamination of Vegetables Grown in Polluted Soil: II. Field and Laboratory Studies on Endamoeba Cysts." *Sewage and Industrial Wastes,* 23:478–85 (1951).

Rudolfs, Willem, Lloyd L. Falk and Robert A. Ragotzkie. "Contamination of Vegetables Grown in Polluted Soil: III. Field Studies on Ascaris Eggs." *Sewage and Industrial Wastes,* 23:656–60 (1951).

Rudolfs, Willem, Lloyd L. Falk and Robert A. Ragotzkie. "Contamination of Vegetables Grown in Polluted Soil: IV. Bacterial Decontamination." *Sewage and Industrial Wastes,* 23:739–51 (1951).

Rudolfs, Willem, Lloyd L. Falk and Robert A. Ragotzkie. "Contamination of Vegetables Grown in Polluted Soil: V. Helminthic Decontamination." *Sewage and Industrial Wastes,* 23:853–60 (1951).

Rudolfs, Willem, Lloyd L. Falk and Robert A. Ragotzkie. "Contamination of Vegetables Grown in Polluted Soil: VI. Application of Results." *Sewage and Industrial Wastes,* 23:992–1000 (1951).

Rolph, Bart S. "Golden Gate Park, a Salvaged Land Irrigated with Reclaimed Water." Paper presented at the 14th Annual California and Pacific Southwest Recreation and Park Conference, Oakland, Calif., February 13, 1962.

Santee County Water District. "Total Water Use." Santee, Calif.: undated.

Seabrook, Belford L. *Land Application of Wastewater in Australia.* Washington, D.C.: U.S. Environmental Protection Agency, 1975.

Sontheimer, Heinrich. "Experience with Riverbank Filtration Along the Rhine River." *Journal of the American Water Works Association,* 72:386–90 (July, 1980).

Sopper, William E., and Sonja N. Kerr. "Cadmium in Forest Ecosystems." Reprint Series No. 90, Institute for Research on Land and Water Resources. University Park, Pa.: The Pennsylvania State University, 1980.

Sopper, William E., and Sonja N. Kerr. "Increased Woody Biomass Production and Land Treatment of Wastewater: An Economic-Symbiotic Relationship." Reprint Series No. 89, Institute for Research on Land and Water Resources. University Park, Pa.: The Pennsylvania State University, 1980.

Sopper, William E., and Sonja N. Kerr. "Renovation of Municipal Wastewater in Eastern Forest Ecosystems." Reprint Series No. 80, Institute for Research on Land and Water Resources. University Park, Pa.: The Pennsylvania State University, 1979.

Sopper, William E., and James L. Richenderfer. "Effect of Municipal Wastewater Irrigation on the Physical Properties of the Soil." Reprint Series No. 82, Institute for Research on Land and Water Resources. University Park, Pa.: The Pennsylvania State University, 1979.

Stoyer, Ray F. "The Development of Total Use of Water Management at Santee, California." Proceedings of the International Conference on Water for Peace, Washington, D.C., May 23–31, 1967.

Thomas, Richard E. "The Soil as a Physical Filter." William E. Sopper and Louis T. Kardos (eds.), op. cit. (see Parizek, Richard R., Chapter VIII).

Vaughn, J. M. "Human Viruses as Marine Pollutants." *Oceanus,* 18:24–28 (Fall, 1974).

Chapter X

Muskie, E. S. "The Economy, Energy and Clean Water Legislation." Joachim Lourbier and Robert W. Pierson, Jr. (eds.), *Biological Control of Water Pollution.* Philadelphia: University of Pennsylvania Press, 1976.

Sharpe, William E. "Water Conservation Devices for New or Existing Dwellings." *Journal of the American Water Works Association,* 73:144–49 (March, 1981).

Sopper, William E. "The Living Filter Project." *Water Pollution Control Association of Pennsylvania Magazine,* 11:6–10 (May–June, 1978).

Sopper, William E. "Surface Application of Sewage Effluent and Sludge." Reprint Series No. 86, Institute for Research on Land and Water Resources. University Park, Pa.: The Pennsylvania State University Press, 1979.

U.S. Department of Agriculture. "Fertilizer Used and Prices Paid." Chart 31, Agricultural Handbook No. 592. Washington, D.C.: 1981.

Van der Ryn, Sim. *The Toilet Papers—Designs to Recycle Human Waste and Water: Dry Toilets, Greywater Systems and Urban Sewage.* Santa Barbara, Calif.: Capra Press, 1980.

Chapter XI

Bukro, Casey. "Itasca Recycling Creates an Oasis." *Chicago Tribune,* October 11, 1981.

Sheaffer, John R. "Commercial Development Uses On-Site System." *Bio-Cycle* (May–June, 1981), pp. 56–7.

Trammell Crow Company. *Comprehensive Resources Management Plan for the Itasca Center (Hamilton Lakes).* Prepared by Sheaffer & Roland, Chicago, 1978.

Chapter XII

Bernstein, Scott. "The Westside Biomass Utility." Feasibility study proposal. Chicago: Center for Neighborhood Technology, 1982.

Center for Neighborhood Technology. "Overview of an Integrated Biomass Utility for an Urban Industrial Park." Chicago: Sheaffer & Roland, 1983.

Comptroller general of the United States. "Large Construction Projects to Correct Combined Sewer Overflows Are Too Costly." Washington, D.C.: U.S. General Accounting Office, 1979.

Office of the Chief of Engineers. "Regional Wastewater Management Systems for the Chicago Metropolitan Area." Summary report and technical appendix. Washington, D.C.: Department of the Army, 1972.

Mann, Charles C. "Digging Big." *Technology Illustrated* (June–July, 1982), pp. 74–80.

U.S. Army Corps of Engineers. Chicago District. District engineer. "The Use of Land as a Method of Treating Wastewater (Its Meaning to the Agricultural Community)." Chicago: Department of the Army, 1972.

U.S. Congress. Senate. Committee on Public Works. "Regional Wastewater Management Systems for the Chicago Metropolitan Area." Committee print, 92nd Congress, 2nd Session, Serial No. 92-24. Washington, D.C.: U.S. Government Printing Office, 1972.

Chapter XIII

Bennett, Truman (1982) "Shades of Immortality." *Ground Water,* 20:390–92 (July–August, 1982).

Bowden, Charles. *Killing the Hidden Waters.* Austin: University of Texas Press, 1977.

Byers, Bo. "Clayton's Plan Won't Hold Water." *Houston Chronicle,* August 2, 1981.

Gray, J. Frank. "Design and Management of an Irrigation System for Municipal Sewage Effluent." Paper obtained from the author at Lubbock, Tex., 1963.

Freese, Nichols and Endress, Consulting Engineers. *Report on Makeup Water for the Upper Canyon Lakes.* Lubbock, Tex.: City of Lubbock, 1971.

Langford, Mark. "Underground Supplies Being Depleted: Southwest U.S. First

Area to Face Water Crisis That Will Confront Entire Nation." *Los Angeles Times,* November 27, 1981.
LCC Institute of Water Research. *Basis of Design Report: Lubbock Land Treatment Research and Demonstration Project.* Prepared by Engineering Enterprises, Norman, Okla., and Sheaffer & Roland, Chicago, 1980.
LCC Institute of Water Research. *Environmental Assessment: Lubbock Land Treatment Research and Demonstration Project.* Prepared by Engineering Enterprises, Norman, Okla., and Sheaffer & Roland, Chicago, 1979.
Lubbock Planning Department. *Development Plan for Yellowhouse Canyon Lakes.* Lubbock, Tex.: City of Lubbock, 1977.
Splinter, William E. "Center-Pivot Irrigation." *Scientific American,* 234:90–99 (June, 1976).
Wahl, Samuel W. "Water Reuse Plans and Demonstrations." Information sheets on Yellowhouse Canyon Lakes, available from the Lubbock director of water utilities. Lubbock, Tex.: 1980.

Chapter XIV

King, Seth S. "Win or Lose, the President Will Be Remembered for His Fight with Congress over Water Projects." *The New York Times,* October 14, 1980.
Wilson, Weston W., and EPA. *Record of Decision, North Glenn Water Management Program, City of North Glenn, Colorado.* Report No. EPA-908/5-5-79-002D. Denver: Region VIII, U.S. Environmental Protection Agency, 1980.

Chapter XV

Landis Sewerage Authority. *Groundwater Assessment.* Study prepared by Sheaffer & Roland, Vineland, N.J., 1981.
Landis Sewerage Authority. *201 Wastewater Facilities Plan.* Plan prepared by Sheaffer & Roland. Vineland, N.J., 1981.

Chapter XVI

Chapin, Mike. "From the Cans and Bottles of Civilization Rose Mt. Hoy." *The Daily Journal* (Wheaton, Ill.), October 16, 1973.
Council on Environmental Quality. Op. cit. (Chapter VI).
Davis, Joseph A., and Kenn Speicher (eds.). *Groundwater Protection.* Washington, D.C.: Water Planning Division, U.S. Environmental Protection Agency, 1980.
Grady, Denise. "Trouble in Atlantic City." *Chicago Sun-Times,* April 11, 1982.
Lappen, Alyssa. "Garbage In, Garbage Out?" *Forbes* (May 25, 1981), pp. 50–53.
Lehr, Jay H. "Artificial Ground-Water Recharge: A Solution to Many U.S. Water Supply Problems." *Ground Water,* 20:262–66 (May–June, 1982).
Lehr, Jay H. "How Much Ground Water Have We Really Polluted?" *Ground Water Monitoring Review* (Winter, 1982).
Lehr, Jay H., and David M. Nielsen. "Aquifer Restoration and Groundwater Rehabilitation: A Light at the End of the Tunnel." *Ground Water,* 20:650–56 (November–December, 1982).
Public Law 96-510. "Comprehensive Environmental Response Compensation, and Liability Act of 1980 (Superfund)." 96th Congress, December 11, 1980.
Shabecoff, Philip. "$38 Million Pact Reached for Midwest Toxic Cleanup." *The New York Times,* November 19, 1982.

"Superfund Gains Momentum in Illinois." *Progress* (Springfield, Ill.: Illinois Environmental Protection Agency), May–June, 1982.
"They'll Ski Down a Mountain of Garbage." *Fortune* (February, 1970), p. 122.
U.S. Congress. House of Representatives. Committee on Government Operations. "Interim Report on Ground Water Contamination: Environmental Protection Agency Oversight." 98th Congress, 2nd Session, September 30, 1980. Union Calendar No. 874, House Report No. 96-1440. Washington, D.C.: U.S. Government Printing Office, 1980.
U.S. Congress. House of Representatives. Subcommittee on Health and the Environment and Subcommittee on Transportation and Commerce. "Hazardous Waste and Drinking Water." Joint hearings, 96th Congress, 2nd Session, Serial No. 96-219, August 22, 1980. Washington, D.C.: U.S. Government Printing Office, 1981.

Chapter XVII

Arlington, Texas, City of. *Feasibility of Land Treatment for the Village Creek Plant.* Prepared by Sheaffer & Roland, Chicago, 1981.
Boffey, Philip M. Op. cit. (Chapter I).
People United to Save Our Homes (PUSH). "The Village Creek Wastewater Treatment Plant." Prepared by Sheaffer & Roland, Chicago, 1980.
Sheaffer, John R. "Reusing Water . . ." Op. cit. (Chapter VIII).
Steinmann, Marion. "Cleaning Up the Delaware." *Context* (Wilmington, Del.: Du Pont), 11:17–19 (No. 3/1982).

PERSONAL COMMUNICATIONS

Chapter I

Jorling, Thomas C., Center for Environmental Studies, Williams College, Williamstown, Mass.
Temple, Truman, press officer, U.S. Environmental Protection Agency, Washington, D.C.

Chapter VII

Baer, Robert G., South Tahoe Public Utility District, South Lake Tahoe, Calif.
Bednarek, Frank, County of Muskegon, Muskegon, Mich.
Demirjian, Y. A., Wastewater Management System, Muskegon, Mich.

Chapter IX

Ruffin, Gale, Santee, Calif.
Stoyer, Ray, Lakeside, Ariz.
Watanabe, Mark, water reclamation plant, Golden Gate Park, San Francisco.

Chapter XI

Eyring, William, Sheaffer & Roland, Chicago.

Chapter XII

Bernstein, Scott, Center for Neighborhood Technology, Chicago.

Chapter XIII

Cowlishaw, Wayne, Sheaffer & Roland, Chicago.
George, Dennis, LCC Institute of Water Research, Lubbock, Tex.
Gray, J. Frank, Lubbock, Tex.

Chapter XIV

McGregor, F. Robert, Sheaffer & Roland, Denver.
Shoemaker, Joe, Platte River Greenway Foundation, Denver.

Chapter XV

Lowenstern, Leon, and William Goelzer, Landis Sewerage Authority, Vineland, N.J.

Chapter XVI

Christiansen, John C., and Jerry Hartwig, Forest Preserve District of Du Page County, Illinois.
Ford, Charles, Sheaffer & Roland, Chicago.
Goldfine, Neil, Municipal Utilities Authority, Atlantic City, N.J.
Goodrich, Toby, Connecticut Department of Environmental Protection, Hartford.
Lehr, Jay H., executive director, National Water Well Association, Worthington, Ohio.
Morekas, Sam, chief of state, regional coordination of the Superfund, U.S. Environmental Protection Agency, Washington, D.C.

Acknowledgments

The authors would like to recognize and thank the following persons for their contributions to this book.

For stimulating many of the ideas found in the foregoing pages: James E. Goddard, Tucson, Arizona, and Gilbert F. White, Boulder, Colorado.

For helping to maintain the flow of countless communications between Chicago and New Milford, Connecticut: Brenda Stokes, Buffalo Grove, Illinois.

For assistance in our research and for checking the completed manuscript: Alma Gilleo, Wheaton, Illinois.

And for his volunteer, highly productive newspaper-clipping service on water problems of the western states: Austin F. Kilian, San Diego, California.

Index

INDEX

INDEX

INDEX

INDEX

INDEX

INDEX

INDEX

INDEX